By the Way

François Carrard

Chiselbury

I am interested in the future,
because the future is where I will spend the rest of my life.
Jean d'Ormesson

Table of Contents

Acknowledgements i

Photographic Credits ii

Preface iii

Foreword by v

Thomas Bach President of the International Olympic Committee v

Prologue vii

1 My Early Years 1

2 A Brave New World 7

3 Striking Out Alone 14

4 Reflections on America 24

5 Back to the Old World 31

6 Some Lessons in Life 36

7 Sweden 40

8 A Lausanne Lawyer 45

9 The International Olympic Committee 50

10 The Court of Arbitration for Sport 58

11 The IOC and its Swiss Hosts 62

12 The Olympic Charter 66

13 Money, Money, Money 69

14 The End of an Era 76

15 Jacques Chirac's Manoeuvrings 86

16 A Most Unexpected Appointment 91

17 The Fall of the Soviet Empire 101

Photographs 102

18 Yugoslavia 142

19 South Africa and Mandela 146

20 The Magic of Lillehammer 1994   152

21 Are the Olympic Winter Games Still Viable?   157

22 The World's Most Exclusive Gentleman's Club   164

23 The Olympic Movement - Family, Sect or Network   170

24 Atlanta 1996, The Centennial Games   175

25 1998 Olympic Disgrace   182

26 A Taekwondo Assault and Attacks by US Politicians   193

27 The End of the Reign of Samaranch   199

28 The Presidency of Jacques Rogge   203

29 Chairman of the FIFA 2016 Reform Commission   207

30 Judges and Referees, a Major Risk for Sport   214

31 The Future of International Sport and the Olympic Games 217

32 Reinventing Olympism   224

33 Glimpses of a Few People   226

    Nelson Mandela   226

    A Bavarian Statesman in Lederhosen   228

    Primo Nebiolo, 'The First'   229

    Lee and Lee   231

    Mink Coat Diplomacy   232

    The King and I   234

    Nelson Paillou, the Chain Smoker   235

    Robert Badinter   237

    Jean-Claude Killy   239

    Fidel Castro   239

    A Brandy with a Cardinal, and Keeping the Beat with a Pope   242

    Helmut Kohl   244

    George W. Bush   245

    Vladimir Putin   245

    Claude Nobs and the Montreux Jazz Festival   247

34 What Else?   249

Epilogue   254

Index   256

Acknowledgements

When François left us his story so that we could remember his remarkable journey, we realised that his legacy to us was far more than a narrative of a life well lived. It was also an account of a man at the centre of events in modern Switzerland, in contemporary music, in sport and in international affairs.

Until we read about the range of his achievements and influence, even we, his close family, had not realised how important he had been in so many areas of today's world. Having done so, we knew that his autobiography deserved a wider audience and had to be preserved for posterity.

We sought help and soon discovered among his friends and colleagues a broad range of skills that helped us create this book, which we hope you will agree is a significant contribution to the history of our times.

Michael Payne worked with François for many years at the International Olympic Committee when he was the Director of Marketing and Television and François was Director General. As well as being colleagues, they became close friends and, in recruiting a team of experts, Michael soon became the driving force to get François' memoir into print.

We are eternally grateful to him and his team. Author and Olympic doyen Stewart Binns, who knew François well, brought thoughtful editing to the manuscript. Theodora Mantzaris, Olympic design specialist, did a brilliant job in making the cover both vibrant and succinct. Stuart Leasor of Chiselbury Publishing then brought the book to life in his marvellous presentation.

We are also indebted to Kellerhals/Carrard, François' law firm, who have lent unending support to the project. To the Montreux Jazz Festival, the love of François' life, who continue to offer friendship. To the Phototech Department of the Olympic Museum for researching and making available an amazing collection of images of François at work.

Finally, we are honoured that Thomas Bach, the President of the International Olympic Committee, who worked with François for many years, agreed to write the Foreword to the book. We know that François would be thrilled to be remembered by the leader of the Olympic Movement and by a fellow champion of Olympism, its crucial values and visionary ideals.

Alba Carrard

Maud and Philippe Gay-Carrard

Anne and Alberto Malo-Carrard

Oscar, Julie and Eliott

Photographic Credits

All Photographs are courtesy of the Carrard family and the Olympic Museum, with the exception of the one of Quincy Jones, at the Montreux Jazz Festival, for which thanks are due to Georges Braunschweig, GM-PRESS.

Preface

Shortly after completing this memoir of his life, François Carrard died on 9th January 2022 at the age of eighty-three. This obituary was posted by the International Olympic Committee on the following day.

* * *

A Doctor of Law from the University of Lausanne, François Carrard spent two years at a law firm in Stockholm before being admitted to the Swiss Bar in 1967, when he joined the firm of Carrard & Associés. He specialised in sports law before becoming the IOC's Director General.

Mr Carrard developed the IOC administration during his time as Director General and made it fit for purpose. With his legal background, he played a crucial role supporting the IOC in driving its fundamental reforms in 1999 and 2000. He also played a key role in the setting-up of the World Anti-Doping Agency (WADA) and the introduction of the first World Anti-Doping Code. In addition, he was heavily involved in revamping the Olympic Charter and in the IOC Commission on Apartheid and Olympism. He was an outstanding communicator for the IOC after being appointed spokesperson for the IOC Executive Board (EB) under President Juan Antonio Samaranch.

He led the IOC through seven editions of the Olympic Games and Olympic Winter Games, from Albertville 1992 until Salt Lake City 2002.

Foreword
by

Thomas Bach
President of the International Olympic Committee

For understandable reasons and quite properly, the headlines in world sport usually belong to the athletes and their achievements. Those who administer sport and make it happen often work in the background, their contributions rarely recognised. However, such was the immense importance of the work of François Carrard, that he became known far and wide as one of the pillars of the phenomenon that is modern sport.

He was made Director General of the International Olympic Committee in 1989 and served until 2003. During that time, I looked on with ever-increasing admiration as his judgement and intelligence led him to become the fulcrum of the organisation during a period of fundamental growth, immense change and profound challenges. Without his extraordinary analytical skills, his lawyer's eye for precise scrutiny and his calm integrity, those years may well have produced less successful outcomes.

Such was the range of his travels and influence, you will find in these pages many insights that will surprise you and you will be amazed by the range of people he met, both in sport and beyond, during his very full life.

Not only did François occupy a pivotal role in the organisation of the IOC, but he also played a crucial role in re-writing the Olympic Charter, in the establishment of the World Anti-Doping Agency and in the creation of the Court for Arbitration in Sport. Not content with one of the most demanding roles in world sport at the IOC, he also made a significant contribution to several other sports, including his role on FIFA's Ethics Commission, and in advising the International Boxing Association and the International Swimming Federation.

I knew François for over thirty years and soon recognised that he was something of a 'Renaissance Man': a gifted linguist, which allowed him to write this book in English, his second language, an outstanding jazz pianist, which led him to become Chairman of the Montreux Jazz Festival and he was possessed of the wit, diplomacy and charm that meant he was asked to be the figurehead of Lausanne's Beau Rivage Hotel, one of the world's most prestigious. His personal and professional gifts were legion: wisdom, insight, warmth, integrity and, most of all, his flawless moral virtue. He loved people and places and had a lifelong curiosity for the world and everything in it. Perhaps most importantly of all, he had a love of life that I found infectious, as did everyone who came into contact with him.

François' memoir is an enthralling read, both an intimate personal account and an important commentary and guide to our contemporary sporting world. I had the great privilege to know him as a good friend and as an outstanding colleague. Like all who knew him, I miss him greatly.

Thomas Bach

Prologue

This book is the testimony of a man who, for more than eighty years, has had the privilege to observe our world from many angles. It is not about what the author may have accomplished, which is of no significance, but about what he has seen and experienced throughout his life. It is about places, incidents and most importantly, about people: their attitudes, behaviours, beliefs and indeed, illusions.

Our stay in this world is ridiculously short. Amidst the vastness of the cosmos and through the countless eons of time, we are infinitely minute and depressingly unimportant. Even on our obscure planet, for the vast majority of us, our achievements are irrelevant. The billions and billions of human beings who have struggled, are struggling and will struggle in the future, either to survive in poverty or to achieve some sort of modest success, will for the most part leave nothing but a pile of ashes or an assortment of old bones. Almost all of us will disappear into oblivion, leaving no legacy and will soon be forgotten. The prospect may not be very appealing, but it is a simple, hard fact. It is true, some of us will leave behind more than others. Great artists, scientists, industrialists, as well as a few statesmen or women, but not usually those who think highly of themselves during their lifetimes, will leave a reasonable legacy. But for the rest of us, there is nothing, no legacy.

Having no choice but to accept my status in this world, I tried to make the best of it. From my earliest days I have been fascinated by people; the people I run into every day; indeed, the people of the world. I love people. During my entire life, I have been dedicated to activities that involve direct contact with human beings. I have watched them, been eager to communicate with them and tried to understand them. And because my professional life has been dedicated to the law, I have had the privilege to occupy various positions which provided me with unique observation posts from where I could scrutinise my fellow human beings.

I am only too aware that, as a humble lawyer, arbitrator, adviser, and sports administrator, I will leave no substantial legacy for the world. However, I have been blessed with two wonderful daughters, two grandsons and a granddaughter. So, on these pages, to help them on their journey through their lives, I have tried to offer some recollections of the world and its myriad inhabitants.

However, what I've tried not to do is describe some of my actions and deeds in a vain attempt to convince any readers of my personal merit. That would be egotistical and futile. The facts in this humble account are as I remember them to the best of my recollection. I did not undertake any research, nor did I check the accuracy of every fact mentioned. So, it may be that some of the background information is not entirely correct. Should that be the case, I ask the reader to accept that any error is accidental.

One final comment regarding the language of the book. For the last fifty years or so, although my professional base has always been in Switzerland, I've worked, read, written, spoken and thought as much in English as in French. So, when I started to write, the words came out in English. Perhaps, if my musings are ever published, my English will be refined by my publisher. However, if it is not, I ask for my readers' forgiveness.

1
My Early Years

I was born on 19th January 1938, in Lausanne, Switzerland. My father, Jean Carrard, was a very worthy lawyer in a small, traditional law firm, established by his father and a partner in 1885. When my grandfather, who I never met, died prematurely in the 1920s, my father, who was born in 1899, felt it was his duty to succeed his father, although he would have preferred to become a magistrate.

My father belonged to a local Swiss French family in the Canton de Vaud, where I can trace my ancestry to the fourteenth century. The Carrards appear to have been mostly local teachers or public notaries. During his student years, my father played a significant role in the local scout movement and like most young men at the time, served in the Swiss army, reaching the rank of captain in the fortress artillery. During the Second World War, although Switzerland was neutral and was never involved in the war, he was proud to serve as the first assistant officer to one of the very few three-star Swiss generals. He was relatively active in politics, serving as a member of the State Parliament of the Canton de Vaud. My father died in 1992. He was about to be ninety-three years old and had been in his office nearly every day until late 1991.

My mother, Erica, née Godall, was fourteen years younger than my father and I was their only child. I was told later that my parents had planned to have more children but abandoned the idea through fear of the possible consequences of the war. My mother was the fourth child of a wine merchant from Catalonia and a Swiss German woman from Thun, near Bern. It was an unusual pairing.

The marriage was not happy and yet produced one son and three daughters over more than twenty years. My Spanish grandfather committed suicide in the 1930s under circumstances which were never disclosed nor discussed in my mother's family. It was hinted that he had lost all his savings during the 1929 financial crisis. Some less charitable souls in the cafés of Thun suggested that he was simply tired of his wife. She belonged to a poor Swiss German family which had moved to the United States, where my grandmother had been born during the second half of the nineteenth century. Having failed, the family returned to Thun even poorer.

Like my father, my mother was active in politics, and, like him, had firm beliefs. While my father was absolutely in line with typical conservative views: free enterprise, individual freedoms and opposed to any hint of socialism, my mother was quite different. She had successively studied pharmacy, music (she was a piano virtuoso, although in my opinion she played too harshly and too loudly) and education. She was an activist for the cause of women's political rights in Switzerland, and when those rights were granted in the Canton de Vaud in February 1959, she was among the first women ever elected to a cantonal parliament. There, she joined my father who had been an MP for some years.

My mother was also actively engaged in consumer affairs. She participated in many initiatives, including launching the magazine 'J'achète Mieux', 'I Buy Better', which still exists. In parliament, my mother was soon disappointed by what she considered to be the passivity and conservatism of her colleagues, including her husband. Realising that she could get little support for her rather radical ideas, she resigned. She had other activities, including being a member of the Swiss Federal Antitrust Commission, and was also a journalist, writing on consumer issues. She was then appointed as a member of the board of directors of Migros, the giant food and consumer goods retailer, on which she served until her retirement. My mother died in 2003 at the age of ninety.

As you might guess from the above, the environment in which I was raised was original and stimulating. On the other hand, ours was a rather middle-class bourgeois home. We lived in small, rather modest apartments. My parents never owned any property until 1953, when my father unexpectedly inherited an old house from a woman musician who was a distant cousin. My parents never really liked the house, which is located in the heart of the most charming village of Cully, six miles from Lausanne. The village is part of a UNESCO World Heritage Site. The house became my home, which I completely restored and with which I fell in love.

Among my most important early memories are the dark days of the Second World War. Switzerland was entirely surrounded by war but proclaimed its neutrality and was prepared to defend it. I was just a baby at the beginning of the war but, as it developed, I remember my parents and their friends would follow the progress of the war by listening to the radio, and I could sense that they were concerned about a possible invasion of Switzerland by the German army.

Their fears were reinforced by some alarming facts. For example, I remember that a nearby house that was occupied by Germans who were related to the German Consul, had its roof covered with large white sheets. The assumption in the neighbourhood was that the German family had been informed of probable air raids and that the sheets served as a sign to alert the Luftwaffe that the house was a German home. There were also numerous times when we all had to spend the night in the cellar which was our air-raid shelter. There were many alerts when we could clearly hear the engines of the aircraft, US or British, in our skies. I also remember the shocking vision and ominous sound of a plane crashing into the French mountains of the Vaud Alps across Lake Geneva. In fact, some Allied planes did bomb Swiss cities, including the suburbs of Lausanne, apparently by mistake, the pilots believing that they were flying over Germany. That is quite a navigation error given that Lausanne is over 150 miles from the German border.

Those and many other incidents created a widespread feeling of anxiety. However, the Germans never came. Some of us believed that they had been impressed by the strength of the Swiss army and feared the potential cost of an invasion. Others were convinced that all the parties to the war had an interest in keeping Switzerland out of the conflict for financial reasons; just think about all the numbered accounts and gold in the Swiss banks. There were also intelligence factors. The country was full of spies from all those involved in the conflict, and it provided an ideal environment for valuable espionage. There were also those who said that we had been spared thanks to Mussolini, who had reservations about having a common border with his ally, Hitler. It was said that he had some sympathy for Switzerland, where he had lived for a while as a young man, spending time in particular in Lausanne. In fact, the University of Lausanne had granted him an honorary doctorate in the thirties. Whatever the reason, and I am no historian, we escaped the war and many Swiss were convinced that we had outsmarted the Nazis.

In 1943, I started at a small private school in Lausanne. It was located next to the railway on which trains carrying war materiel rolled by, and on some of the trains were the first Americans we had ever seen. They were GIs on leave. We found them very impressive in their olive-green uniforms, which were totally new to us. We were used to the uniforms of the Swiss army, similar to those of the Germans, which looked old fashioned and impractical. The GIs, suntanned, smiling and chewing gum, waved at us from their windows. They threw chocolate bars and tablets of gum at us. Among them were some black men, another first for us. At that time, there were few black faces in Switzerland, except on some advertisements promoting cocoa or a variety of chocolate called 'Negro Head'. How times have changed.

For young schoolboys, those encounters were our first contacts with the outside world, the world of those who had just won the war. They were heroes, superstars, and we were just fascinated by them. They walked confidently, laughed loudly and talked and behaved differently. They also brought new sounds, such as the music of Glenn Miller.

During the whole war, most Swiss considered themselves superior to their neighbours. We thought we were smarter than everybody else, living on an island of stability, security and prosperity and, to our obvious benefit, our bankers knew how to manage simultaneously both Jewish and Nazi funds. At the beginning of the war there had been, particularly in German Switzerland, some support for the German qualities of organisation and discipline. But the Germans had lost and, as often happens, the Swiss quickly distanced themselves from the losers. The Americans and the British were different and, as the victors, commanded considerable respect. They had shown courage and deployed formidable materiel and human resources.

The end of the war meant that the Swiss had to brace themselves for the challenges of a new world. That required a fundamental change of mentality. Not only did the Swiss feel superior to the rest of the world, but they had also developed a sense of selfishness and cynicism on their artificial island in the heart of a devastated Europe. I clearly remember that in Lausanne, on the beautiful Quai d'Ouchy by Lake Geneva, passers-by could hire fixed telescopes to watch the devastation wrought by the Germans just a few miles away across the lake in France's Haute-Savoie. It made us feel sympathy for the French and contempt for the Germans but reinforced our arrogance. Such feelings, not entirely abandoned to this day, caused many miscalculations by Swiss politicians and representatives on the world stage. For example, over too many years, Switzerland decided that it need not join the United Nations and could conduct its global policy on its own. Very recent events have shown how naive and outdated was such a view. Fortunately, the country and some of its leaders appear to have realised that times have changed.

However, Switzerland remains a unique country as far as its democracy and political institutions are concerned. In some respects, it is extraordinary that they still survive. With a population of about eight million people, not even the equivalent of a very large city in today's world, Switzerland has four languages and twenty-six cantons, which are not only relatively autonomous but still sovereign in many respects, just like the states of the US. Switzerland is probably the oldest real democracy in the world. It was founded in 1291 by three states and grew throughout the centuries. The current Swiss constitutional system is inspired by the US Constitution while retaining many Swiss traditions and values.

By 1945, we were proud that we had a state-of-the-art automatic dialling telephone network, the most efficient public transportation system, the finest chocolate and the best watches. We had central heating and hot water in most homes, electricity throughout the country, first class education, excellent health care and our people were hardworking and thrifty. With post-war peace, our 'island' became less insular. Until then, the only foreigners we had seen, rather than met, had been either poor refugees who were temporarily sheltered in Switzerland or soldiers from various armies who were detained in camps or schools.

I remember very well my mother taking me to a school in Lausanne in which several hundred Russians from the Red Army were housed. I was impressed by their smart uniforms, with their heavy, grey winter great coats and deep red collars and epaulettes. I envied their striking leather boots and loved hearing their emotive songs. At the time, many people were afraid of a possible takeover of Western Europe by the Soviet armoured divisions, which were only 150 miles from Switzerland's eastern border. In order to be prepared for such an eventuality, my mother was learning Russian. She insisted that I learn some basic words, just in case! So, I knew how to say hello, thank you and goodbye in Russian when she took me to the fence of the school where the Soviet soldiers were. In exchange for a few bars of Swiss Nestlé chocolate, she would practise basic conversation with the soldiers.

In the summer of 1945, my first trip abroad with my parents was a day trip to Annecy. Annecy is a lovely French city about twenty-five miles from the Swiss border near Geneva. My assumption was that everything and everybody would be poor and dirty and that we would be exposed to various alien germs and diseases. I still remember my impressions when I boarded a French train, a foreign train. It looked different. So did the French people. Their clothes were not like ours, nor were their shoes; they even had different haircuts.

The smells were not necessarily bad, but different. Ever since then, I have been sensitive to fragrances and odours in places like hotel lounges, shops and on people. During communist rule, the smell of public places and shops in the Soviet Union and other communist countries was particularly pungent. On the other hand, I particularly enjoyed the more attractive scents which characterised the shops and buildings of the USA, which I immediately identified with the urban realism of Norman Rockwell's paintings.

Ever since that Annecy trip, I have found it fascinating to travel, to watch and to meet other people; to try and understand them and, in short, to cherish them. My entire life has been dedicated to dealing with people and to focus on human relations in many places in the world, under many challenging circumstances and for different causes or purposes. But back in 1945, to me, a foreigner was a different creature. I had a lot to learn.

2
A Brave New World

The end of World War Two was the beginning of a new era, an era, it was hoped, of peace and prosperity, not only for Europe but for the whole world. And so it was, at least for a while. For a young schoolboy like me, they were wonderful years as my friends and I opened our eyes to an entirely new world: new cultures, new habits, new products; every day provided another opportunity to enjoy something unexpected, something different.

For me, the most fabulous discoveries were in music, in particular jazz. My mother had enrolled me in some classical piano classes at the Lausanne Music School, but I dropped out after a few lessons. My passion was jazz. My formative years were the era when Afro American musicians toured Europe and we rushed to their concerts. The biggest star of them all at the time was Louis Armstrong. I never forgot the magical experience when I had the great good fortune to see and hear him live for the first time. It was in Lausanne, in a movie theatre called the Métropole, which is now a concert hall.

Armstrong had with him fantastic jazzmen like Earl Hines on piano, Arvell Shaw on bass – who was rumoured to spend a lot of time in Montreux with a girlfriend, which made him nearly 'one of us' - Jack Teagarden on trombone, Barney Bigard on clarinet, Sydney Catlett on drums and the spectacular singer Velma Middleton. They were our stars, our icons.

Those days were also my senior school years. The curriculum during eight years of college and gymnasium was strict and typically classical, involving compulsory Latin, optional Ancient Greek or English, German, mathematics, French, philosophy and science. Sport was practically non-existent in most Swiss public schools, its practice consisting of about two hours weekly of so-called physical education divided into gymnastics and some very short football or other ball games. My school had been built in the late thirties, which characterised it as modern. It had showers but we couldn't use them. The almighty school caretaker didn't want to clean them and had prohibited their use by cutting off the water supply. We tried to convince our principal to allow access to the showers, but in vain. The caretaker was the real boss.

Anyone who wanted to practise sport more seriously had to join a sports club or use municipal facilities outside school hours. Fortunately, we lived near an Olympic-size outdoor swimming pool in Lausanne, which was used by several swimming clubs. My mother, concerned that her only son might fall under the negative influence of street gangs, decided that I should join the CNL, the 'Cercle des Nageurs de Lausanne' (Lausanne Swimmers Circle).

I was a rather good swimmer but not particularly fond of the idea of spending several hours training every day. However, I had no choice but to enrol. Now, looking back, I remember them as very pleasant times. The training was boring and consisted of ploughing through the water for miles and miles in an uninspiring pool. The club had decided that breaststroke would be my specialty and that I should also be a goalkeeper on one of its water-polo teams. And so it went on until 1955, when I was seventeen. The CNL members became a wonderful group of friends, some of whom I still meet today, more than sixty years later. We would train together, travel together and compete together. There were also very attractive girls in the club and soon, for some of us, they were the days of our first romances.

As far as competitions and results were concerned, I performed reasonably in a number of regional competitions. My best result was a third place at the French Swiss Championships. As the goalkeeper of the junior water-polo team, I enjoyed a number of victories, some of them quite challenging as we played several games at night in the cold water of Lake Geneva. I was particularly proud when I was called up for a game on the Senior Varsity CNL team, which at the time was the Swiss national champion.

There was no swimming during the winter, as there were practically no indoor facilities around Lausanne in the fifties. So, winter sport for me was divided between outdoor skating, which provided an ideal opportunity to meet girls, and like many Swiss youngsters, skiing.

For young children, the structure of sport has not substantially changed in Switzerland and in many European countries during the last fifty years. While our school systems go through reform after reform in every aspect of the school curriculum, sport continues to be neglected, and the huge educational value of sport is ignored. Very expensive school buildings are constructed, but with insufficient sports facilities. The politicians don't seem to understand that important principles and values can be encouraged through the practice of sport in schools. They are standards that are as essential for the development of well-balanced young people as the subjects taught in classrooms. It seems to me that at the moment, only the Anglo-Saxon people and governments have understood this, which is a pity.

Apart from school and sport, the life of young Swiss teenagers like me was divided between family life, usually during holidays, and a social life with friends, mostly school friends. During the weekends, apart from the usual teenage parties, a few friends and I loved to attend jam sessions held in various bars and cafés on Saturday nights and Sunday afternoons. There were concerts given by artists like Count Basie, Erroll Garner, Oscar Peterson, Dizzy Gillespie, Duke Ellington, the Modern Jazz Quartet and many more who were touring Europe and performed in Lausanne.

Whenever I was at home during the evenings, I would never miss the daily Voice of America Jazz Hour on AFN Munich, the American Forces Network in Germany. It was regarded as one of the best jazz radio programmes in the world, and fans like me would immediately recognise the beautiful, deep voice of the anchorman, Willis Conover. Thanks to him, a man I would never meet, I discovered several great artists, in particular Dave Brubeck, whom I deeply admired, and who performed beautifully until his death in 2012. When I was much older, I was fortunate to meet him backstage in Washington DC and again in Montreux.

Those early years encouraged me to try and play some jazz piano by ear, which I still do very modestly. My passion for jazz has never faded and I cultivate it not only by listening to jazz records every day at home and in my car, but also, when travelling, by seizing every opportunity to spend time in clubs such as the Blue Note in New York, Tokyo or Milan, the Village Vanguard in New York, the Basement in Sydney, Ronnie Scott's in London and many others in Scandinavia, Russia, China and even Azerbaijan, a country with an amazing musical and jazz culture. Finally, despite the sad loss in 2013 of its founder, heart and soul and chief executive, my great friend Claude Nobs, I enjoy every single moment of my office as chairman of the Montreux Jazz Festival.

During the fifties, while Switzerland watched, more convinced than ever that it was by far the finest nation of them all, Europe was rebuilding itself stone by stone. We were encouraged in our complacency by the fact that many foreign friends and visitors expressed a sincere admiration for our achievements. Here was a small country, without any natural resources other than the beauty of its landscapes, which had succeeded in developing its industry, its services and its social peace. Swiss banks were becoming very prosperous, attracting many foreign customers eager to avoid paying taxes in their own countries. Our bank secrecy system, established by law, with its numbered accounts, where the customer's identity was only known by a very limited number of senior bank officials, was one of the smartest inventions by the so-called Gnomes of Zürich. For their very best clients, bank officials would even travel abroad disguised as ordinary tourists or businessmen to meet their clients in circumstances not unlike clandestine meetings between spies.

Our major industrial groups, like Nestlé, Ciba, Geigy, Schindler, Oerlikon, ABB, Omega, Longines, Tissot and Rolex, to name but a few, were universal brands enjoying worldwide reputations for the quality of their products and services. And there was Swissair, the iconic flagship of air transport. Wealthy Italians, Spaniards, Greeks or Portuguese and many others would never fly out of Europe without boarding their favourite Swissair planes in Zürich or Geneva.

Switzerland was also considered as a haven of security and the crime rate was very low. There was hardly any violence in the streets. While foreign immigration had been increasing since the beginning of the twentieth century and was at about 20%, it was relatively well controlled, thanks to an efficient police administration assisted by citizens eager to voluntarily contribute to the enforcement of law and order.

Many foreigners were attracted by what they considered to be the good life in Switzerland. The very favourable tax regime offered to non-working residents in some Swiss cantons, especially around Lake Geneva, Lake Lucerne and the Alps, attracted movie stars like Charlie Chaplin, Sofia Loren, James Mason, William Holden, David Niven, Yul Brynner, Peter Ustinov, Audrey Hepburn and many others. They were highly appreciative of the fact that their privacy was respected in Switzerland. Authors like Graham Greene, Norman Krasna and Georges Simenon and painters like Balthus or Oscar Kokoschka enjoyed the peace and quality of life which were characteristic of Lake Geneva.

Like most Swiss, in spite of my early interest in the outside world, my instinct, when confronted with any foreign person or thing, was that I had the privilege to belong to a superior people who knew more, shared the highest values and thus enjoyed better lives than the rest of the world. This feeling distorted our perception of the world at large. It would take many years and some very serious setbacks, like the Swissair collapse in 2001 and the UBS and Credit Suisse disasters of 2008, for the Swiss to begin to understand that they were not as perfect as they had been led to believe.

Although my background was distinctly bourgeois, my father was a respected lawyer, nearly all my friends, with whom I had great fun, did not belong to that circle. In fact, I felt like I had one foot in the bourgeois world and the other in a world of totally different people, socially, politically and culturally. As my parents were not intrusive at all, I felt free to conduct my life as I pleased. My father, while being personally quite conservative, was the most tolerant and understanding person I have known. His respect for others, whoever they were, was impressive. He never tried to impose his own views on others. In terms of studies, he simply thought that it would be good for me to pass the baccalaureate and perhaps go on to university, and he was prepared to support me to that effect. But had I decided to drop out of school and take a simple job, he would not have objected.

His concept of education was that children should be raised like horses. As we know, a newly born foal is soon able to walk, so its mother will limit her care to watching the foal from a distance. My father believed that the education of children should abide by the same principles, which he translated as follows: give a lot of autonomy to your children while keeping a discreet eye on them. As for my mother, fortunately for me, she was so busy with her numerous political, journalistic and social activities that, provided my grades in school were good, which was usually the case, she left me in peace. Those family circumstances enabled me to live a happy life.

My parents' financial circumstances were quite comfortable. They were not rich, but my father got a decent income from his work as a lawyer, to which my mother added more funds from her activities. We lived more simply than many other families, and I consider that I was not spoiled. In 1947, at the insistence of my mother, my father agreed to buy a small second-hand car. It was a yellow, four-door, four-cylinder Peugeot 202, which became our first family car for trips abroad, and in the summer of 1948, my father decided that we would drive to the French Riviera and spend a week there.

However, my father liked to improvise and wanted to keep an alternative open, which was to spend a week not on the French Riviera but in the Swiss Alps. My mother was, therefore, instructed to pack both the necessary light clothes for the Riviera and warm for the mountains. As for the departure date, it would be decided without notice, on the very eve of the move. So, my father came home for dinner and declared that we would leave at 2:00am that night so as to avoid traffic on the roads. Once at the wheel of the car, my father would wait, in the middle of the night, until another car drove past. If the car arrived from the left, we would go to the left, which would mean going towards the Swiss Alps. If, on the other hand, the car came from the right, we would drive towards Geneva and then onwards to the French Riviera. Fortunately for me, the random car, which we recognised as belonging to the local milk supplier, arrived from the right, so the French Riviera was our destination.

After a very tedious ten-hour drive, there were no motorways in those days, we arrived at Juan-les-Pins, where we spent our first night in a modest hotel by the sea. The resort was packed with tourists, mostly French. We found the landscape beautiful and loved being by the sea, a special treat for us Swiss, who have no sea. The food was delicious, and I discovered seafood for the first time in my life.

As for the French people, our relationship with them was not easy. Many of them looked down at the Swiss as a primitive peasant nation, thinking and speaking slowly and heavily. Also, the Swiss appeared to the French as prosperous and conceited. To us Swiss, the French looked rather poor and dirty. It was well known that France had too few bathrooms, while the Swiss took great pride in their cleanliness. On the whole, the relationship between the French and the French-speaking Swiss was, and still is, a love-hate relationship between neighbours.

From Juan-les-Pins, we drove to Monte Carlo in Monaco, which was a very different experience. We stayed at a modest hotel in the middle of the city, the Hotel de Russie. Coincidentally, approximately twenty-five years later, I was to represent clients of mine in purchasing the hotel, which they needed for an important real estate development. The atmosphere in Monte Carlo was different from that in France.

Monaco is a separate sovereign state and what immediately impressed us at the time was that, contrary to what seemed to prevail in France, there was a distinct aura of prosperity in Monte Carlo. Of course, there was the legendary Casino and the distinguished Hotel de Paris, where all the rich and famous of the world would stay. It was quite a lesson in modesty for us Swiss to realise that our allegedly perfect country was not necessarily the most impressive place on earth and that there was an outside world, that had not been entirely destroyed. Many years later, I had the occasion to remember those evenings in Monte Carlo, to where I often travelled professionally, and became a frequent guest of the Hotel de Paris. When I think back to those moments in Monte Carlo, they were the origin of my taste for luxury hotels and now I have the privilege to chair the board of some of the most prestigious hotels in Switzerland, including the world-famous Beau-Rivage Palace and the Lausanne Palace. In any event, our short stay in Monte Carlo definitely made me aware that there was another world beyond Switzerland and that that world was growing and changing rapidly.

3
Striking Out Alone

In 1954, at the age of sixteen, I had my first opportunity to travel abroad without my parents. Through some friends, I was invited to stay for a few weeks with an Italian family in Rome. It was a great experience in every respect. The journey itself, twelve hours by train, was fascinating, particularly because I spent all those hours with a most interesting man. He was a communist member of the Italian parliament and mayor of a small city in northern Italy. Fortunately for me, he spoke fluent French and gave me an intriguing and, to my surprise, a reasonably objective description of his country's situation. The whole trip was like attending a seminar in political science, delivered by a man who had vast historical and political knowledge. I didn't meet him again but never forgot those unexpectedly inspiring hours.

In Rome, I stayed with an interesting family. The father was an air force colonel who was serving at the Italian Ministry of Defence. The mother was a highly educated daughter of a famous Venetian professor of medicine. One of their two sons was about my age and preparing for the Italian diploma which would give him access to university. They were all cultivated, dynamic and curious about everything. Thanks to them, I discovered not only the many extraordinary ancient sites of Rome, but also a number of other cities and landmarks throughout Italy. I was particularly lucky to be escorted on all those visits by a young professor of history, who was as entertaining as he was scholarly.

I spent more than a month with them, learning more history during those weeks than during all my years in school. I also discovered the fascinating ruins of Ostia Antica, the harbour city of Ancient Rome, while one of the most striking visits was to the Etruscan tombs. I had never realised the importance of the Etruscans as Rome's rivals, long before the Romans conquered them on the way to building their mighty empire. Apart from the daily excursions and historical visits, which I absorbed with great enthusiasm, my friends also showed me modern Rome's social life.

I was invited to many dinners and parties, which were totally different from what I was used to in Switzerland. Roman parties were much livelier than Swiss ones. The hosts and guests were gracious and friendly, the food more varied, the women were much more elegant than their Swiss counterparts, and there were some very beautiful girls. I remember that one night I fell madly in love with a gorgeous Roman woman who drove me home in her tiny Fiat Topolino car. Nothing ever happened between us. She was probably close to thirty years old, and I was sixteen. I didn't dare express my feelings to her and she probably didn't even notice me. I never saw her again but ever since, I've always associated Rome and Italy with passion and charm.

When I got back to Switzerland, I found my country dull and boring, and had a different perception of the outside world. It encouraged me to look for more new experiences outside an environment which appeared to me too narrow. This reflection may appear immature and superficial, but I know for a fact that my Rome experience had a decisive influence on my subsequent attitude towards life.

Then, unexpectedly, I got a few opportunities to spend some long weekends in Paris, which I thoroughly enjoyed. In 1953, my mother had attended a convention of the International Union of Family Associations in Lisbon, Portugal. There, she had met the chairman of the Union, a conservative, Catholic French businessman, father of seven, living with his family near Paris.

My mother was a very serious woman, probably unhappy in her marriage with my father who was fourteen years older than her. Their life as a couple seemed monotonous and boring, which didn't really affect me as I had my own rather independent existence. Nevertheless, it came as a totally unexpected surprise when I later learned that the French father of seven and my mother had fallen in love in Portugal and embarked on a secret affair that was to last for several years.

The two spouses ignored the situation for quite a while, while my mother, who needed excuses to travel to Paris to meet her lover, somehow managed to convince my father that it would be good for my education to know more of Paris. So, I had the chance to make several trips to the city with my mother. Each of the visits lasted a few days. We would be greeted at the station by her lover, who pretended to be just a friend, and my mother and I would stay in separate rooms, usually at the Hotel du Mont-Thabor. As soon as we reached the hotel, I was on my own, free to go out in the evenings. Paris by night was mine at the age of sixteen.

I saw a number of fascinating shows, plays and operas, including Gershwin's Porgy and Bess, which was a sensation running for the first time in Europe and which left a deep impression on me. I also attended jazz clubs, in particular the Club du Vieux Colombier where a resident combo was clarinettist, Claude Luter, playing with the great soprano saxophone player, Sydney Bechet. I had a few friends in Paris, in particular some nice girls whom I'd met during some international swimming competitions and with whom I visited many places, mainly on the Left Bank. Those excursions were another opportunity for me to see that the world outside Switzerland was not only different, but very stimulating and exciting.

Just for the record, a few years later, my father discovered piles of letters, one per day, which my mother had received from her French lover. He reacted very decisively, telling her that she had one day to end her affair or face an immediate divorce. She chose to stay and, although she was probably very unhappy, managed over the years to regain my father's trust and become a close friend to him until he passed away in 1992 on the eve of his ninety-third birthday.

In early 1955, as I was expecting to obtain my 'baccalauréat ès lettres' which would give me automatic admission to any European university, I began to think about my future. I definitely wanted to leave Switzerland. At the time, the impact of my mother's affair was still evident, and my parents were considering a divorce, which was for me another good reason to distance myself from Switzerland for a while. Knowing that I loved Italy, my father suggested that I could go and study law at the University of Bologna, a highly reputable institution. I was quite tempted by the idea, in particular because at the time, I was attracted to a Bolognese girl.

At the same time, I had applied for an American Field Service (AFS) scholarship. A few weeks later, I received the news that the AFS had granted me a one-year scholarship to attend the final year as a senior in a Southern California high school. This was to change my life forever. I didn't hesitate for one second and gave up any possible academic and romantic plans in Bologna and decided on Southern California.

My AFS scholarship provided for a one-year stay with a Californian family, tuition as a senior in a public high, the travel costs to and from Europe and, at the end of the year, a month-long trip through the USA by Greyhound bus. Each student was also entitled to a monthly allowance of twelve US dollars as a contribution to personal expenses. The AFS had begun as an American volunteer ambulance corps during the Great War. It was transformed into an idealistic international educational institution organising exchanges of young students from various countries to US families and vice-versa.

I arrived in New York on a glorious August morning at sunrise. I will never forget the extraordinary sight of the New York skyline. It was simply breathtaking; everything, everyone looked so different and made for a fascinating scene. Throughout the immigration and other inspection formalities, which lasted about two hours, most of us felt overwhelmed. There was definitely a sense that something important was happening in our teenage lives. We were entering the New World. Another life was beginning, and I will never forget my first day in New York.

After an AFS briefing, we were free to wander around Manhattan. I suggested to my two roommates that we should go to Harlem and find a place to listen to some jazz. So, we boarded a bus on Broadway which took us all the way up to Harlem. I clearly remember that as the bus was driving uptown, the people onboard gradually changed. At the beginning of the ride, the crowd was racially mixed but by the time we reached the upper end of Central Park, all occupants except the three of us were African Americans. We got off the bus in the heart of Harlem, probably around 115th Street. To our surprise, the street was dark and rather silent, until we heard the sound of a gospel choir in a small church. The street was deserted and when we entered the church, we found an African American congregation celebrating a service. We were the only whites.

The minister, who was standing at his pulpit, was amazed to see three young visitors. To our surprise and embarrassment, he suspended the service and asked us the purpose of our visit. We were totally unprepared to answer his question. However, under the glare of the entire congregation, I mumbled something about being European students who had arrived in New York that very day and had thought to make Harlem our first destination to listen to original African American music. We got an enthusiastic round of applause and the minister welcomed us warmly. He invited us to sit with the congregation, which we did, and resumed the service. We were fascinated by the people around us, by the minister who was also conducting an impressive choir and by the music, which was pure gospel. At the end of the service, we were offered some refreshments. As we were about to look for some way to get back to our hotel, our hosts told us that there were no more buses at that time, but kindly escorted us to a subway station, giving us the necessary directions to reach Times Square. We were treated like old friends. Thus, our very first night in New York was an extraordinary experience. We had spent it in a Black church in Harlem.

On the morning of the next day, I flew with my fellow students whose destination was, like mine, California. Our flight landed at Burbank Airport on what was a typical August day in the Los Angeles area. The sun was hot but filtered through a hazy layer of smog. I was welcomed by Peg Fairfield, the American woman who was to be my 'foster mother' for one year. She was a slender woman in her early forties, warm and spontaneous; I immediately felt comfortable and welcome. We then drove to what was going to be my home. Her car was a brand-new four-door, two-tone, blue and green Oldsmobile, with a powerful, but silent eight-cylinder engine, air conditioning and soft suspension. For a European teenager accustomed to small cars, that first ride was amazing.

Home was a very nice family bungalow in La Cañada-Flintridge, a small city fourteen miles to the north of Los Angeles in the foothills of the Verdugo Mountains. It was a typical four-bedroom, three-bathroom Californian home with a large well-kept garden with orange and lemon trees, a swimming pool and a garage for two cars with a basketball hoop on its door. The view towards Pasadena and Downtown Los Angeles was breathtaking.

Besides Peg, a matriarchal but warm American housewife, my foster family consisted of its father, Wally, a sales manager for a ball-bearing company, and three sons, Bill (sixteen), Dick (thirteen) and Bob (eight) and their dog, Tyco. Bill shared his room with me during the entire year. He proved to be very gracious about it, and we became like two brothers. Unfortunately, Bill passed away at the end of July 2016, at the age of seventy-seven. Throughout more than sixty years, although we were geographically separated and only saw each other occasionally, whenever we met, we had instantly behaved like brothers. Indeed, the whole family treated me like their fourth son; an extraordinary privilege.

As I now reflect upon that exceptional period, the environment into which I was so suddenly plunged could be characterised as a mixture of Norman Rockwell's imagery and that of the movie 'The Truman Show', an American dream as imagined by many young Europeans in the fifties.

After a few days dedicated to settling in and meeting the family's neighbours and close friends, the time came to prepare for school, which was the John Muir High School in Pasadena, ten miles from home. Nearly all the youngsters of my age had their driver's licence, the legal age was sixteen, and most of them, including my brother Bill, had their own cars, which they drove to school. In the Los Angeles area, the ownership of a car was not a luxury, but, to all intents and purposes, a necessity.

My first visit to John Muir High School was to meet a senior class counsellor, John McSweeney, who was to guide me and organise my curriculum. The meeting was very friendly, and it was then that I discovered that, contrary to the rather rigid curriculum I'd known in Switzerland, I was offered what appeared to be a long menu from which I could choose a number of optional classes. Following Sweeney's advice, I decided to take up English, US history, government, Spanish and public speaking, as I would be expected to give a few public speeches and presentations as a foreign exchange student. In sport, which was a daily compulsory period, unheard of in Switzerland, I chose swimming.

Before the actual beginning of the school year, my counsellor had insisted, supported by my family, that, for practical reasons, as nobody could be expected to correctly pronounce François, my French name, I should adopt a new name. So, for one year, I became 'Frank'; another big change.

A few days later, school began. The first thing that struck me was that the students went to their teachers and not the other way around. In Switzerland, students were assigned for the whole school year to specific classrooms in which they followed all their courses. They would stay in the same classroom in which each student kept his desk, in which all books and other papers and personal junk were stored, while the teachers moved from room to room for each lesson. At John Muir, I had to attend a different class and meet different students for each lesson. And the classes were mixed, which, for a youngster who had spent the last eight years in boys-only Swiss schools, was a real treat.

There were many rather pretty girls around, and I had to learn the social rules of the relationships between American boys and girls. I was surprised to discover that in America, relations between boys and girls followed distinct patterns. 'Going steady' was a formal status which meant specific rituals like holding hands in public, escorting your girlfriend to her classes and being introduced to her parents. You could exchange Hollywood-style kisses in your car while watching a movie in a drive-in theatre but what was called, 'going all the way' was regarded as taboo by the vast majority of the teenagers and parents.

Although I had no interest in 'going steady', I couldn't escape the prospect. For instance, after meeting an attractive girl and inviting her to some parties or movies two or three times, the topic was raised by her. "Frank darling, my friends and parents are wondering if we've decided to go steady. I discussed this at length with my best girlfriend and with my mom. They both think you're terrific, but we understand that in a year or so, you'll go back to Europe. Therefore, we all think that it's best that you and I don't go steady." That thoughtful outcome suited me perfectly.

Most Americans had no idea where Switzerland is. They vaguely imagined a cold land of mountains but probably couldn't differentiate between Switzerland and Sweden. Nearly all of them couldn't have cared less about anything happening outside of the US. Every day, I would read the Los Angeles Times, but to find some foreign news, I would have to move to pages four or five where the information was very meagre. Some locals wondered whether I lived in an Alpine chalet, together with cows and goats, and a local magazine wanted to feature me on its front page in my lederhosen. Sadly, I had to disappoint them, as I'd never worn lederhosen in my life, which the editor refused to believe.

Looking back at my time at John Muir High, I found it very well depicted in the movie 'Grease', which I saw many years later. The dress codes, the hairdos, the cars, the attitudes and the relations between boys and girls were very well portrayed in the film.

Another particularly interesting aspect of life in John Muir was the relationship between African Americans and white Americans. At the time, the proper word to designate African Americans was 'Coloured'; as the word 'Negro' had been recently dropped as derogatory. John Muir had between a quarter and a third African American students, and one of its alumni was African American baseball legend, Jackie Robinson, who broke the sport's 'colour bar' in 1947. I was quite impressed that the coexistence between whites and non-whites appeared to be smooth. I had read and heard so much about racism in the US that, at first, I was very pleasantly surprised by the apparent harmony. However, I soon realised that beneath the surface of the apparently easy coexistence, the situation was in fact quite different.

Once the students had left school for the day, they wouldn't mix together; they would live in different parts of the area and there were no mixed couples. Any white girl seen with a coloured boy would be scorned as promiscuous. At the weekends, the school dances were usually attended by the whites only. The coloured students were not formally excluded; they simply didn't appear. And yet, at school, there was no perceivable tension of any kind. On the contrary, my observation was that the relations between both communities were usually quite relaxed, and even friendly. One specific element which, in my view, contributed substantially to such apparent friendliness was sport.

Until I experienced it, I was completely unaware of the importance of sport in American schools. In Swiss schools, like in many other European countries, except in the United Kingdom or in some authoritarian states, sport was, and unfortunately still is, almost totally ignored. So, I was deeply impressed by the organisation of the Physical Education Department at John Muir. There were facilities for all major sports, with plenty of equipment for the students and there were showers, locker rooms and clean towels. All this was absolutely unheard of for me, and I was totally amazed by what appeared to me to be an extraordinary organisation. However, within a few weeks, I discovered that the resources at John Muir were not exceptional at all and that, in fact, there were other high schools with even more luxurious facilities.

My next surprise linked to school sport was to witness the collective enthusiasm for sporting competitions. I began to realise the meaning of sport in school not only as part of the curriculum, but also as a value and reference to the overall standard and reputation of the school. Attendances at events was significant and it was at those events that I noticed friendly relations between the black and white communities. African American students excelled in several important disciplines, particularly in team sports like basketball and football, and the entire school was proud of their achievements. That status was also enhanced by the fact that even with a large majority of whites, the students elected a black boy as student president.

These and other facts led me to conclude too quickly and too superficially that while there was still racism in the southern states, such a plague didn't exist in Southern California. I would later have a number of opportunities to revise my exceedingly simplistic judgment on an issue for which I was not prepared. Indeed, it took me many more years to understand what racism really meant and I still regret that, for fear of complications with my foster family, I didn't try to socialise with some of my African American classmates. I recall in particular a most charming African American girl who sang blues music and whom I accompanied on piano; tempi passati…

Sport at John Muir offered me some wonderful opportunities. I joined the swimming team and, after a couple of months of very hard training and practice under a very competent coach, I was accepted on the school team, which meant joining the sporting elite on the campus, identified by very recognisable jackets emblazoned with a large 'A'. My status was further enhanced thanks to my getting a brand-new 'crew cut', thus giving up my European hairstyle.

I was one of very few breaststroke swimmers and the coach wanted me to be part of the 4x100 yards medley relay team. The training was much harder than what I'd known in Switzerland, at least two hours per day after school. We participated in many interstate school competitions, and I was surprised to see that on a number of occasions, there were several hundred spectators and even several thousand when we swam at the finals of the Californian Championships, where we ranked fourth. Incidentally, this marked the end of my short career as a swimmer. Indeed, when I returned to Switzerland, in the autumn of 1956, the training facilities appeared to me to be so poor, particularly in the cold winter season, that I gave up. Later, when I was at the University of Lausanne, there was no opportunity to practise swimming: no pool, no coach and no competition. The USA and Switzerland were two very different worlds in nearly all aspects of life.

Throughout the following fifty years, I kept contact with and met my foster brothers and I visited California on several occasions. On one occasion in 1994, during the FIFA World Cup, when the final between Brazil and Italy was played in the Rose Bowl, where I had been cheering for my school in 1955, I took the opportunity to pay a brief visit to John Muir. However, when I was invited to the fiftieth reunion of my class in 2005, after pondering the pros and cons for quite a while, I decided not to attend. I had the feeling that, after fifty years of zero communication with my former classmates, it would be a huge shock, beginning with the challenge of even trying to recognise them.

I remember flipping through the pictures of the boys and girls of my class in the 1956 School Yearbook. Handsome young men and pretty young girls, as they were then, I realised that instead of those images, I would be meeting senior citizens in their late sixties, many of them distinctly rotund, some bald or with white hair, and maybe even a few with walking sticks. And I certainly didn't want to hear about those who had already died. I was simply horrified by such a prospect, and, somewhat cowardly, to buy myself an excuse, I accepted a professional commitment in Italy on the day of the reunion. Needless to say, I adopted the same tactic when invited to the sixtieth class reunion.

I am still convinced that reunions, held after more than a couple of years, become occasions to be avoided. For me, the same applies to looking at old photographs of family, friends and myself. I hate looking backwards, which is the reason why I never take any pictures. My memory acts as a filter which eliminates those moments, events or people that are best forgotten. On the other hand, the most precious moments are stored away and kept vividly alive in my memory.

4
Reflections on America

While my American school was a unique opportunity to gain insight into American people and their lives, there were many other enriching experiences available to me. One of those was particularly dear to me: jazz and the world of entertainment, of which it formed a not insignificant part. To my amusement, I noticed that my Californian friends seemed surprised that a young Swiss could have any knowledge of anything else but Swiss yodel.

When some of my friends found out that I loved jazz and that I was a very modest but enthusiastic amateur piano player, they thought that the idea of a small jazz combo led by a Swiss musician might draw some attention and some success. Therefore, with three friends whose names I will never forget: Bill Yaryan on alto saxophone, Paul Magdaleno on drums and Art Toor on bass, we formed a group named the Frank Carrard quartet. In fact, we had the nerve to claim that the source of our inspiration was no less than the music of Dave Brubeck, who was becoming a world-famous jazz pianist and composer.

We got a few dates to play for dances, collecting up to twenty-five dollars per head, which was very generous. We also won a contest on a show, on KLAC Radio Los Angeles, hosted by famous anchor, Alex Cooper. The climax of my mini career as a jazzman took place when I was invited, together with some other amateur musicians from John Muir, to perform live on a TV show hosted by one of the most famous jazz producers in the world, Gene Norman. Somewhere in my mind, I was probably dreaming of a career in the entertainment industry. That never happened, but, even today, I sometimes wonder whether I should have tried my luck.

During my stay, when I had some free time, I couldn't resist watching television. In Switzerland, very few people had TV sets in their homes. The main media, apart from the printed press, was the radio. In America, the media was in private hands, while in Europe it was controlled by governments, including those countries which, like mine, claimed to be liberal states promoting free speech and free enterprise.

I am certainly not an advocate of private media at any cost, and I support solutions such as the general approach in the United Kingdom, which allows competition between a strong BBC and viable private channels. However, I find that the current situation in Switzerland, where the federal state radio and television agency enjoys a nearly total monopoly, is unacceptable. The main consequence of the lack of competition is that, as in most state-run agencies, civil servants are in charge, which unavoidably leads to poor management, little creativity, a waste of resources and an arrogant bureaucratic state of mind.

As far as American sports were concerned, I never really enjoyed baseball. I was told that in order to really enjoy it, you had to be born in the USA and understand its cultural dimension by spending long evenings in stadiums while eating hotdogs and hamburgers and drinking sodas. I tried but never succeeded in really liking it. On the other hand, I immediately loved American football and the atmosphere of its games, including the cheerleaders and marching bands. I also enjoyed basketball games and was amazed by the sport's popularity.

During my year in California, I also had the opportunity to visit a number of interesting places and enjoy other new experiences like camping, riding horses in the desert, hiking through the Sequoia National Park, driving on US Highway One up to San Francisco, visiting the southern part of Arizona around Tucson and various trips to Palm Springs, Long Beach, Lake Arrowhead, San Juan Capistrano, Lake Tahoe, Sacramento and San Diego. I had the opportunity to visit several studios, including the Walt Disney Studio and, shortly after its opening in Anaheim, Disneyland, which was then considered a revolutionary theme park. At the time, the movie icons for the youth of California were James Dean and Natalie Wood, especially after the release of their 1955 coming-of-age film, 'Rebel Without a Cause'.

As the end of the school year neared, preparations for the graduation ceremony progressed. Once more, I was surprised. There was no possible comparison between the grandiose Pasadena Rose Bowl graduation ceremony and the short, rather casual function during which I had obtained my Swiss baccalauréat. I couldn't believe my eyes and ears at the seriousness and solemnity of the ceremony, with the music, choirs and formal speeches and addresses with most families in attendance.

As I was about to leave Southern California, possibly forever, my feelings were confused. I had regrets about leaving my foster family and many friends and sad to be leaving a wonderful country with a nearly perfect climate. On the other hand, I was looking forward to going back to the Old World and more particularly Lausanne, where I had my roots. As for my parents, I was curious to see whether they were over their problems. We had only communicated by mail, exchanging frequent letters. When I look back to those times and compare them with today's society of immediate, relentless communications, I am not convinced that we have yet mastered the incredible technological developments the world is undergoing.

Apart from having acquired some additional language skills, my Californian experience provided me with what I consider to be a strong basic knowledge of the USA and the American people, their mentality, their habits, their rituals, in short the American way of life.

My understanding of the American way of life was sometimes forced upon me through unexpected incidents. For instance, I remember that, on one special occasion, the entire student body was gathered in the main auditorium. The hall was absolutely packed, and an important politician, a US senator, had been invited to deliver a keynote speech. As was the case on a number of occasions, the gathering began with the entire audience rising to their feet and pledging allegiance to the US flag. It was a serious US ritual which I knew perfectly. Being a foreigner, I felt it was inappropriate for me to pledge allegiance to the US flag, so, out of respect, I would simply stand up and remain silent. All my friends understood, but on that day, I was in the front row of the auditorium. When everybody, including, of course, the senator, who was facing the audience from the stage, rose for the pledge, I stood up respectfully and listened politely. Of course, I didn't say anything and my right hand was not on my heart.

Almost immediately, I saw that the senator had noticed me and was giving me a very ominous stare. As soon as the pledge was over, the senator, in front of the entire student body, probably more than a thousand students, said that he'd noticed that some 'jerks' felt they could ignore the respect owed to their flag and country and ordered me to leave the auditorium. Without thinking, I reacted spontaneously and said very loudly that I was not a jerk, that I was a foreign exchange student from Switzerland and that my personal attitude was not disrespectful. He mumbled something which nobody understood, and I sat down.

The episode taught me two things, namely that Americans are particularly sensitive about anything patriotic and also that I had learned a lot about public speaking. Before my stay in California, should a comparable incident have happened to me in Switzerland, I wouldn't have dared to react in a similar way.

Living the American way of life for a whole year in a typical Southern Californian family in 1955-1956 was a unique experience. It provided me with an opportunity to see how genuinely the Americans are convinced that not only is the American way of life superior to any other, but that it should be adopted by the rest of the world.

After I graduated, it was time to prepare for departure and return to Switzerland. The AFS had organised a one-month trip by Greyhound bus through much of the USA. Many buses brought all the exchange students from around the country, all of which would arrive on the same day in Washington, D.C., where we would all be welcomed by the US Secretary of State, Foster Dulles, before going to New York and then back home.

The farewells with my US family were very emotional, but the sadness was eased by the excitement of the huge tour that awaited us. Our bus included about thirty foreign exchange students, all based in California, escorted by a couple of American teachers to act as chaperones, which turned out to be a challenge. Despite the fact that they had to cope with a group that had instantly recovered its non-American behaviour, including the rules of engagement between boys and girls, which resulted in a couple of torrid entanglements, they eventually survived graciously.

We were to make stopovers in various places throughout the US, where we would be assigned to spend two or three nights with local families, who would take us to various places of interest. The main stops were to be in Arizona, Utah, Nebraska, Indiana, Illinois, New York State, Pennsylvania and Virginia. During the trip, I experienced an unforeseen encounter. The various AFS chapters, which organised our local stays, had received the list of our names in advance. The plan was that boys should stay with local families with boys and girls with families with girls. When I left California, I gave up my American first name 'Frank' to become François again. Someone had, mistakenly, added a final 'e' to my name on the list, thus turning me into a girl with the name Françoise. The consequence was that at each stop, I was welcomed by girls, not boys, which had some amusing consequences. For instance, I never forgot the faces of my friends upon our arrival at Lincoln, Nebraska, when they saw me picked up by a gorgeous blonde girl driving the latest Cadillac convertible. Two days later, after she drove me back to the bus, I couldn't stop myself from giving deliberately vague answers to their probing questions.

In Washington, all the AFS students were reunited. We were given an inspiring speech by Senator J. William Fulbright, a leading liberal and internationalist, and Secretary of State John Foster Dulles gave a reception.

From Washington, all the buses drove to New York, where we were all directed to the army facilities of Governor's Island to spend the last couple of days of our stay in the US. With some friends, I rushed to Manhattan to get some last impressions. Once more, I was lucky to hear some great jazz. I remember the then famous drummer, Cozy Cole, playing on an elevated counter behind the barmen at a bar on Times Square. Shortly afterwards, most of us boarded a train for Québec where a small ship, the Arosa Kulm, was waiting on the Saint Lawrence River. It took us about ten days to sail back to Zeebrugge, Belgium.

When I disembarked, I had five dollars left in my wallet and was slightly concerned that I wouldn't be able to afford a train ticket to Switzerland. Fortunately, my father and one of my uncles were waiting for me on the pier. It was the end of a most extraordinary experience. It would take many years to decode all the messages I had received during that unique period of my life. For instance, during my rather insulated stay, I hadn't realised how violent and brutal American society can be. Nor did I notice how difficult life could be for the poor and for those who were still being discriminated against and left behind.

As is everyone else, Americans are only too aware of the many awful wars and genocides that have taken place around the world in modern times: Vietnam, Yugoslavia, Chechnya, Iraq, Afghanistan, Syria, Myanmar, Sudan, Uganda, to name just a few. Terrorism is still striking daily in the most horrendous ways; while we still remember its most dramatic strike, on 11th September 2001, in New York. The numerous multiple killings which have taken place in a number of public places and schools in the USA have sparked an encouraging awakening of public opinion, in particular among young Americans.

On the other hand, global terrorism has changed US policy in world affairs. Since 9/11, the US has developed a national security and anti-terrorism policy whose limits are disconcerting for the rest of the world. While everyone agrees that terrorism is a plague that should be eradicated, there is a growing apprehension that major powers, particularly the US, are seizing the opportunity of the fight against terrorism to seriously reduce individual rights and freedom.

For example, one of the most disappointing failures of President Obama's tenure as president was his inability to close Guantanamo Bay detainment camp. The camp is a permanent reminder that the US, when it considers it to be in its own interest, does not hesitate to grossly violate fundamental principles of law, justice and human rights. Guantanamo is a striking illustration of the worst aspect of US politics. Upon his inauguration, President Obama, who was undoubtedly deeply shocked by the existence of Guantanamo, signed an order to shut down the camp. Because of the unwillingness of his own legislature, he never managed to enforce his own presidential order. Of course, it came as no surprise that his successor, Donald Trump, decided to keep the detainment camp in operation.

I have now reached the conclusion that, though I still trust and love the American people, at least most of them, I have serious doubts about their government's policies and actions. Prompted by Trump's 'America First' policy and justified by the fight against terrorism, all political, military, financial, fiscal and legal actions undertaken by all branches of the US government under his administration were part of a vision that was a new form of imperialism.

Trump didn't rely on anyone's advice and only believed in his own judgement, or rather, his own instinct. There is no doubt that the 2016 presidential campaign in the US frightened Americans themselves. Veteran political observers considered that US politics descended to its lowest possible level. The primaries, the debates and the campaign were mostly disgusting and absurd. The amounts spent by the candidates were obscene. The insults exchanged were scandalous. The incompetence of the major political parties was shameful. Yet, after a campaign and an outcome that could have led to an immediate uprising and possible civil war in many other countries, the election was free and fair, and democracy has prevailed despite Trump's unpredictable and frightening outbursts.

His replacement, Joe Biden, notwithstanding Trump's infantile suggestions that the 2020 election was rigged, has swung the political pendulum back the other way. Even so, America is more divided than since the dark days of its 1860s civil war, and Trump and Trumpism are still alive and kicking.

Despite my personal fondness for the American people, it is really sad that many people from around the world don't feel comfortable when they arrive in the US. I must say that I sometimes share those uneasy feelings when I arrive in the States. I appreciate that things have changed drastically since 9/11. Nevertheless, I hope that the current situation will improve and that, as a foreigner, I will once again feel truly welcome, not only by my many personal friends, but by their nation.

5
Back to the Old World

Fifty years ago, the USA was the world's most formidable superpower. It had won the Second World War and imposed its Pax Americana on most of the world. It had funded the reconstruction of those European countries ruined by the war through the Marshall Plan, a major initiative worth $13 billion, worth $115 billion today.

At the end of the war, the Americans were acclaimed as heroes and saviours. Many people outside the US dreamed of moving to the States, getting a green card, and starting a new life; it was the American Dream, a hope that still inspires people to this day. As for the Americans themselves, they were proud of their achievements, considering themselves as the ultimate model of democracy, freedom and free enterprise in a nation blessed by God. Armed with that conviction, they soon led the free world in another fight, the Cold War against the Soviet Empire. Communism was an evil that should be fought at all costs.

Europe was divided by the Iron Curtain, beyond which the Soviets and its Warsaw Pact allies had amassed military forces which could have conquered the whole of Europe in a matter of days were it not for the protection of the United States through NATO. Interestingly, over time, the warmth felt for Americans faded. In many left-oriented intellectual circles, it became politically fashionable to criticise America and the Americans. Of course, US policy was far from innocent and, first and foremost, served the interests of the US economy. Thus, the relationship between Americans and Europeans gradually evolved into a complex mix of reciprocal mistrust, corrected by more positive feelings when and where they reflected mutual interests. This was illustrated by the Cuban Missile Crisis in October 1962, when Europe realised it was dependent upon the US for security.

As had been the case during the war, during the tensions of the Cold War, the Swiss tried to make profitable use of the situation for themselves and their sacred neutrality. The Swiss business community, in particular its major financial and industrial decision makers, made substantial efforts to develop relationships with both camps. The sympathies of the business establishment were clearly leaning towards the US but, as always, the official line was to remain neutral.

The world was changing very quickly around us, but just like during the war, most Swiss quietly carried on with their business without too much concern for the dramatic changes which were taking place elsewhere. We were comforted by the fact that most of the tourists visiting Switzerland, including US visitors, looked very pleased with what they ate: cheese and chocolate; bought: watches, and saw: gorgeous landscapes. We were once more rated as the cleanest and most prosperous country in the world. Security and safety were prevailing everywhere. Our trains ran on time and our other services, including our banks, could claim to be among the best, if not the best, in the world. As always, we pretended to be the modest citizens of a tiny country, but in our hearts, we felt that we were the best in the world.

It was in such a general climate and environment that, in October 1956, upon my return from California, I enrolled in the law faculty of the University of Lausanne which, at the time, enjoyed an enviable reputation. After having spent a year in a lively environment on a modern US campus, I then found myself in the ancient buildings of an academy which had been established in 1537. The buildings of the law school were distributed around the old city of Lausanne, a neighbourhood not without charm. However, apart from a very modest cafeteria and an equally modest secretariat, there were hardly any common premises. Nobody welcomed the new students, there were no counsellors or advisers of any kind. Students just had to show their qualifications to the secretariat, pay their tuition fees, which were very modest, and that was it.

I received a paper listing the courses which I was expected to attend and found that my first class was Roman law, to be held on a Thursday morning at 8:00am. Having found the appropriate classroom, I walked in on time and found myself sitting with about twenty students. The attendance was obviously low because a number of students were not bothering to attend courses. And the laws of Ancient Rome were not an attractive topic. It was the so-called 'academic freedom', under which, to qualify for exams, students were only required to produce a paper signed by the relevant professor certifying that they had attended the required course. While some professors were demanding and would only sign for students they knew had attended diligently, most of the professors couldn't have cared care less and blindly signed the papers presented to them. Of course, the real tests were the exams, which could be pretty tough.

So there I was, sitting on an old wooden bench in an ancient classroom, wondering what the hell I was doing there with a group of strangers. Why had I left California and why hadn't I applied for a scholarship to Stanford, that most wonderful university of clever and beautiful people? And why was I studying law? My mother had suggested that I study pharmacy, because she thought that the studies were not too arduous and that pharmacists were making a lot of money easily. I didn't have the slightest interest in studying pharmacy. In fact, I was rather tempted to study music and become the next Dave Brubeck, but I knew I didn't have the talent for that. So, eventually, I opted for law, in spite of the reservations expressed by my father, who was himself a distinguished lawyer.

Suddenly, an elderly, well-dressed, distinguished gentleman rushed into the classroom and all students stood up out of respect. He quickly nodded, sat at his desk and began by saying, "Before the summer vacation, I interrupted my course at the point where we were trying to determine whether the 'mancipatio' was a legal act having the effect of actually transferring title or merely serving as a guarantee for such transfer. This is a fundamental issue dividing the most reputable scholars of the world into two opposed schools of thought. And I shall demonstrate that, contrary to my Italian or German colleagues, who are entirely wrong, the 'mancipatio' is not an act of transfer of property but an act of guarantee, as is the case when the seller of a slave knocks such slave with a stick called 'festuca', thus guaranteeing the transfer of property…"

I was totally devastated by what I heard, which I still remember perfectly. I hadn't understood a word of it. The professor concerned was Philippe Meylan, a leading world authority on Roman law. I'd expected a few words of introduction, perhaps an outline of what the course would cover for the semester, what we would be expected to achieve or some advice about available textbook or other publication that we could read. Nothing!

The class lasted two hours that morning and was entirely dedicated to scholars' disputes over the mancipatio. At the end of the period, Professor Meylan rose from his chair, nodded and disappeared as quickly as he'd arrived. By then, I was terrified and giving serious thought to bringing my legal studies to an immediate end. Fortunately, I went to the cafeteria, where I met some old friends, who helped me reconnect with the real world, among which were a few charming young ladies. I missed the second period, making what I considered to be an appropriate discretionary use of my newly acquired academic freedom. My friends knew a nice students' café nearby, where the food was good, and so was the wine; life began to be enjoyable again. I subsequently began to understand the presentations by Professor Meylan. He really was a most distinguished scholar, and I even ended up liking his courses.

Having gradually adapted to my new condition, I found that the time spent at the University of Lausanne was becoming pleasant and stimulating. Like many other students, I took part time jobs to improve my finances. They included private tutoring for young schoolboys and girls, being a temporary high school teacher, swimming pool attendant and translator, where I could use my English.

Once I got used to the fact that there was no campus life and that the university was scattered throughout the city, my life as a student became quite enjoyable. I liked to go to the library of the law faculty, not only to study, but also because it was a daily meeting point for many students, including a number of attractive young ladies. From there, we would spend hours drinking coffee and putting the world to rights. I was living in an apartment in Lausanne which was rented by my parents, who only used it occasionally, and so I had an independent existence.

There was one activity which I really missed after John Muir: competitive swimming. There were no facilities for swimming at the university, and my former swimming club in Lausanne offered no training opportunities in winter. So, I quit training for competition and turned to other sports: skiing in winter and tennis in summer.

Thanks to my John Muir experience, I enlisted in the university student body activities, ending up, after a few years, as president of the Lausanne University student body association. The office, which of course was carried out on a volunteer basis, with the assistance of a part-time paid secretary, turned out to be demanding in terms of time, but fascinating. There were many political movements in Lausanne fighting for various causes. Some wanted more facilities and resources from the government to improve the university, while others advocated radical political changes such as salaries for all students. We had movements fighting hard for causes like the liberation of African colonies.

One of the most important movements at the time was the FLN, the Front de Libération Nationale, the movement that demanded Algerian independence from France, which was officially established in Switzerland. Its activities were supported by a strong Algerian student community in Lausanne, supported by many others in the Lausanne student body, but there were also students who backed conservative French opinion.

In California, all student body activities, admittedly at high school level, were non-political and exclusively dedicated to campus life. Lausanne University was another world, hosting an important community of student activists, located in the heart of Europe, which, ten years after the end of the war, was facing serious threats again. In the autumn of 1956, Soviet armoured divisions invaded Hungary and crushed an attempt by the Hungarian people to free themselves from communist rule. The repression was brutal, and we were all suddenly reminded that in a matter of hours, the Soviet army would be able to reach Austria and Switzerland.

The Cold War had reached a peak as refugees fled from Hungary, mainly through Austria. Mass demonstrations were organised with significant student participation, including in Lausanne. The explosive situation led to numerous heated political debates. Oddly enough, while there was no doubt that the Soviet invasion of Hungary should have been unanimously condemned, it was disturbing to note that there were many young people who tried to justify, if not the invasion itself, at least the values, not only of communism, but also of the Soviet system. I was shocked by the anti-American feelings expressed, not only by left wing extremists, but also by more moderate socialists and social democrats.

I remember that later, during the sixties, I had a few opportunities to visit East Germany and Czechoslovakia as a private tourist. Each time I crossed the Iron Curtain and left the West, I felt like I was entering another planet. Everything was so different, beginning with the attitude of the border guards – the Vopos, so-called People's police, who made you instantly feel guilty of some undefined yet serious crime. Such feeling would not leave you until you got back to the West.

6
Some Lessons in Life

One of the charms of the University of Lausanne was its cosmopolitan environment, which provided me with opportunities to meet many foreign students and get acquainted with their different cultures. It was also a valuable source of experiences which gave some lessons for life. Among the many memories, an apparently minor episode taught me a lesson which I've never forgotten. One of my friends was a Moroccan student. He was an intelligent, well-educated and kind young man with whom I would sometimes share a cup of coffee.

One day, shortly before the upcoming Easter vacation, he asked me whether I could lend him three hundred francs, a modest sum by today's standards but a significant amount for me at the time. He told me that because of temporary Moroccan currency restrictions, he had not received his monthly allowance and feared, as a North African, that if he didn't pay his rent for his room, he would be expelled. He promised that the money would be returned within two weeks at the latest. I withdrew the money from my savings and handed it to him, for which he thanked me profusely.

After two weeks, I hadn't got my money back. Some weeks later, I saw him by accident across a street, at which point, he ran away and disappeared. I never saw him again at the university. I then learned that he'd gone back to Morocco without leaving any address. I cursed him and blamed myself for being naive and decided that I had paid the price for an important lesson.

Seven or eight years later, I was a young lawyer in Lausanne when the office operator told me that there was a call for me from a friend from Morocco. I took the call, which was from my debtor. He immediately told me that he'd never forgotten his debt, that he was in Geneva with a Moroccan diplomatic delegation and that, if I would accept, he would like to come to Lausanne to reimburse me with interest and to invite me for lunch, which, of course, I accepted. During a most pleasant lunch, he explained to me that when he'd borrowed the money, he hadn't known that the delay in getting his allowance was in reality the beginning of a serious political crisis which caused him to rush back to Morocco.

I then reminded him that I'd seen him across a street, that he'd obviously seen me and had run away. So, I asked him why he hadn't come up to me to explain the situation. His answer totally surprised me, "Because I was mad at you!" Obviously, his answer led me to ask him to clarify. Once again his answer was not what I expected, "I was very mad at you, because you were a witness to the fact that I had failed to comply with my promise and thus lost face. You knew that I'd broken my word, and that was unacceptable to me. A man of honour can't be seen breaking his word. And I hated you for witnessing that. It was therefore out of the question for me to face you at the time. Until this day, I never came back to Switzerland. The best proof that what I am saying is most important is that after many years, I traced you, found you and that I can now fully regain my honour. I know that our origins are different. So are our cultures."

I had learned a lesson that I have never forgotten. In any society, men and women should be spared the humiliation of losing face. Since my Moroccan episode, I always try, in all circumstances, professional and private, to avoid causing any loss of face. This is particularly important in international negotiations. For instance, when dealing in Asia, in particular in Japan, questions should be formulated so as to avoid leading to a negative answer.

By the way, nearly sixty years later, my relationship with my long forgotten Moroccan friend was suddenly revived in 2016 when he wrote to me after seeing me on a television programme broadcast in Morocco. We started corresponding and exchanging pictures from the old days. Better late than never!

After a couple of years at the University, I felt the need to begin a more active professional life. At the age of twenty, I had met a very attractive Scandinavian girl with whom I fell in love. She had been studying in Lausanne and, rather than returning to Sweden, decided to stay, a decision founded on our relationship. Being intelligent and qualified, she found a job as personal assistant to a well-known industrialist. At the same time, I was deeply involved in my studies and student body activities. She had entered into another world, the corporate world. Over the months, our relationship deteriorated. I was suggesting student weekends in cheap youth hostels and travelling by train. However, her boss drove a Jaguar and asked her to accompany him to London or Paris and stay in five-star hotels. It was bound to happen; they became lovers and our relationship was over.

I was sad, frustrated and angry, thinking that if I'd had enough money to match some of my competitor's generosity, I wouldn't have lost her. As a result, I decided to stop spending weeks and months on legal studies. I couldn't have cared less about the mancipatio, nor about student affairs. It was time to stop what appeared to me to be a futile pursuit and to get a job. I came across an ad published by Procter & Gamble offering a very interesting chance for a career beginning with training in marketing. The job was based at Procter's international headquarters in Geneva, an ideal location, and the initial salary was very attractive, turning a relatively modest student into a promising future executive. I applied and got through all the initial tests, which resulted in an interview with a fairly high executive, Brian F. Dennis, an impressive personality I will never forget.

He welcomed me into his office and told me that based on my file and the results of my tests, there was a high probability that I would be offered the job. I tried to hide any emotion as he went on to ask me why I wanted to interrupt my studies. I told him my reasons. He replied that he understood me perfectly and added that, if I got the job, I could expect a nice career with P&G. Then, quite suddenly, in a very smooth and quiet tone he suggested that it would be the worst mistake for me to abandon my studies. Without any further discussion, he told me to go home and think the whole matter over during the upcoming weekend. I was upset by the sudden change, not in tone, but in substance, and wanted to discuss it further. He smiled and gently dismissed me, advising me to think really seriously and to call him back on Monday morning, at which time the job would probably be mine if I hadn't followed his advice.

I went back to Lausanne and had a difficult weekend. The man had impressed me; he was obviously a strong executive and yet he had treated me as if I were his son. I felt confused, I was so close to achieving something way beyond studying, and the very person who was ready to grant me what I was hoping for was telling me to give up. After a very long weekend, on Monday morning, I rang Dennis and told him that I was withdrawing my application and continuing my studies. He said that he was happy that I'd made the right decision. I never met him again.

The episode may appear trivial, but it was one of those very few decisive moments which determined the course of my life. To that point, I had gone through two other similarly pivotal moments. The first was my decision in 1955 to 'go West' to California for a year. The second was my choice, a year later, to go back to Europe and give up my plan to apply to Stanford or any other US university. I never had any regrets over those preferences. Life is a succession of crossroads. Sometimes you have a glimpse of what lies ahead, sometimes not. It then often becomes a matter of luck or fate. However, chances are not distributed fairly and whatever our circumstances may be, there are people who somehow know how to grasp whatever opportunities are offered to them, and others who are totally unable to seize them.

As for me, I gave up any hope of becoming the future CEO of Procter & Gamble and went back to law school and my student routine, which was soon to include a new, mandatory activity, namely serving my country in the Swiss army. By the way, the love that I lost had taught me another lesson in life, and although she and I went our separate ways, we became and remained

7
Sweden

While I was going through the agony of writing my thesis for my doctorate, and as I had no more classes to attend, I worked almost full-time at an accounting and auditing firm which had hired me. It was an excellent opportunity to acquire practical experience in an area about which I had only a limited knowledge.

My first assignment was part of the auditing of a mountain restaurant in a ski resort. More specifically, I was put in charge of a part of its inventory, namely counting all plates, cups, spoons, knives, forks and including the entire kitchen equipment, and the contents of the cellar. At the end of two hectic days, after filling out various forms and reports, I realised that I knew nothing. Being a future doctor at law was one thing, becoming an auditor was quite another. After that first assignment, I got the opportunity to be involved in various other aspects of the auditing profession, which helped me be more practical in my academic work, which I was to complete in 1964.

During that time, I was dividing my hours between my daily audit job, my work on my thesis and my social life in Lausanne. I began thinking of a professional future. As I had always been very interested in international relations and was longing for more travelling abroad, I considered becoming a diplomat and applying for a position in the Swiss Foreign Affairs Department. I went to Bern, the Swiss capital, where I was received by an officer in charge of human relations at the department. The office was sinister, and so was the man. He gave me such a stern and boring description of a possible career in the Swiss foreign service that I abandoned any ambition of joining any form of federal public service. I had to look for other options. Unfortunately, my passion for jazz had to be put aside as it was obvious that I didn't have the talent to pursue a life as a professional musician.

Remembering my nearly successful earlier attempt with Procter & Gamble and just as I was considering opportunities in the corporate world, a totally unexpected opportunity came up. During coffee breaks at the university cafeteria, I ran into a very nice Swedish man who was studying French. He was in his forties, very friendly and eager to get to know younger students and was a great art collector and friend to many major artists. During our conversations, he told me that he had left Sweden and moved to Switzerland with his young wife and four children for tax reasons. He told me that his tax case in Sweden was being handled by a famous Swedish lawyer, who was looking for a young legal assistant who spoke good English and was capable of assisting on international legal matters involving, in particular, Swiss law.

He asked me if I would be interested, in which case he would arrange a meeting with his lawyer on the occasion of his next visit. I liked the idea, not only from a professional standpoint, but also because, at the time, I was fond of a Swedish girl, not the one I mentioned earlier, but one who had recently left Lausanne for Stockholm. So I agreed to meet the lawyer and we had a meeting during a train ride through Switzerland, at the end of which I agreed to join his Swedish law firm for an initial period of several months. It was a decision, just like my year in California, that would have a decisive influence on my entire life.

In June 1963, I joined Advokatfirman Henning Sjöström in Stockholm, a highly reputable firm that is still active to this day. Henning Sjöström was one of the most impressive personalities I have ever met. He was forty years old and one of the most famous lawyers in Sweden, mainly specialising in high-profile criminal litigation. He was also one of the most glamorous Swedish personalities, getting daily coverage by the media, in particular in their people's sections. He was handsome and fit, had been a national javelin champion and was still practising several sports, including tennis and boxing. His physical stature was impressive. His extraordinary blue eyes were piercing and his voice was loud and clear; he was even a talented opera singer. He had a fantastic network of clients and friends, but he also had enemies, especially among colleagues who envied him. His style and atypical methods drew criticisms from various sides, but he didn't care and would never hesitate to accept apparently desperate or unpopular cases.

My first working day with Sjöström was indeed atypical. I arrived in Stockholm by car, having had the opportunity to convey a friend's car from Lausanne to Sweden. The trip had lasted several days in a hot summer, and I reported to Sjöström's offices when I arrived. It was late afternoon, the weather was gorgeous and the location superb. The office address was Strandvägen, a prime location on the city's harbour where ships and ferries plied their trade, and I had been told that I would be housed in a bedroom which was part of the office. I was so excited, what an adventure.

Tired after a long drive, I was welcomed by a receptionist who showed me to my room and told me that Mr. Sjöström was out of town until the next day but that I was expected to begin my work immediately and meet with a professor of law who was waiting for me. It was seven in the evening, and I was a bit surprised to be put to work immediately. I had hoped to take a shower and have my first stroll in Stockholm. As is the case in midsummer in Sweden, the sun was still bright and the air hot and work was the last thing on my mind. The professor I met was a well-known Swedish academician who specialised in financial law. He'd been asked by Sjöström for a legal opinion on a matter which involved a number of international issues and some research on Swiss law. The professor explained the case to me and gave me a file to study immediately, expecting that after a couple of hours, we would discuss the issues together.

I will never forget that first night in Stockholm. I sat in a beautiful office, glimpsed a unique sunset at around midnight, with an equally striking sunrise at about 2:00am, while the professor and I reviewed the complex arguments for a draft legal opinion. We worked until 5:00am, at which point I fell on my bed totally exhausted. I must say that at that point, I began to wonder whether I'd made a wise choice in going to Stockholm.

Everything changed the next day with the arrival of Sjöström himself. He called me to his office and welcomed me warmly and asked me about my first assignment. When I told him about my surprise, he laughed loudly, a response I was to hear so many times from then on, and told me that the professor, who was a legal genius, was just supposed to meet me and hand me the file which could be discussed later.

Sjöström himself was very friendly and I immediately warmed to him. He showed me around and introduced me to his staff. His main legal associate at the time, Leif Silbersky, who later became a famous criminal lawyer in his own right, was away on leave for some time and I was to use his office. It was a beautiful room with a splendid view overlooking the harbour in which cruised majestic ocean liners and huge commercial vessels. The firm's offices served both as a workplace and as residence for Sjöström and his wife when they were in town. They also rented a beautiful manor by a lake located south of Stockholm, less than one hour away by car or train. Like many Swedes, the Sjöströms split their time between town and country. Apart from my guest room in the Stockholm apartment, a small wooden cabin on the country property was at my disposal so that I could live a typically affluent Swedish life. Depending upon my work or private agenda, I could commute by train or ride in Sjöström's own car, a Ford Thunderbird and later a Rolls-Royce, which made my life particularly comfortable. From day one, I felt part of the Sjöström family. He was about fifteen years older than me and always treated me like a young brother.

The workload assigned to me was heavy, but varied and interesting, especially for a young beginner. While Sjöström was focused on his high-profile criminal cases, the rest of his staff were handling the other files, which were typical of a general law practice. His notoriety, which was enhanced every week in the Swedish media, brought him a number of celebrity clients, mainly movie stars, authors, musicians and other artists. With his wife, he entertained them, at his country place. As part of the family, I was at many of the parties which often lasted the entire weekend.

At that time, the Swedish film industry was universally celebrated. It was the time of Ingmar Bergman and all the actors linked to him. Many of them used to visit the Sjöströms, which provided me with unique opportunities to meet them on a personal level. It was fascinating for a young foreign lawyer to enter a world which was totally new and stimulating. Some of the most popular events at the Sjöström house were midsummer's eve, a huge celebration in Sweden, and 7th August, the opening night of the crayfish fishing season. To this day, I still maintain close ties with the friends I met then.

At the office, a number of the cases I was asked to assist with were claims for substantial damages resulting from a drug named thalidomide, taken by pregnant women, which caused severe and irreparable physical birth defects to their children. The cases were handled together with several high-profile international lawyers in the United States, the United Kingdom and Germany. Thus, I was fortunate to be in touch with law firms all over the world, and to have the opportunity to meet several interesting people.

The work at Sjöström's was so interesting and challenging that after a few weeks, without realising it, I had become a young lawyer. Not only that, I discovered that I loved it. Sweden was a very special country, a unique blend of tradition and conservatism, mixed with very progressive political and social ideas. At the time, in Sweden, as in the United Kingdom, cars drove on the lefthand side of the road, which was changed overnight in 1967, an incredible achievement.

At the beginning of the dark and cold season that inevitably follows summer and autumn, I decided to return to Switzerland, where the completion of my doctor's degree was awaiting. Thankfully, Sjöström suggested that I could carry out some of my work for him from Switzerland, which I did. We also agreed that our co-operation would continue and that I would return to his Stockholm office after a few months, which I also did. In fact, the agreement was extended until, having obtained my doctoral degree, I formally enlisted as an intern in Lausanne to prepare for my admission to the bar, which happened in early 1967.

After my admittance to the bar, my new status as an independent lawyer in Lausanne changed my status with Stockholm, but a new relationship developed based on friendship. When Sjöström died in October 2011, a few months before his ninetieth birthday, I felt a deep loss. He had been an older brother, a mentor, a colleague and a close friend. His wonderful, intelligent and beautiful second wife, Kerstin, who was also a practising lawyer, and my family are still good friends.

As I think back to those years, there is no doubt in my mind that my decision to become an independent lawyer was directly inspired by my Swedish experience. Previously, I had many doubts about my future. My father had always discouraged me from becoming a lawyer. I don't think he ever really enjoyed his practice which, although well considered, remained essentially the general practice of a local Swiss lawyer in a small city, Lausanne. However, I was fascinated by the profession, and I thought, perhaps foolishly, that it could be as exciting in Lausanne as it was in Stockholm.

As I began work in Lausanne, I already had a few Swedish clients who wanted to settle in Switzerland, and I also had mandates in Europe for Sjöström and some of his clients. That's how, thanks to, and in spite of, my father, to the American Field Service and California, to a wise Procter & Gamble executive and to Sjöström, I became, and still am today, a happy independent lawyer in a successful firm, instead of having been a dull diplomat or a mediocre jazz pianist.

8
A Lausanne Lawyer

Having received my doctor's degree in late 1964, I married my wife, Alba, a very talented painter, in September 1966. We have had two wonderful daughters together and, fortunately, she still puts up with me.

I completed my internship and was admitted to the Bar of the Canton de Vaud and of Switzerland in early 1967. In spite of the reluctance of my father, who was by then sixty-eight-years old, I thought that joining a family firm which had been established in 1885, was a great opportunity. Its offices, an apartment in an old building in the heart of Lausanne, had a modest staff of three lawyers and three secretaries and, to this day, I am still grateful to my late father for his support and understanding.

I began with a few clients of my own, mainly Swedes in Switzerland, and I also handled a few international cases for Sjöström and his firm. There were also various cases typical of any law firm: private or public litigation, criminal defence, divorces, administrative issues, wills and probate. Because the Swiss Supreme Federal Court was established in Lausanne, and not in Bern, the Swiss capital, our firm also specialised in international arbitration and gave assistance to foreign individuals or companies hoping to settle in Switzerland. This provided very interesting opportunities for me. A prerequisite was an excellent command of English, which I could claim, and which was not as common as it is now.

My first international case was, thanks to my command of English, as a personal assistant and translator for the Swiss chairman of an international arbitration tribunal in charge of the resolution of a major dispute between some major contractors and the Egyptian government. The issues were about the huge costs of the relocation of the Ancient Egyptian temples at Abu Simbel in order to make way for the construction of the Aswan Dam and the creation of Lake Nasser. The stakes were high, the case was fascinating, and it gave me my first real access to the institutionalised world of international arbitration. I quickly discovered that, even to this day, it is a very select club. The rules of procedure were simple, flexible and tailored for the nature of the case, in accordance with the wishes of the parties and their advocates, and would, hopefully, be quicker and cheaper than going before state courts.

Today, in many cases, international arbitration does not comply with its original purpose. It has become far too costly for the parties concerned, and the files are huge and consist of thousands of submissions, documents, endless exhibits and unnecessarily long hearings. The whole system has, in fact, been developed for the benefit of 'the club' and its members, and not in the interests of the parties.

Although the main headquarters of international arbitrators are now in London and Paris, with a number of other major cities like Stockholm, Hongkong and New York trying to welcome club members, Lausanne is currently out of the mainstream of international arbitration. However, it has recently regained a role on the international arbitration scene thanks to the Court of Arbitration for Sport (CAS) , which established its permanent headquarters in Lausanne in 1984. Conceived by Juan Antonio Samaranch, President of the International Olympic Committee, CAS currently handles hundreds of sports-related disputes every year including disciplinary appeals in issues like doping and in commercial disputes in several sports. Originally linked to the IOC, CAS is now independent, both organisationally and financially.

In the late sixties, our firm was busy assisting foreign individuals and firms, including multinationals, to settle in or around Lausanne. The Lake Geneva area is beautiful and has always attracted foreigners, among them film stars, authors, composers and musicians. What was also decisive in attracting the rich and famous was Switzerland's favourable tax levels, allowing non-working foreign residents to be taxed, not on their actual assets and income, but on the basis of so-called 'presumed living expenses', an amount which should more or less correspond to not less than five times their rent.

Our firm did assist a number of foreign celebrities, like Charlie Chaplin, Peter Ustinov, Graham Greene and Coco Chanel. We would help them obtain the required resident's card, and other legal issues like the purchase of houses and the hiring of staff. As far as I was concerned, I brought a number of Swedish and Danish clients whom I'd known in Stockholm.

Times have since changed significantly and, under pressure from a number of foreign governments and international institutions, Switzerland is progressively renouncing most of its laws and regulations that provide special tax and administrative status to foreign investors or immigrants.

However, attacks on Switzerland's secretive banking practices are both logical and understandable. The reaction of the Swiss authorities is rather weak and reveals a lack of vision. There is no clearly defined policy, neither in parliament nor in the executive branch of government, the Swiss Federal Council. The general motto seems to be no more than to try and convince the foreign negotiators of Swiss good will, which is obviously naive. As a consequence, Switzerland's credibility is currently very low, both inside and outside the country.

The current situation in terms of Switzerland's attitude toward the rest of the world has become a matter of most serious concern, and I am not very optimistic about any short-term improvements. What Switzerland currently lacks is serious, responsible, high-level leadership. We have honest administrators, but we need much stronger leaders. Unfortunately, Swiss democracy is such that it favours mediocracy. And there is worse. In early February 2014, the Swiss people, with a majority of less than 51%, adopted a new constitutional amendment restricting immigration into the country. The result of the vote is that the Swiss authorities are even weaker, inasmuch as Switzerland will be unable to comply with some of its international obligations, in particular regarding the free circulation of people. We are in a difficult political time. My hope is that my country will bounce back. Time will tell.

Apart from my main areas of practice, like most lawyers engaged in general practice, I also did my share of courtroom work. I took up a few criminal defences and also handled civil cases. While I liked the atmosphere in the courtroom and enjoyed arguing and pleading my cases, I always, or nearly always, felt a sense of frustration for my clients. Any case or dispute which ends up in a court is the end result of a failure which should have been avoided with a better outcome for the parties. Fear of the judge is the beginning of wisdom. That is a fundamental principle in which I strongly believe.

Apart from my local practice, I was handling a number of international cases at a distance for Sjöström. One of them was a very original legal situation, that of Radio Syd, a radio station located on a ship situated in the Baltic Sea beyond any territorial waters. At the time, any form of radio advertising was prohibited in Sweden and

Denmark. However, the owner of Radio Syd, an entrepreneurial woman with a strong personality, had found a creative way of broadcasting highly popular programmes, including a lot of highly paid commercials. Our task was to assist Radio Syd in acquiring a legal status that would protect it from various forms of harassment by the Swedish authorities.

I remember very well sailing across a stormy Baltic Sea on a dark and cold winter night. But when I reached the ship, the contrast was striking. Lighting, music, warmth, a great Scandinavian buffet and excellent drinks had been prepared, and I was welcomed by an enthusiastic young team. We managed to conceive an appropriate legal status for this very unusual enterprise. However, the Swedish government applied very high international political pressures which, if I remember correctly, resulted in the enforcement of an international convention regulating radio frequencies. I believe that the ship was eventually moved to The Gambia.

In parallel to my legal work, I undertook some volunteer community activities, one of which that kept me rather busy, was to serve as president of the Vaud chapter of the Automobile Club of Switzerland (ACS), which numbered more than six thousand members, some of whom were quite active. I was elected at the age of thirty, becoming the youngest Swiss president and decided that I would retire at the age of forty, which I did, then becoming the youngest retiree. During those ten years, I developed a substantial network of private and public relationships, including politicians.

A substantial part of my role was to lobby for car owners and drivers while, because the ACS was the governing body for the sport, another covered motor racing. One of my most exciting experiences was, because circuit races were prohibited in Switzerland, to preside over the organisation of a Formula 1 Grand Prix in Dijon, France. It was my first substantial involvement in sports administration and granted me access to the unique F1 environment. I ended up being appointed advocate to the Grand Prix Drivers' Association when it was chaired by the famous French Ferrari driver, Didier Pironi, who became a good friend of mine. Didier was a doubly unlucky man. In 1982, when leading the F1 drivers' championship by thirty-nine points, he crashed into the back of Derek Daly's Williams' car.

He nearly lost both legs in the accident and never drove in F1 again. However, four years later, he'd recovered sufficiently to begin a career in offshore powerboat racing. Then tragedy struck again. On

23rd August 1987, Pironi was killed in an accident in the Needles Trophy Race near the Isle of Wight, in England, that also took the life of his two crew members: journalist Bernard Giroux and his old friend Jean-Claude Guénard. Their boat, Colibri 4, rode over a large wave caused by an oil tanker, causing the boat to flip over. Pironi was just thirty-five years old.

9
The International Olympic Committee

My first involvement with the Olympic Movement and with the International Olympic Committee happened in the most unexpected and surprising circumstances. One late afternoon, at the end of November 1979, I received a phone call from a courteous but somewhat aloof woman who introduced herself as Madame Monique Berlioux, a former French swimming champion, Olympian and Director of the IOC. I had probably heard her name before, but at that moment, it didn't mean much to me.

She explained to me that she had been advised by the IOC's usual international legal advisers that it was necessary to call on a local Lausanne lawyer for a minor procedural matter. She added that my name had been mentioned by one of their advisers and asked me if I would be prepared to take care of the small problem. Her tone was quite polite but clearly hinted that as a local lawyer, I was not playing in the same league as the IOC's usual international lawyers.

I was, of course, intrigued and told her that if the matter was within my competence and if there was no conflict of interests, I would be prepared to accept. She then very briefly told me that all I would have to do was send a letter, which had already been drafted, to a Lausanne judge, informing him that the IOC was availing itself of its immunity of jurisdiction. As the matter was somehow urgent, she proposed to send her personal assistant to visit me and bring me the entire file, to which I agreed.

At the end of the day, the said assistant arrived at my office with a file from which he extracted the draft letter to the judge. I then discovered that the IOC was being sued in the Lausanne Civil Court by the IOC member for Taipei, Mr. Henry Hsu, and by the National Olympic Committee (NOC) of Taipei. Both parties considered that two recent decisions by the IOC should be declared null and void, namely a decision to recognise as China's National Olympic Committee the organisation established by the People's Republic of China on the mainland and a decision ordering the Taipei based organisation to change its name into Chinese Taipei Olympic Committee.

I should add at this point that the island of Taipei, now called Taiwan, was and is the home of the Republic of China, a country which became independent of communist mainland China at the end of China's civil war in 1949. Needless to say, mainland China claims that Taiwan is a part of the People's Republic.

My instructions were to explain to the court that it had no jurisdiction over the IOC, which, as an international organisation enjoyed an immunity of jurisdiction in Switzerland. I must confess that at that moment, I had no idea about the IOC's legal status. Berlioux's assistant was very insistent. I read the draft letter which I was supposed to sign, and it looked convincing. In support of the IOC's position, the assistant handed me a copy of the Olympic Charter, which contained a rule specifying that the IOC was an association established pursuant to international law.

I thanked the assistant and informed him that I would need to undertake some research to check the legal basis of the claim for immunity and that I would be ready the next day. He was not best pleased and obviously impatient. However, reluctantly, he agreed and left. The next morning, I looked for legal material relating to the IOC's status and found nothing. Having studied the Olympic Charter, a document which has since then occupied a significant place in my life, and reached the conclusion that it was a purely private instrument, I called up the Swiss Foreign Affairs Department in Bern, where one of my best friends was in a senior position in charge of international law. The department kept an updated list of all organisations, embassies and other agencies which were entitled to any form of immunity. The IOC was not mentioned anywhere.

Having completed my research, I called Berlioux the next day and told her that I had reached the unavoidable conclusion that the IOC was, like thousands of other Swiss groups, charities or clubs of any kind, a private entity characterised as an 'association' governed by Swiss civil law. It was not entitled to any form of immunity, contrary to the apparent opinions of her international advisers. The competent court for both claims was undoubtedly the Lausanne Civil Court. As a consequence, I explained that I would not send a letter claiming a non-existent immunity, as that would make fools of both me and the IOC. Finally, I advised that the IOC should actively prepare its defence on the merits.

Berlioux was shocked to find out that the IOC was not what it claimed to be, and worse, that it was nothing more a private club and told me that she would have to think the matter over. I assumed that meant that she was going to ask for a second opinion, which was perfectly understandable. One or two days later, she called me back and asked me if I was still willing to assist the IOC and prepare a defence on the merits. I accepted and this was the very beginning of a relationship with the IOC which, after a number of unexpected but fascinating developments, is still continuing today.

As soon as I received the entire file, I found out that the pending procedure in Lausanne was the judicial expression of what appeared to be a major political dispute into which the IOC had become embroiled, that is, the long-running dispute between two 'Chinas' over the sovereignty of Taipei (Taiwan). Of course, Beijing was delighted to be acknowledged by the IOC, and to have its National Olympic Committee recognised. But it would not accept that there could be a second organisation, based in Taipei, claiming that it represented China. The IOC's decision to acknowledge mainland China's People's Republic was a major political blow to Taipei. Not only that, Taipei was directed by the IOC to give up its historical name and its own anthem and flag. Taipei felt betrayed by the IOC, considering that it was violating the Olympic Charter and moving away from its mission by making purely political decisions.

Taipei and its IOC member, Henry Hsu, had launched a formidable legal battle. They had set up a very strong legal team, headed in Lausanne by a most distinguished lawyer, Alain Wurzburger, who later had an impressive career as a member of the Swiss Supreme Court. For its part, the IOC found itself in a most uncomfortable situation as defendant in a case caused by a bold decision reached through a postal ballot of its member, which was not the most appropriate way to come to a decision on a major geopolitical issue.

In fact, the recognition of Beijing made a lot of sense. The Olympic Movement and the international sports community couldn't ignore the People's Republic any longer. After all, its population had just topped one billion people! It was also time to deal with the fiction that Taipei represented the whole of China, when at the time its population was less than eighteen million. On the other hand, the new status imposed on Taipei by the IOC was viewed by many as representing an excessive concession to Beijing. Subsequent events had left the IOC, with a very narrow margin for finding a legally and politically acceptable solution.

In early December 1979, as an opening gambit in their legal battle, Henry Hsu and Taipei requested that the Lausanne judge grant an injunction authorising the Taipei delegation to participate in the impending Olympic Winter Games in Lake Placid with its own flag. But, for procedural reasons, I was fortunate in being able to report to Berlioux and to Lord Killanin, the IOC president, that the Swiss courts would not cause a problem for the IOC at the Lake Placid Games. However, the legal battle was also engaged in the US courts, where a New York State Supreme Court justice ruled that the delegation from Taiwan could use its own name, flag and anthem at Lake Placid. The ruling was stayed by The State Supreme Court's Appellate Division.

While the courtroom battle was pretty fierce, there were also some more relaxed moments. For instance, during a public hearing in Lausanne, the judge ordered both sides to show him the respective flags of Taipei, the Republic of China, and of the People's Republic of China. My opponent immediately displayed a copy of Taipei's flag, in A4 format, which was the standard size for documents produced in court. In my own file was an A4 envelope which had been delivered to me the night before by the Chinese embassy and which contained the country's red flag. Having very little time to prepare the hearing, I just had time for a quick look in the envelope and could see that the flag was clearly red.

When I actually opened the envelope for the first time in front of the judge and a packed courtroom, I realised that the flag was made of extraordinarily thin silk and that its size far exceeded the standard A4 format. Much to the amusement of everyone, including the judge, like a magician, I kept pulling more and more silk out of the envelope until a huge red flag almost filled the entire courtroom.

Both the Swiss and US rulings, together with the departure from the Lake Placid Games of the Taipei delegation, allowed the IOC to gain some time. But they were provisional decisions which had not ruled on the merits. Fortunately for the IOC, the next date was the 1980 Summer Games, which were going to be held in Moscow. There was little fear of enforcement in the Soviet Union of a court decision which would have been unfavourable to the IOC and to Beijing, even if the latter was not officially a party to the dispute.

Before the Moscow Games in July 1980, the case went on in Lausanne through various arguments and submissions. It seemed clear to me that the Lausanne judge, while remaining impartial, would favour a negotiated settlement and I reported that to Killanin and Berlioux.

On 15th July 1980, IOC member in Spain, Juan Antonio Samaranch replaced Lord Killanin as president of the IOC and immediately decided that finding a solution to the 'Two Chinas' dilemma would be one of his priorities. As soon as he arrived in Lausanne, he asked me to meet him so that I could give him a full report on all aspects of the case. Having listened very carefully, he told me that he was going to look for a settlement. While appearing flexible on his approach towards the Taipei NOC, he was adamant that an IOC member should never be allowed to sue the IOC.

Samaranch was a true diplomat and had all the skills and experience needed to negotiate his way through the nuances of international politics. He had served in political positions in Spain under General Franco and in his country's new democratic government. When democratic Spain decided to establish diplomatic ties with the USSR, its first ambassador to Moscow was Samaranch. More importantly, the contrast between him and his predecessor at the head of the IOC was striking. Killanin's style was like that of an Irish gentleman's club chairman, whereas Samaranch was a politician. He was also passionate about sport, which he knew inside out, and leading the Olympic Movement was his life's ambition. He would dedicate himself to it for the rest of his life.

Samaranch knew that the 'Two China' dispute had to be resolved quickly. He couldn't contemplate a global Olympic Movement without the full participation and support of the whole of China. But he was also smart enough to seek a solution which would not exclude the Taipei NOC. So he began to negotiate personally with all involved. During the subsequent meetings, he knew how to be persuasive and firm; yet he also knew how to listen. Finally, after many months of meetings and discussions, he managed to outline a final settlement. My instructions from him were to draft the shortest possible settlement, and to convince my opponent that it had to be the solution. And so, after some lengthy arm-twisting, we had an agreement.

The settlement, which is still in force today, was signed on 23rd March 1981 by Samaranch on behalf of the IOC and by the president of the newly named Chinese Taipei Olympic Committee (CTOC), Shen Chia-Ming. The substance of the settlement is included in four short articles, of which the first two concern the name, Chinese Taipei Olympic Committee (CTOC), and its new flag and emblem. The third article confirms the CTOC's right to participate in all future Olympic Games with the same status and rights as every other NOC. The fourth and final clause specifies that the IOC will assist the CTOC in its applications for membership or reinstatement in the various international federations within the Olympic Movement.. The settlement agreement was never communicated to the court and remained confidential. It has always been strictly observed by all three interested parties, Taipei, Beijing and the IOC. It is remarkable to observe that as I am writing these lines, the 1983 settlement is still in force. This is due to the exceptional diplomatic skills of Samaranch, to his patience and understanding of Chinese culture and to his insistence on using a very succinct text for the agreement.

Seven years later, on the occasion of the Opening Ceremony of the 1990 Asian Games in Beijing, I saw the entire packed arena rise and give an extraordinary standing ovation to the Taipei delegation when they walked into the stadium behind their flag, as included in the settlement which I had drafted. I must confess that at that moment, I felt a profound sense of pride. For once, as a lawyer, I could witness the positive outcome of a major case in which I had played a constructive part. That feeling was repeated on a number of other occasions, in particular in Beijing eighteen years later, during the extraordinary Opening Ceremony of the 2008 Olympic Games in the Bird's Nest Stadium when the team from what was by then called Taiwan made its entry. My involvement in the Two Chinas case from late 1979 until March 1983 taught me five main lessons.

First of all, I learned that in late 1979, the IOC was operating without clear knowledge of its own legal status. I was stunned to discover that the senior IOC members and its administration believed that the IOC was somehow above national laws and that, by self-proclaiming itself as subject to international law, it enjoyed a special legal status.

Nobody had seriously checked, and the general impression was that there could be no legal issue with the IOC's legal status because it had been in existence since 1894 as a highly distinguished club, unconcerned by trivial matters like is own legal standing. Amazingly, that arrogant stance was even shared by distinguished lawyers who were themselves members of the IOC and on its Juridical Commission. When I first became aware of that rather unusual legal position, little did I realise that I would be actively involved in the review of most major legal IOC instruments and rules, and later on, with the entire revision of the Olympic Charter, a task in which I was still involved in 2014.

The second lesson I learned was that while the IOC's business was sport and not politics, politics constantly intruded on national and international sport. Thus, it was inevitable that responsible sports leaders had to deal with the world of politics and to stay close to governments in order to ensure the protection of sport and the athletes of the world.

The third lesson concerned the personality of Samaranch. I soon discovered that he was constantly thinking ahead and trying to anticipate the future. While fully involved in a specific problem yet unsolved, he was already considering what consequences could result from any solution. His attitude was always to try to transform a crisis into an opportunity. A typical example of such sense of his foresight was to be found in the circumstances surrounding the establishment of the Court of Arbitration for Sport (CAS)and the World Anti-Doping Agency (WADA). Both were created from Samaranch's initiatives and will be the subject of chapters later in this book. Another example was Samaranch's permanent quest for an upgrading of the political and legal status of the IOC through its recognition by governments and the international community as a true international organisation rather than being seen as a private club.

The fourth lesson was that a very important political settlement can be embodied in a very short written instrument. In the Two Chinas case, my opponents' lawyer, Alain Wurzburger, and I managed to convince our respective clients to accept that the text of the settlement be strictly limited to the absolutely essential clauses.

The fifth and most important lesson concerned China and the Chinese people: their obstinacy, their patience, their consistency, their intelligence and ultimately, their wisdom. Nowadays, as the United States and Russia are clearly embarked upon a new, extremely dangerous cold war, and as the European Union is painfully striving to develop convincing projects and fails to reach unity, China appears to be progressing and increasing its global influence in a most efficient way, in particular through substantial investments in key sectors of the world economy. Facing Europe's decadence and America's derailment, China is steadily moving towards becoming tomorrow's world leader. True, it is facing some problems of its own, is becoming distinctly bellicose and is guilty of very serious human rights issues. I nevertheless consider that all young people should prepare themselves in terms of education, culture, psychology and knowledge of China. I hope that I will be able to convince my grandchildren to travel to China to try and understand Chinese people and even learn Chinese.

10
The Court of Arbitration for Sport

The Court of Arbitration for Sport (CAS) was established in Lausanne. In October 1980, three months after Samaranch's election as IOC president, he summoned me to his office. He told me that he wanted to avoid the repetition of legal actions filed by IOC members or NOCs against the IOC. He asked me whether there were any options. I told him that an appropriate alternative might be an institutional form of arbitration dedicated to sport. I briefly explained to him the differences between arbitration tribunals and ordinary courts and mentioned the example of the Court of Arbitration of the International Chamber of Commerce (ICC). He was interested by my suggestion and asked me to prepare a report and to include a proposal.

On 27th October 1980, I sent him an eleven-page letter in which I recommended the creation of a "…sort of International Arbitration Court for Sport which could constitute the supreme body in charge of settling all disputes between the parties who would accept its jurisdiction." I added that in the sports world such an institution could acquire a notoriety and authority comparable with that enjoyed by the ICC Court of Arbitration over the international business, commercial and financial community.

Having studied my proposal very carefully, he called me back to his office to ask me for more explanations and details. He then told me that he would pass my letter on to Judge Kéba Mbaye, a senior IOC member for Senegal and vice president of the International Court of Justice. At the time, Mbaye was becoming Samaranch's closest and most trusted legal and political adviser and friend.

Kéba Mbaye was a very distinguished man, a legal academic, apart from his many accomplishments in sport, and at the IOC, he served as vice president of the International Court of Justice and was Honorary Chief Justice of the Supreme Court of Senegal from 1964 to 1982. He was also President of the International Commission of Jurists from 1977 to 1985 and Commissioner from 1972 to 1987. His published works include, 'The Realities of the Black World and Human Rights', 'Family Law in Black Africa and Madagascar', and 'Human Rights in Africa', 'The International Olympic Committee and South Africa, Analysis and Illustration of a humanitarian sport policy'.

Years later, Mbaye told me that, initially, he wondered whether my proposal was realistic but that on second thoughts, and after Samaranch told him to go ahead with the creation of CAS, he set to work and elaborated the statutes and other legal documents which provided for its establishment. It began its work in 1984 and Mbaye was its first president, and I had the privilege to be named among the very first CAS arbitrators, a function in which I served until 2009.

CAS can deal with any disputes submitted to it which are directly or indirectly connected to sport. The scope of the cases it hears can therefore be wide-ranging and include anything from commercial disputes regarding sponsorship agreements or contractual provisions in an athlete's contract, to issues like doping allegations concerning individual athletes. Sanctions handed down by worldwide governing bodies to their members are also challenged in front of CAS, as, for example, when a football club is given a worldwide transfer ban by FIFA, the governing body of football. In general, the following governing bodies and individuals can approach CAS for a judgement: individual athletes, clubs, sports federations, the organising committees of sporting events, sponsors of sporting events and sporting federations, television companies which own, or which aspire to own the rights to certain sporting events or properties.

Importantly, an arbitration award given by CAS is final and binding on the parties from the moment it is communicated and is usually enforced in accordance with the New York Convention on the recognition and enforcement of arbitration awards, to which more than 125 countries are signatories.

Since its creation, CAS has grown to become everything we envisaged in 1980. It has become a respected international arbitration institution which handles several hundred cases each year. While its headquarters remain in Lausanne, the world capital of sports administration, CAS also has permanent or temporary branches, for example in Australia, Asia, America, and Africa.

However, the success of CAS has brought new challenges. Over the years, CAS has become the standard court of appeal for nearly all international disciplinary sports sanctions. In that capacity, CAS acts de facto not as a real court of arbitration but more as a court of appeal. This raises more and more issues, particularly as far as procedure is concerned. At its beginning, CAS was not conceived as a disciplinary court of appeal, there were very few formal appeals thirty years ago, but as a friendly mode of amicable dispute resolution. The CAS workload has escalated dramatically.

In 1986, there were only two disputes brought before CAS, while by 2015 that number had grown to over six hundred.[1]

Today, there is an obvious need for a unified, simplified, fast, systematically enforceable method of administering sports justice. It needs all necessary powers, including the authority to issue subpoenas, recognised, not only by sports organisations, but also, where needed, by governments. Ordinary state courts should not be burdened with disciplinary sports matters. There is an opportunity for sports organisations and governments to act together once more to find a simple, practical solution by upgrading the CAS appeals division into an International Sports Court of Appeal, duly recognised as such by the International Community. This could be achieved for instance by amending the UNESCO Convention against doping, which was adopted in record time. If there is a will, there is a way. While it is essential that CAS decisions retain the authority to be legally enforceable in the entire world, which requires the support of all governmental and judicial authorities, it is absolutely not necessary that sports arbitrators and judges be part of public court systems. In such a context, the Olympic Movement could make a very original and creative contribution to society at large.

The circumstances of the origin of the creation of CAS perfectly illustrate the vision, style and method of Samaranch and his constant quest for solutions for the future. He didn't want to wait for the Two Chinas cases to be settled before launching a revolutionary project like CAS. Such was the man.

Today, after more than three decades since its establishment, CAS is in need of a fundamental reform. This is quite normal. CAS is a victim of its own success and of the growing culture of litigation affecting sport. CAS procedures tend to become more and more complex and lengthy, essentially because of the imagination and creativity of lawyers who are taking advantage for their clients, and

---

[1] Since François wrote this summary in 2015 the CAS workload has increased even more substantially. In 2021, there was a genuine surge in the number of disputes that were adjudicated by CAS, when a total 957 disputes were brought before it. That was an increase of almost 60% compared to the previous year. In total, the statistics show that CAS has handled 7869 disputes since its modest start in 1984, the large majority of which were filed in the last five to ten years.

themselves, of the many loopholes offered by the flexibility and vagueness of international private arbitration procedures.

The result is soaring legal costs, which in turn create a new form of discrimination between poor and rich athletes and between wealthy and impoverished sports bodies. The problem is not simple but must be tackled quickly. If the issue is not addressed quickly, sports litigation, which is growing very fast, will, in the absence of arbitration organisations, be taken over by the state courts. This would not be a good idea. State courts are already overwhelmed by the number of ordinary cases submitted to them. Sport litigation is a very specific area which can best be dealt with by judges who, while remaining absolutely independent, must rely on a deep legal background and on a profound understanding of the world of sport.

CAS is definitely the most qualified institution to take care of sports disputes. However, it must quickly draw on its more than thirty years of existence and make the necessary adjustments. In that context, the IOC has a key role to play by having its representatives launch the necessary reform process.

11
The IOC and its Swiss Hosts

During the early years of his presidency, Samaranch asked me to assist him in improving the legal and political status of the IOC in Switzerland. It turned out to be another fascinating challenge. As I explained earlier, the previous leadership of the IOC assumed that the IOC was a recognised international organisation which could claim immunities and privileges in Switzerland. It was, to say the least, a naive notion at best.

The reality was completely different. The IOC was an entity comparable to a private club or other not-for-profit society. Given the IOC's role and status in the world, Samaranch thought such a status to be ridiculous, and shortly after his election as IOC president, he transferred his domicile from Spain to Lausanne. He quickly developed a close relationship with the Swiss authorities at all three political levels, federal, cantonal and municipal, and engaged in lobbying in order to be granted a more appropriate Swiss status.

He enlisted as supporters a number of prominent public personalities, and the negotiations with the Swiss Federal authorities soon began. I was asked to prepare submissions and documented opinions in support of the IOC's request. The task was extremely difficult because the applicable law didn't apply to a private entity like the IOC. The Swiss government could only consider recognising intergovernmental institutions in charge of the enforcement of international treaties like the International Red Cross. In spite of the assistance of some leading Swiss politicians, including the Swiss ministers of foreign affairs and finance, we met very stern opposition from a number of senior civil servants who essentially feared that any improvement of the IOC's legal status would create an unfortunate precedent which the hundreds of non-governmental organisations established in Switzerland would immediately use in order to obtain administrative and fiscal advantages. However, Samaranch was adamant. He felt that the IOC should obtain at least what he characterised as semi-diplomatic status in Switzerland, which would be more in line with the status of the IOC in many other countries.

After several rounds of negotiations, it appeared that there wasn't sufficient legal basis for the Swiss government to grant any specific official 'semi-diplomatic' status to the IOC. Creating a legal basis would involve going through the entire legislative process in both chambers of the national parliament and would take years. On the other hand, it was clear that other countries, including Monaco and France, the IOC's country of origin, would be prepared to welcome the IOC and grant it a status more in line with its actual international status.

However, Samaranch was determined to keep the IOC in Switzerland. As it proved to be legally impossible, a solution was found at the highest level by the Swiss president himself, Kurt Furgler. Instead of an agreement, Furgler created a unilateral decree by the government, the Swiss Federal Council, under which the IOC would be recognised as an existing legal entity and would benefit from various tax and administrative exemptions. The decree, adopted in July 1981, was not exactly what Samaranch had hoped for; nevertheless, it recognised the importance of the IOC in Swiss law and acknowledged the IOC's specific role in world affairs. Throughout the entire negotiating process, we were supported by leading members of the national parliament and federal government from Lausanne, in particular Georges-André Chevallaz and Jean-Pascal Delamuraz who both served as presidents of Switzerland.

Samaranch was a pragmatic negotiator who understood that he'd benefited from the best political support at the highest level and that the solution imagined by Furgler had to be accepted. He nevertheless made it immediately clear that he considered the federal decree as a first step and that the legal obstacles, which had characterised the process, could be removed so that the status of the IOC could be upgraded in a not-too-distant future. However, it would take more than nine years to achieve.

Also in 1981, I was instructed to represent the IOC in a bitter litigation in the Geneva courts. An American licensee, Stanley Shefler of Intelicence, claimed that the IOC was in breach of an agreement, signed by Berlioux, which granted the licensee worldwide rights over Olympic symbols. The problem was that in several major territories, including in particular the USA, the relevant National Olympic committees considered that any licence over symbols required their consent. That had not been given, thus freezing the licensee's operations. The latter was claiming scores of millions of dollars in damages. After many hearings and tough negotiations, during which, sadly, Mr Shefler died, we managed to settle the case for a fraction of the amount claimed.

My growing involvement with those and other legal issues for the IOC taught me a lot about the structures, operations and leading personalities of the Olympic Movement. I also discovered the ongoing rivalries and power struggles within the organisation. My original instructions were given by Berlioux, with distant oversight from the then president, Lord Killanin, who was overviewing the organisation mostly from Ireland, relying almost entirely on Berlioux.

The situation changed drastically after the election of Samaranch in 1980. The new president was going to be a full-time president, albeit as a non-paid volunteer. He took up residence in Lausanne, at the Lausanne Palace, the traditional IOC hotel, and when not busy with the IOC or travelling abroad, commuted between Lausanne and his family home in Barcelona.

It soon became obvious to many observers, including me, that the relationship between Berlioux and Samaranch was deteriorating. At the time, I had to be careful in managing my professional relationship with both of them. Each expected me to report directly to them, which was not always easy. Both were prone to think of me as a personal ally, which I tried to avoid as my duty was to serve the institution and not the individual.

During the entire Samaranch presidency, one of his major concerns was to maintain very close relationships with all Swiss political authorities. He would dedicate a lot of time and resources to his personal contacts with Swiss statesmen and political leaders. For instance, he paid a personal one-day visit to each of the twenty-six Swiss cantonal governments, by which he was always received with dignity and treated like a head of state. In actively pursuing those relationships his goal was to see the IOC achieve the status of a fully recognised international organisation. Indeed, another step was taken with the execution, in November 2000, of a specific agreement between the Swiss Federal Council, namely the Swiss government, and the IOC. The agreement incorporated the main administrative exemptions granted to facilitate the performance of the IOC's mission.

The significant element was that the agreement, which is still in force, has placed the IOC on a higher level than most other non-government organisations. In 2009, during the presidency of Samaranch's successor, the Belgian Jacques Rogge, the IOC was given observer status at the United Nations, confirmation of its status as an international presence. Furthermore, a new law was passed in

Switzerland that came into force in 2008, bringing new opportunities for a further upgrading of the IOC's status.

As soon as he was elected, at the end of 2013, the new IOC president, Thomas Bach, began negotiations with the Swiss government. They have resulted in a further improvement in the relationship between Switzerland and the IOC. However, we should never underestimate the growing political difficulties which most international sports organisations, including the IOC, are facing in many countries. That includes Switzerland, where many politicians express their mistrust and don't recognise the special status of sport.

It is of growing concern for many sports leaders. During many years, in particular in Europe, sports leaders have been striving to obtain from their governments a binding recognition that sport needs legal confirmation of autonomous status. I have been involved in some of those early negotiations with ministers and other representatives of the European Union, the purpose of which was to find an acceptable wording for the insertion of an adequate status of sport within the authority of the European Union.

My conviction today is that in spite of many efforts, no current solution is really satisfactory for the sports movement. The public authorities, in particular the European Commission, are very careful about ensuring that sports organisations comply with directives and regulations relating to the free circulation of people, goods and services. The legitimacy of a number of international and national sports federations is more and more frequently challenged in courts, sometimes successfully, by outside private sports events organisers. This trend is intensified by the appearance of new sports and other forms of events, games, pastimes or competitions like X-sports or, more importantly, E-Games and E-sports.

12
The Olympic Charter

In the summer of 1983, Samaranch appointed me as a member of a small commission charged with a fundamental revision of the Olympic Charter. The commission was chaired by a distinguished Canadian judge, James Worrall, and included Judge Kéba Mbaye from Senegal, Swiss IOC member Raymond Gafner and IOC member in Romania, Alexandru Siperco. All members of the commission had a legal background, except Siperco who was an original, independent personality, historian and author. He was a very cultured man with an in-depth knowledge of the history of the Olympic Movement. He was spending most of his time in Lausanne, having imposed his almost permanent presence in the IOC headquarters where Samaranch allowed him to use an office. He was very intelligent but often confusing when expressing his opinion, which always took an inordinate amount of time.

The task of the commission was made harder due to the fact that while Worrall spoke only English, the other members of the commission were all more fluent in French than in English. The prevailing version of the Charter was to be in French, which is not easy with an English-speaking chairman. Apart from translation issues, we were also facing different legal cultures, often resulting in fundamental legal differences. Samaranch had advised the commission that he was not in a hurry. Such lenient advice was taken to heart, and it eventually took seven years for the commission to complete its work and submit a complete draft in French and English for approval by the 1990 IOC Session in Tokyo.

During those seven years, the commission gathered for several two or three-day meetings each year. On those occasions, each rule and byelaw of the Olympic Charter was discussed at length and reviewed in great detail. I was probably the member with the best command of both the French and English languages. So, apart from expressing legal views, I often also served as a translator at the request of the other members. As the work of the commission progressed, it actually became a drafting committee and, apart from discussing legal issues, we also debated political questions. Worrall was often worried when hearing proposals made by Siperco, who was relentlessly creative. As the latter belonged to a communist state,

Worrall was generally defensive when considering Siperco's suggestions. His apprehensions were even transcribed into a nickname he would jokingly use when addressing Siperco. The nickname was 'KGB', to which Siperco, who had a good sense of humour, did not object.

Mbaye was a senior African leader deeply concerned by all possible forms of racial discriminations; Siperco had a rather authoritarian vision of the role of the IOC; Gafner and I had to see to it that the commission's proposals were compatible with Swiss law, which governs the IOC and the Olympic Charter. All those factors, combined with the many compromises which had to be reached, often after intermediate meetings with Samaranch himself, explain the relatively mediocre style and language of the Charter, which perhaps should be described as a sort of legal patchwork.

Thanks to my participation in the work of the Worrall commission, I began to acquire an in-depth understanding and knowledge not only of the Olympic Charter, an unusual legal instrument, but also of the IOC, its structures and those of the entire Olympic Movement. I was also becoming familiar with some key players of a unique institution, which would be of considerable help when, in 1989, I was asked to take up the office of IOC Director General.

One of the first challenges encountered during the revision of the Olympic Charter was to define the Olympic Movement. In previous versions of the Charter, reference was often made to both the Olympic Family and to the Olympic Movement. While 'family' expressed the idea of a close relation, 'movement' had a wider meaning. 'Family' is a word which has been used in many sports organisations. It might have been appropriate in the past, in particular to describe relatively small sports organisations dealing with specific sports, but today sounds quite old fashioned.

Whenever I hear an international sports leader publicly boasting about the unity of the great 'family' of the sport he or she leads, I can't help smiling. Of course, the word disguises the truth; most governing bodies are full of intrigue, plots and even ferocious internal fights.

So, I much prefer 'movement' as a descriptive term. In the existing Olympic Charter, the Olympic Movement is now defined as follows: "The Olympic Movement is the concerted, organised, universal and permanent action, carried out under the supreme authority of the

IOC, of all individuals and entities who are inspired by the values of Olympism. It covers the five continents. It reaches its peak with the bringing together of the world's athletes at the great sports festival, the Olympic Games. Its symbol is five interlaced rings…Belonging to the Olympic Movement requires compliance with the Olympic Charter and recognition by the IOC." To any layperson, the jargon is probably impenetrable, the Olympic Charter a mysterious document, the IOC a secret society. While nearly everybody in the world recognises the five rings and has heard about the Olympic Games, very few have any idea about the Olympic Movement and the IOC.

13
Money, Money, Money

During the years 1983 and 1984, Samaranch and Berlioux involved me in a number of items, including some legal advice relating to the first contracts of what became known as the TOP programme, which marked the beginning of a new economic era for the IOC.[1]

When Samaranch took over the IOC, its commercial operations were in a parlous state. To sort it out, he enlisted the help of Horst Dassler. Dassler's link to the Olympics had begun in 1956 when, as a twenty-year-old, he was sent to Australia by his mother, Käthe Dassler, Adidas' head of sales, to distribute to athletes at the Melbourne Olympics, shoes made by the family sports company, Adidas. Not only did the athletes receive free shoes, the boxes in which they were given contained wads of 'hospitality' dollars. It was, to say the least, a novel tactic at the time.

Dassler's father, sports shoemaker and supplier of boots to the German army, Adolf Dassler, had founded Adidas in 1949. Following an argument, his brother Rudolf set up camp on one side of the Aurach River in Bavaria, founding the rival sports shoe company Puma, while Adolf set up Adidas on the other side. So, for a time, the remote German town of Herzogenaurach, with a population of just 18,000, became the capital of the world's sports goods industry.

Thanks to Horst Dassler's Australian visit, four years later, at the 1960 Rome Summer Olympics, 75% of all track and field athletes were wearing Adidas shoes. Over the years, Dassler had built up close relationships with the leaders of the International Sports Federations. With lavish hospitality of varying degrees of generosity, he helped them understand the potential of partnering with companies like Coca Cola, to help promote and fund their sport around the world. Initially with UK-based sports marketing agency, West Nally in the 1970s, and then with his own agency, Swiss-based ISL in the 1980s, Dassler showed remarkable vision in how sport could be financed for the future. He created the foundations of event marketing and pioneered the partnership between commerce and sport.

---

[1] For the detail in this section about the IOC's finances, I am indebted to my old friend Michael Payne, former IOC Marketing Director, who was one of the main architects of the TOP programme.

He courted world leaders and was probably better known in Moscow and the Kremlin than many heads of state. As a result, the whole Soviet team, as well as nations like East Germany, wore Adidas. Dassler maintained a dedicated intelligence office at Adidas headquarters in Herzogenaurach to track sports leaders and political elections. For those seeking success in any sports industry election, whether for the presidency of FIFA, or the selection of an Olympic host city, Dassler's support was crucial.

In 1983, Dassler had submitted his ideas on the development of an Olympic marketing programme with a short video to the 86th IOC Session in New Delhi. The presentation delivered a stark message to the seventy-eight IOC members in attendance.

"You, the International Olympic Committee, own the most valuable and sought after property in the world. Yet the Olympic rings   are the most unexploited trademark in existence. No major corporation in   the world would tolerate such a situation."

When the quiet Dassler spoke, the industry listened. His long-standing sporting links meant he was well placed to play a crucial role in   exploiting the Olympic brand. In May 1985, he went to Lausanne to sign a mould-breaking marketing agreement with Samaranch. For an event that would revolutionise the fortunes of the Olympic Movement, everything was remarkably low key. There were no speeches, no champagne flowed and no members of the media were there except for a lone photographer.

During that time, I met Dassler. It was also when I had my first meetings with Dick Pound, a Canadian IOC member, who had been appointed by Samaranch as chairman of the newly created IOC marketing commission, a major office set up to oversee the IOC's commercial revolution. Dick was to maintain that role throughout Samaranch's presidency until 2001. I was immediately impressed by his personality. He definitely was, and still is, one of the brightest individuals and leaders of the Olympic Movement.

He had been a finalist in the 100 metres swimming at the 1960 Olympics in Rome and also possessed exceptional intelligence. He was known as a remarkable lawyer in Montreal, specialising in tax law, a professional life which he successfully pursued, combined with an important academic career, which led him to the office of Chancellor of the renowned McGill University in Montreal.

Samaranch's choice was not accidental. He knew that the United States' economy would play a decisive role in the future development of the Olympic Movement. He also knew that the IOC needed to resist attempts by the US sports movement and corporate world, to achieve control of the Olympics and of the Olympic Movement. There would be difficult and tough negotiations ahead with the US and Samaranch knew that as a Spaniard with little experience of North America, modest language skills and scarce knowledge of the US business community, he needed a very strong and independent representative for the IOC. Pound was his choice, and it proved to be a perfect one.

Throughout all the years during which I was to serve as IOC Director General under Samaranch, he always told me that he regarded Pound as being by far the most intelligent and competent IOC member. In fact, during many years, he considered him as his most likely successor. However, Pound's excellence at negotiating and delivering favourable deals for the IOC was not matched when he had to politically manoeuvre within the IOC. His fierce independence, his open and often shatteringly candid statements to the world's media on Olympic policies, particularly when he disagreed with the politically correct party line, and his sarcastic comments about some of his colleagues, would eventually alienate Samaranch. In fact, Pound's forceful demeanour cost him the IOC presidential election in 2001 as successor to Samaranch. He was heavily defeated by Belgian IOC member Jacques Rogge.

However, that didn't prevent Pound from continuing to play a major role in the IOC and in the Olympic Movement, of which he remains a prominent, independent voice, a voice that doesn't please some of his colleagues, including the current president, Thomas Bach. Pound was the leading force behind the launch of the World Anti-Doping Agency, which he subsequently chaired for eight years and over which he still exerts a strong influence. He is still considered throughout the world as the champion of the fight against doping in sport. During many years, he was considered by the US sports and business community as a formidable obstacle to their aspirations to exert control over the Olympic Movement.

Although Dassler's view about the commercial exploitation of the Games was accepted by the majority of IOC members, implementing a global sponsorship programme was a monumental task. In fact, it was thought by many that it couldn't be done. Indeed, purists thought it shouldn't be done. Many inside and outside the Olympic Movement were concerned that using the Olympic rings to generate revenue was a slippery slope that would undermine the moral values of the Olympic Movement.

Not only that, would-be sponsors of the Games faced a complex labyrinth of vested interests. Although a Games' organising committee could grant marketing rights to its Games, those rights couldn't be used outside of the host country without the express approval of each National Olympic committee, and the NOCs controlled all Olympic marketing rights for their territories and could effectively veto any programme by a Games sponsor.

Gaining access to a territory quickly evolved from a simple request for approval to a long drawn-out and expensive negotiation, which, in effect, meant that any company wanting to develop a global programme had to enter almost two hundred separate agreements with all the world's NOCs. Solving the problem involved persuading all NOCs to sign up for a single marketing strategy. In many ways it was like the political challenge of unifying all the members of the United Nations or the European Community around a single policy.

The IOC's basic marketing concept was remarkably simple, on paper at least. It was to bundle all Olympic rights together: the IOC, the Winter Olympic Games, the Summer Olympic Games and all the National Olympic committees into a single four-year exclusive marketing package, offering companies one-stop shopping for their global Olympic involvement.

The programme operated under the secret code name 'TOP', which, initially, stood for absolutely nothing. Later, the sheer complexity of it all meant that TOP soon stood for 'The Olympic Puzzle' in the minds of those involved. Only after the project was fully established did the TOP code name become 'The Olympic Programme'. Later, to reinforce the partnership element, it was officially re-christened as 'The Olympic Partners' and within the marketing industry, 'TOP' became a brand name in its own right.

There was just one problem: neither the Games' organising committees nor the NOCs wanted to sign up. There wasn't a long queue of companies wanting to exploit the potential of a global Olympic association and Dick Pound kept telling Samaranch that the concept would never work.

"The difficulties of persuading the organising committees and the NOCs were such that I believed the programme would never get off the ground, least of all in time for the 1988 Games in Seoul."

Samaranch responded,

"Right, you're responsible for making it work."

Even after a couple of years of development, Pound was still far from sure that TOP would ever make it.

"This is a trial," he told journalists. "If it works, great. If not, we'll go back to the old way."

The first challenge was to get the NOCs to sign up for a centrally co-ordinated marketing programme and give up all their marketing rights in select sponsorship areas. Although few NOCs had a really developed marketing programme, the proposal was seen as a threat to their control. It meant ceding authority back to the IOC, and worse, working with an untried marketing agency. Few NOCs were happy.

The biggest battle was with the United States Olympic Committee (USOC), which protected its control over the Olympic trademarks in the US territory like a guard dog. As many of the prospective sponsors were US-based, participation of the USOC in the TOP programme was absolutely critical. Over three years, monthly meetings were held with the USOC. This was still the Cold War era and the USOC Executive Committee members wanted to know on what basis Olympic organisations in communist countries would receive sponsorship revenues from TOP. To American sports leaders, the idea that funds from US corporations might be used to help fund communist sports training was difficult to swallow.

However, slowly but surely, the NOCs were brought on board. All were offered a modest $10,000 payment spread over three to four years, and an additional $300 for every athlete they sent to the 1988 Games. About twenty NOCs which had some form of established marketing programme were offered financial guarantees by ISL to buy out their rights. Some of those ran into millions of dollars.

Some NOCs signed up quickly with little comprehension of what the TOP programme was all about, while others, with long drawn-out arguments about the real economic value of their territory, took upwards of fifty individual rounds of negotiations. In the end, the vast majority of NOCs existing at the time, signed up, 154 out of

167. Only thirteen NOCs refused, most, like Afghanistan, North Korea and Cuba, for political reasons.

Convincing the NOCs to sign up to the concept of TOP was only half the battle. To make any sense at all, the IOC needed the money at the heart of the deal and for that we needed big global sponsors. A list was drawn up of more than forty-four potential product categories to which exclusive sponsorship could be sold. Coca-Cola committed itself to Samaranch from the outset and joined the programme. Kodak and FedEx also signed fairly quickly but then months passed and no other interest appeared.

Companies like American Express refused to believe that all the NOCs would agree. They were sure that in the end, the rights would be broken up and that they would then be able to cherry-pick their key territories. Samaranch appealed directly to Amex chairman, James Robinson, without success. Amex was certain it had no competitors who could step up to the programme. Elsewhere, despite the fact that the next Games, 1988, would be in Seoul, none of the big Korean companies came forward. The situation in Japan was much the same.

By late 1985, with just over two years to go until the Seoul Games, things were looking precarious. After nearly three years of effort, only three partners had signed up. It became clear that if at least two more partners hadn't materialised by the summer of 1986, the TOP programme would have to fold, and with it the IOC's attempt to create a marketing strategy.

However, market forces and a little good fortune came our way. The new management team at Visa, the US credit card giant, was exploring how to move Visa upmarket, an area dominated by arch-rival American Express.

Visa wanted to create a unified international programme that all of its 20,000 member banks across 150 countries could use. Visa's advertising agency liked the idea of a campaign showing Olympic venues and athletes, ending with the tag line, 'And bring your Visa card, because the Olympics don't take American Express'. There was to be much haggling about the price. American Express had paid the '84 Los Angeles Games organising committee $4 million and the IOC wanted $14.5 million from Visa for global TOP; its board eventually agreed.

Suddenly, the IOC had momentum. Out of the blue, 3M, the sprawling conglomerate making more than 50,000 different products, expressed its interest. It was also looking for a programme to unite its disparate worldwide workforce of 85,000 employees across fifty divisions. 3M had never been involved in any major sports sponsorship programme, for the simple reason that no programme had ever offered the necessary scope. However, TOP did exactly that and 3M was soon the fifth TOP partner. The announcement by two major global companies, companies that had no track record of sports marketing, galvanised the market and provided the IOC with the necessary critical mass to drive the programme forward. Four more companies joined TOP in the following months: Dutch electronics giant, Philips, US publisher, Time-Sports Illustrated, Matsushita-Panasonic and Brother Industries from Japan. In total, the first TOP programme attracted nine leading multinationals and generated around $95 million.

Sadly, Horst Dassler died suddenly in April 1987 at the age of fifty-one. He never saw his original vision for the future of Olympic marketing fully realised. However, he helped to establish the foundations of a programme that revolutionised the IOC's financial fortunes and changed the basis of sponsorship for the whole sports marketing industry.

14
The End of an Era

One of my other early tasks was a somewhat delicate employment issue, which marked a watershed in the history of the IOC. In February 1984, just before the Calgary Winter Olympic Games, I was invited to submit the Olympic Charter Commission report to the IOC Executive Board. My stay there was short, but while there, I noticed that the atmosphere was noticeably tense between the pro-Berlioux faction and those supporting Samaranch. However, my client was, and always would be, the IOC, not one of its political blocs. Not surprisingly, I was being briefed and receiving instructions from both sides and it was far from easy to remain loyal to the institution, rather than become involved in political manoeuvring.

A few months later, Samaranch asked me to advise him on the content of the IOC's contract with Berlioux, which he gave to me, asking that I keep it in my firm's safe. While he didn't mention anything about his intentions, he wanted an analysis of the rights and obligations of both parties. For the first time, he expressly asked me to keep the matter entirely confidential, which, of course, I did.

Obviously, something was in the air, but Samaranch never came back to me on the subject until the events which took place, totally unexpectedly, in June 1985, during the meeting of the IOC Executive Board and Session in East Berlin. As I had in Calgary in 1984, I was invited to submit a report on the revision of the Charter to the Executive Board. In those days, there were severe travel restrictions for getting into East Germany, in particular by air. In order to facilitate the IOC members' and staff's travel, the IOC had chartered a special direct Swissair flight from Geneva to East Berlin. Upon boarding the plane, I met for the first time a number of IOC members who were totally unknown to me. Samaranch was sitting in the first-class section with a few vice presidents and other senior members. The rest of the passengers, including Berlioux, IOC members, staff and advisers, were in the economy section.

The atmosphere was tense. However, Samaranch spent a lot of time in the economy section, greeting everybody and chatting with many members or staff, including me. He appeared to be relaxed. At East Berlin's Schönefeld Airport, all passengers were welcomed in the usual Soviet fashion, very politely but coldly. The immigration formalities were conducted relatively swiftly, but everybody had to wait in an uncomfortable lounge overheated by a burning hot sun until the very last passenger was finally cleared.

Typical communist refreshments were on the table, soda water and chemical-tasting juices at room temperature. Everybody was sweating. Samaranch, who had diplomatic status and was being treated as a head of state, was taken away in a limousine, while the rest of us were taken in buses without air conditioning to the Palasthotel, the IOC's hotel, a modern but charmless complex with a conference centre, which was known as the 'Stasi nest', where foreigners could be bugged and monitored. It was the first time that I participated as an insider in a full IOC Session. My only previous experience had been as an outsider, when an IOC Session had been held in 1984 in Lausanne at the Beau-Rivage Palace, of which I was chairman of the board, when my involvement had been only peripheral and limited to some protocol functions. The East Berlin Session also provided me with my first real opportunity to be introduced to many IOC members in my official capacity as IOC legal adviser, and I enjoyed it.

My time in East Berlin was divided between walking through the city, which I found fascinating, and meeting participants to the Session in the various lounges, lobbies and bars. The weather was beautiful and extremely hot. During my walks, I went into a few shops, where I was the only stranger. Foreign tourists were expected to shop in duty-free shops reserved for them, but I wanted to see where local people shopped.

I found a bookshop, but after only two minutes, I couldn't bear the atmosphere. There was no air conditioning and it had an overwhelming aroma of the pungent sweat of people, blended with the sour smell, which I later found to be characteristic of many communist countries, of dirty floorcloths soaked in buckets of cheap chemical cleaning products. For me, it became the characteristic odour of most communist buildings, which I would recognise for many years throughout the Soviet empire, and which, to this day, hasn't disappeared from old buildings in remote former Soviet republics.

Famously, as in the best Cold War espionage stories, travel to East Berlin involved arrival in West Berlin and special access via the legendary Checkpoint Charlie, the most public entry to East Germany at that time. For anyone who has walked through the notorious crossing between the Western World and the Eastern Bloc, it is quite an experience. The affluence of West Berlin, its neon luminance, top restaurants and glitzy cafes was a striking contrast to the run-down drabness of East Berlin, with its empty streets and dilapidated buildings which still bore the scars of the Second World War. The Red Army had captured the most famous of Berlin's sites, but no tourists gawped at them, there were no souvenir shops or ice cream stalls to service them.

I stayed in the Palasthotel. Although better designed than most East German buildings, the Palast was an enormous concrete and glass block of over 1,000 beds. It was as well appointed as anything could be in the Eastern Bloc, but its food was far less sophisticated than the international cuisine just yards away on the other side of the Berlin Wall.

What I didn't realise at the time was that the hotel was nicknamed the 'Stasi nest' because it played an important part in the Stasi-surveillance of all foreigners who entered East Germany. At all times, there were four Stasi officers employed in monitoring the hotel. With Stasi recording suites on the fifth floor and using cameras and microphones, the spooks kept the reception hall, lifts, corridors and several rooms under strict surveillance. Twenty-five to thirty rooms in the hotel were technically equipped for the 'necessary monitoring' of especially 'interesting' guests. However, I doubt I was one of them. On the other hand, I am sure that President Samaranch, of course, a former Spanish ambassador to Moscow, was one of the 'interesting' guests, as must have been several of the variety of sheikhs, princes, princesses, generals and prominent businessmen among the IOC membership.

Because I was fed up with having no access to media other than the official communist newspapers, I decided to cross the border every morning to buy newspapers in West Berlin. Thanks to the courtesy and vigilance of the East German authorities, I was assigned an official East German black limousine and driver and went through the famous Checkpoint Charlie. I had all the required official documents for quick clearances and things went smoothly, although the government car was duly searched at length each time. Very few cars were crossing the border then and I was amazed by the number of tourists, particularly Americans, standing on the western side of Checkpoint Charlie eagerly taking numerous pictures of anyone crossing, including me. As I was sitting alone in the back of my official limousine with East German licence plates, I sensed that the tourists were giving me a hostile look, probably thinking that I was some sort of communist fat cat. It was an uncomfortable feeling.

During those cross-border rides, I took the opportunity to talk with my driver. There is always something to be learned from conversations with drivers anywhere in the world. Of course, exchanges might be limited when you're in the hands of official drivers, in particular in totalitarian states. However, in the case of my East Berlin driver, he was quite open and happy to talk. At the time, as far as standards of living were concerned, the difference between East and West Berlin was spectacular, and my driver was fully aware of it.

I asked him whether he was tempted to leave East Germany, which could have been relatively easy for him as he had various opportunities to cross over. His answer was very clear and candid. First of all, he and his family enjoyed a better standard of living in East Berlin than in any other East German city. He and his wife had two teenage children, who had the opportunity to study in good schools. He also told me that he had heard from friends who had escaped to West Germany that they were disillusioned by their experiences. It seemed that after a short period of welcome, they were transferred to refugee camps where life was very dull and with little hope of obtaining a promising job. He was well aware that, while the standard of living was much higher in the West, the chances of success were first reserved for the West Germans and not for refugees. So, while conscious of the gloomy outlook offered by the communist regime, he preferred to maintain his modest but apparently safe status. Both of us could not have envisaged that about four years later, the entire communist world would collapse. Nor would either of us have imagined that a little later, a woman from East Germany would be chancellor of a reunited Germany.

On the day I was to present a report to the Executive Board, an unexpected change to the agenda happened. As I waited, I saw the entire staff, including Berlioux, leave the meeting which was to continue in camera. Suddenly, there was drama in the air. Berlioux looked furious and walked away to her office in the hotel. I suspected there'd been a major clash but couldn't yet measure its significance. The Berlioux entourage appeared extremely agitated. After a while, Berlioux returned to the meeting room, and left again shortly afterwards.

Berlioux had been forced to resign after the IOC's German Sports Director, Walter Tröger, had informed the board that he couldn't continue to work under Berlioux. The meeting was then suspended and, while I was still waiting to be called for my report, Tröger, whom I scarcely knew, came to me, obviously concerned. He briefly explained to me what had happened and told me that he expected the IOC, including me as its lawyer, to protect and defend him in case there was any litigation. Although I didn't know what had happened, I tried to reassure him.

The power politics of the hierarchy of the IOC was, at the time, way above my pay grade. Even so, I know it was a brutal decision. Berlioux had served the IOC since 1960 and was quite rightly called the 'Iron Lady'. Her life had been totally immersed in sport. The daughter of a swimmer, Suzanne Berlioux, Monique studied at the Sorbonne, where she got a degree in literature. She was French champion in the 100-metre backstroke at the Club des Nageurs de Paris from 1941 to 1944, the Racing Club de France from 1945 to 1952, except 1949, when she won the title under the colours of CP L'Isle Adam. In 1942, 1943 and 1945, she won the Traversée de Paris in women's swimming, succeeding her older sister. When she later became the IOC's Director, she ran the organisation with efficiency, but she was from a different era and not in tune with the way in which sport was changing through the significant influence of television, sponsorship and money.

By way of complete contrast, Samaranch understood how sport needed to grab the opportunities available to it. Also, he was ruthless in his ambition to transform the IOC. From the demise of Berlioux, Samaranch had the free hand he wanted. Mind you, his determination was relentless and didn't lack cunning. He was convinced that she had to go before the 1984 Los Angeles Games but knew he didn't have enough support within the IOC membership, among whom she had friends. He also tried not to alienate Berlioux too much. Apparently, when he was running for president, he promised her that, like his predecessor, Lord Killanin, he wouldn't be an agent for change and would run the IOC from a distance, from his home in Barcelona, like Killanin did from Ireland. However, as we now know, Samaranch introduced change on an extraordinary scale. Not only that, as soon as he was elected, he moved into the Lausanne Palace Hotel and hardly ever left throughout his long presidency. It had been a bitter battle; indeed, there have always been rumours that both protagonists had one another's rooms bugged!

Soon after the Executive Board decision, Samaranch ordered me to join him in his office. He was calm but tense and asked me to bring him Berlioux's contract. I told him that I didn't have it with me in East Berlin and he realised that he hadn't informed me of his intention to dispose of Berlioux's services in Berlin. He then asked me how much time it would take for me to bring the contract to his office. It was Friday evening and the contract was in my firm's safe in Lausanne, which, apart from me, was only accessible to a couple of other people.

The weather all over Europe was beautiful and hot and everybody was beginning to enjoy a wonderful weekend. There were no mobile phones then and I had to begin a frantic telephone search to find a partner in my law firm who could access the safe, and a reliable assistant who could fly with a copy of the contract to East Berlin the next morning. There were no direct flights and whoever was flying needed an immediate visa.

With the remarkably efficient assistance of Samaranch's staff, I managed to locate the contract and find an assistant who flew to West Berlin the next morning, where she was picked up by an official East German driver who cleared her and her bags through Checkpoint Charlie into East Berlin. She had planned to eat a raclette in the Swiss Alps with friends on that day but suddenly found herself in the heart of East Germany where she arrived like a secret agent, a role for which she was totally unsuited but which she performed perfectly. She missed her raclette but got a unique chance to discover East Berlin.

As soon as I had Berlioux's contract in my hands, I took it to Samaranch, who ushered me into a meeting room with Kéba Mbaye, with whom I served on the Charter Commission, and Berthold Beitz, the IOC member for West Germany. Beitz was a most prominent and highly influential man with a formidable personality. He had been the head of the Krupp industrial group and had been recognised and honoured by the Israelis for his courage in saving the lives of at least eight hundred Jews while working for Shell Oil in Ukraine during World War Two. Indeed, after his death in 2013 at the age of ninety-nine, the World Jewish Congress named him as, 'One of the great Germans of the past century'.

As I sat in the meeting room, Samaranch explained to me that the Executive Board had decided to negotiate a settlement of Berlioux's forced resignation. He told me that the negotiations would be conducted directly by Mbaye and Beitz, the latter having full authority to conclude a deal. He further told me to repeat the advice I had given him previously on the legal status of the contract under Swiss law. He then said he would call me back for a meeting with Berlioux and her own Paris lawyer, M. Bloch, who had flown to East Berlin. As I left the room, I began at last to understand that the crisis was not accidental but that the whole sequence of events had been very carefully planned by Samaranch, who had chosen the cast, location and timing of a drama for which he had written a sophisticated script.

At the time, Samaranch was often criticised by some German and French media. Although representatives of many media were in attendance for the Session in East Berlin, the overall exposure would be somewhat reduced and, more importantly, delayed until after the end of the crisis. In those days, communications from communist countries were not impossible but were slow and more complex. So, the timing, over the weekend just before the Session began, was shrewd. The cast of the drama had been equally well selected. Samaranch knew that Berlioux had many supporters within the IOC, but by removing himself from the negotiation and delegating full authority to two of the most prestigious IOC members, he would avoid any personal recriminations. In addition, in order to show to the German media that Berlioux's departure was not his unilateral decision, he engineered it so that the matter would be essentially settled by Germans in Germany: Tröger and Beitz, in Berlin.

It all happened exactly in accordance with Samaranch's plans. Under the authority of Beitz, a fair and generous settlement was reached, in line with the contract of 'Madame', as she was called by the entire IOC staff. Her lawyer, Bloch, and I reviewed the drafting of the settlement, which brought an immediate end to Berlioux's tenure. Beitz granted her two favours: the right to hold a joint press conference with him and the right to personally take her leave from the Session at her own volition.

Samaranch instructed me to attend both 'events' in order to ensure that Berlioux, who was understandably furious, would not create an incident. The press room was packed with media which didn't have much else to report from East Germany on that day, but the press conference was conducted without incident. Much more interesting, and a novelty for me, was the final act of the drama, which took place during the IOC Session. All the IOC members, close to one hundred, were seated as Berlioux entered the vast room, walking at a solemn pace. The atmosphere was very emotional and tense. The two prestigious French IOC members, Count Jean de Beaumont and Maurice Herzog, the world-famous alpinist and former sports minister under French president, General de Gaulle, both of whom have passed away since then, stood up and, one after the other, took the floor to pay an eloquent tribute to the woman who had been the true and only IOC boss for many years.

She then walked through the rows and shook hands with every single IOC member. They stood up as she walked by and some of them hugged her, knowing that her actions were a symbol of defiance against Samaranch, who, watching the scene from his presidential chair, looked distinctly irritated at what had become a pompous farewell ceremony. Despite his displeasure, he knew that, regardless of the support formally displayed by the members for Berlioux, he was the winner. The drama would have been complete if Berlioux could have walked out with the Berlin Philharmonic playing Brünhilde's Immolation Scene from Wagner's Twilight of the Gods.

As soon as Berlioux had left the meeting, Samaranch immediately took full control of the Session and moved to the agenda. East Berlin and East Germany had been a perfect location for the staging of a dramatic act in the history of the IOC and the Olympic Movement. It had been fascinating for me to be a witness to an event which had been totally unforeseen, and in which I even unexpectedly was to play a minor part. By then, I felt I had begun to better understand the IOC.

In order to replace Berlioux, at least temporarily, Samaranch had decided to call upon one of his Swiss colleagues and friends, Raymond Gafner, a senior IOC member. Samaranch knew that at all times he could absolutely rely on Gafner's loyalty. An unusual character, Gafner was in his late sixties and a highly respected figure in Switzerland. He had retired from his position as director of the main State and University hospital in Lausanne and, as an IOC member, he would serve on a voluntary basis. He had played an important part in the Swiss Olympic and sports movement, first as an active athlete, he had been a goalkeeper of the Swiss national ice-hockey team, then as a volunteer sports administrator, in particular as president of the Swiss National Olympic Committee.

He had served in the Swiss army, reaching the rank of colonel and had lofty political ambitions, believing that he should have become

Swiss president. As he never succeeded in fulfilling his political ambitions, he was obviously frustrated and probably saw his appointment at the head of the IOC administration as some form of compensation and late international public recognition. That was soon obvious as he immediately raised the issue of what his title should be. Eventually, after much haggling, he was given the title of 'Administrateur-délégué' the French equivalent of CEO or managing director.

In my view, the episode threw light on two aspects of Gafner's character: on one hand, he was a man of total dedication and loyalty at the service of the Olympic Movement; on the other hand, he possessed a number of repressed ambitions, not only political, but also the desire to be a recognised author. He published many texts, including military subjects, and would later publish, with the IOC's support, novels with a sports and Olympic background, which unfortunately, didn't attract many readers.

As soon as Gafner took over the IOC administration, he had to restructure it, which he did quickly, with the help of the newly appointed IOC Secretary General, Françoise Zweifel, who had been his personal assistant when he was head of the Olympic Museum. Gafner was also in charge of the building of the new IOC headquarters in Lausanne. He performed all these tasks most diligently, in an environment which, at first, was not very pleasant. There were still a number of employees who were loyal to Berlioux and who didn't accept what they considered to be a revolution. It took Gafner and Zweifel some time to restore a better working climate at the headquarters.

Some of Berlioux's supporters ended up leaving the IOC. A few others rallied to Samaranch's and Gafner's camp, including, for a while, Berlioux's personal assistant who, confirming a persistent rumour, made a spontaneous confession to Samaranch, telling him that he had been ordered by Berlioux to install microphones and other listening devices in Samaranch's office.

The transition was not easy but was nevertheless completed within a few months. Samaranch had feared that Berlioux would publish a book that would be very negative about him, but she never did, probably because the terms of her settlement had been carefully drafted to discourage her. After leaving the IOC, Berlioux moved back to Paris, where she worked for Jacques Chirac when he was the mayor of Paris. She died in 2021 at the age of ninety-one. So, after

Berlioux's departure from her formidable reign, Samaranch had a free hand to shape the IOC for the future of sport that he knew was about to dawn.

15
Jacques Chirac's Manoeuvrings

In October 1986, the IOC held its annual Session in Lausanne, and I was invited to attend as legal adviser. The agenda was of particular importance to Samaranch because the IOC was due to choose the host cities for the 1992 Winter and Summer Olympic Games. There were seven candidates for the Winter Games and six for the Summer Games, including favourites, Paris and Barcelona, Samaranch's hometown. The other bidders were Belgrade, Birmingham and Amsterdam.

To insiders, including myself, it appeared obvious that Barcelona, which had produced an excellent bid, would win, even if other candidates, including Paris, were quite impressive. Each candidate city had brought to Lausanne large delegations, including famous movie stars like Gina Lollobrigida, or lyric performers such as the diva, Montserrat Caballé, in an effort to sway the votes of the seventy or so IOC members who were to make the decision. Lavish parties and dinners were thrown by the delegations which also brought with them political leaders who would actually present in person their country's candidature.

Apart from Paris, the French also had Albertville as candidate for the Winter Games, competing against six other venues, including close rival, Sofia, and Italian resort Cortina. The French delegation included Jacques Chirac, who was not only prime minister of France, but also mayor of Paris. He stayed for a couple of days at the Beau-Rivage Palace, the five-star hotel of which I was chairman of the board. Upon his arrival in Lausanne, Chirac was informed that a senior IOC member, on whose vote he counted, had been invited by Samaranch not to attend the session, which infuriated Chirac. The member concerned was none other than the former prime minister of Tunisia, Mohamed Mzali, with whom France entertained a special relationship. The situation was delicate. A few weeks earlier, Mzali, who had been the designated successor to Tunisian President, Habib Bourguiba, had been abruptly removed from office, and in fear of being arrested or worse, he had escaped from Tunisia in secret and fled to Lausanne, where he arrived as a clandestine refugee seeking political asylum. The news of his escape made headlines in the international media, which did not disclose Mzali's location.

Samaranch immediately called me and instructed me to organise Mzali's stay and help him to obtain the necessary authorisations to stay in Switzerland. Being the counsel to the IOC, I decided that Mzali should have his own personal counsel and called up an old friend, Maurice Rochat, who was a senior lawyer and a Swiss political figure. In view of the personality of Mzali and the possible impact of his arrival on relations between Switzerland and Tunisia, Rochat and I immediately made a personal call to a close friend, a member of the Swiss government, Jean-Pascal Delamuraz, who would later become Swiss president.

Delamuraz met with us and Mzali on the same day at Rochat's home, and Delamuraz assured Mzali that he would be under the protection of the Swiss government. However, it would be appropriate not to disclose Mzali's location for a while, because of the unavoidable diplomatic turmoil which could be expected. A few days later, the Tunisian government found out about the IOC's and Samaranch's role in assisting Mzali and demanded that Mzali be immediately deprived of his IOC membership. Samaranch would not, of course, consider such a step. However, in order to restore some political calm and also to increase Mzali's personal security and protect his privacy, he advised him to move from the IOC Session in Lausanne to Montreux.

As soon as Chirac learned the facts, he protested and asked for a personal meeting with Samaranch. He believed that Mzali's removal from the Session was nothing but a sordid manoeuvre to favour Barcelona by depriving Paris of what he considered to be a certain vote. Samaranch had no intention of meeting with Chirac, which surprised me, as he usually welcomed all opportunities to meet political leaders.

So, I was very surprised when Samaranch called me and asked me to meet Chirac immediately. He told me that he'd told Chirac that, unfortunately, he couldn't meet him but that he was dispatching me as his personal envoy. He also said that, in addition to being the IOC's counsel, the fact that my mother tongue was French and that I was the chairman of the hotel in which Chirac was staying, would enhance my status in the mind of one of France's political heavyweights.

So I rushed to the Beau-Rivage where Chirac greeted me most courteously at the door of his suite and invited me in for a one-on-one conversation. He was warm and friendly and began by congratulating me as Beau-Rivage's chairman for the excellence of the hotel's services. At all times, he addressed me as "Monsieur le Président", a title which he would never have used toward a simple lawyer. Samaranch's assessment as to my temporary personal status had been correct and I was astonished to be treated on an equal footing by the prime minister of France, in a meeting which lasted nearly an hour. The subject of our conversation was, of course, the Mzali situation. Chirac gave me a broad lesson on geopolitics, in particular French policy in North Africa. For him, Mzali was a prominent political figure, not only in Tunisia, but also in all other Maghreb countries.

His escape was the signal that major political events would soon take place in that part of the world, and France had plans which included a very important role for Mzali, exceeding by far the Olympic dimension and of crucial concern for France. He insisted that I would soon see Mzali as a major political leader for the whole of North Africa. His own political career, his sense of democracy, his vast cultural credentials and his excellent connections within the Islamic world, including Saudi Arabia, would all lead to Mzali's rise, an eventuality firmly supported by France.

Having concluded an impressive and enthusiastic discourse on realpolitik, Chirac turned to the real issue, Mzali's status and the IOC Session, which would begin the next day. Chirac explained that he thought it intolerable that Mzali be deprived of his right to appear and vote at the forthcoming IOC Session, that Mzali was a member in good standing, which was true, and that it was a manoeuvre by Samaranch to ensure Barcelona's victory over Paris. The French intelligence service, which was among the best in the world, estimated that one or two votes would swing the vote.

So, he demanded that Mzali, whose vote would, of course, be in favour of Paris, be admitted to the Session. Should that be refused, France would not hesitate to make an international diplomatic incident of such a refusal, which would of course be worsened if, by any chance, Barcelona and Samaranch won. Chirac's tone was still very polite to me, but much more aggressive when speaking of Samaranch. I immediately replied to Chirac that, as a lawyer, I entirely shared his opinion that Mzali was a full IOC member, in good standing, and that legally he had every right to attend the Session and vote. I then proceeded to explain to him that, while I didn't doubt that France had an excellent intelligence service, the evaluation of the probable outcome of the vote by the IOC insiders was entirely different from theirs.

Most neutral observers, including myself, were convinced that while France had an excellent chance of winning the Winter Games for Albertville, Barcelona would overcome Paris easily for the Summer Games. I offered him my view that the IOC was not an ordinary international organisation, but more a sort of gentleman's club, not usually swayed by international politics.

Barcelona, which had produced an excellent bid, was President Samaranch's hometown, and, naturally, a majority of the members of the club would be inclined to vote for their president's hometown. I then told Chirac that Samaranch didn't need to enter into any manoeuvres to interfere with the vote as he knew well in advance, like most of us, that Barcelona would have a comfortable majority. I also reminded him that, as far as Mzali was concerned, Samaranch had been the first to assist and protect him.

Chirac looked surprised at my evaluation of the probable outcome of the vote. He thanked me for my explanations but repeated, in a more moderate tone, that he had to insist, as a matter of principle, that the IOC should allow Mzali to attend the Session. I promised him that my recommendation to Samaranch would be to accept his request and I left, with him, very politely, escorting me to the hotel's lift.

I immediately went back to Samaranch and reported my conversation with Chirac. He asked me what I thought of the situation. My answer was that legally, Chirac's position was correct and that, as Mzali's vote would probably not be decisive at all, it was better for the IOC to avoid any risk of a possible diplomatic incident with France by allowing Mzali to attend the Session. Samaranch agreed and immediately ordered his staff to make the necessary arrangements for Mzali's transportation from Montreux to Lausanne the next day.

He also told me to call Mzali to inform him of the decision and to explain to him that, in view of the uncertain political situation, Samaranch was asking him to be very discreet, to refrain from any statements to the media and to return to Montreux immediately after the Session in order to avoid the press crowds. Mzali seemed relieved and pleased.

The next morning, Mzali attended the Session, where Chirac unexpectedly appeared to present not only the Paris bid, but also the Albertville bid. According to what had been previously communicated to the IOC, the French plans had been that Albertville's candidature would be represented by its leaders, the skiing legend, Jean-Claude Killy, and the powerful French regional politician, Michel Barnier, who was later to pursue a high-profile political career in French and European politics as Foreign Affairs Minister under Chirac's presidency, and European Commissioner in charge of the Brexit negotiations.

It was expected that Chirac would focus on Paris' bid, as prime minister and mayor of Paris. I still wonder whether my conversation with him and the prospect of a nearly certain loss for Paris could have caused him to change his plans overnight and appear also for Albertville in order to return to France with at least one victory to his credit. He had been known as rather opposed to Albertville's bid, which he saw as a potential danger for Paris.

Anyway, Chirac spoke eloquently for both bids and Albertville won, with Chirac receiving last minute credit for its success. Barcelona defeated Paris in the third round by a substantial margin as expected, forty-seven votes to twenty-three.

Mzali's vote didn't have any impact. As to the discretion which had been expected from Mzali, he deliberately managed to appear prominently in all photographs in the very middle of the front row of the IOC membership. He was launching his own political campaign and later moved to Paris, where he lived rather modestly in exile for many years.

At the end of his life, he was allowed to return to Tunisia by President Ben Ali, who was himself later overturned after the revolution in his country and died in exile in Saudi Arabia. Mzali never played the political role which had been described to me at length by Chirac. Indeed, recent Tunisian history has shown that France's policy has not been particularly successful. Mzali died in Paris in 2010.

16
A Most Unexpected Appointment

In February 1988, during the Calgary Winter Olympics, Samaranch called me to the lounge located at the arrival of the downhill race. He asked me whether I would accept the role of IOC Director General, the head of its administration, as Raymond Gafner, who was soon going to be seventy, was to reduce his workload to focus on the construction of a new Olympic Museum on Lausanne's lakeside at Ouchy.

I was astonished. While I had become more and more involved in various aspects of the IOC's activities for the last eight or nine years, and while I knew that Samaranch was considering looking for a new CEO for the IOC, he had even asked me if I had any names of potential Swiss candidates to suggest, I had never imagined myself in a role other than that of legal adviser.

I answered that I felt honoured by his offer but, being totally unprepared for such a drastic change in my career, I couldn't give him an immediate answer. I needed time to assess all the consequences for my professional and private life. I had a rather successful practice as a lawyer and director of companies, and it would be difficult for me to consider abandoning my law firm. I also had to consider the impact on my family, as the position would imply a lot of travelling abroad. Samaranch's answer was that I was already quite involved with the IOC and that he considered that I could keep my position as partner in my firm as well as some important other positions which I held. He added that I would not be considered as an employee but could retain an independent status. I would be paid an annual retainer but would not be integrated into any pension scheme, that I would be expected to dedicate at least half of my time to the IOC and that he and I would be free to terminate the relationship at any time if either of us felt it wasn't working. Finally, he said that he hoped that I could accept his offer.

"If you accept, you'll not become rich, but you will have a very interesting life."

He then asked me how much time I would need to give him an answer. My answer was that, at the age of fifty, it would take me up to three months to sort out all the aspects of my professional and family life. It was an unusually long timeframe, and I expected a negative answer, which would have closed the subject. But his answer was the second shock of the day.

"OK, three months, but no more. And while you may of course discuss this with your family and partners, please don't talk about this conversation with anyone within the IOC."

The next three months were not easy for me. On the one hand, Samaranch had offered me a position which would make many envious, and I knew enough about the IOC to appreciate how fascinating the job would be. On the other hand, I was, and still am, fiercely protective of my independence. As a lawyer, I always made sure not to depend on any single major client, and I didn't want to leave the firm. And then there was my family. Being a realist, my wife sensed that our family life would not be improved by the prospect of an additional professional burden. But also, being wise, she knew that if I refused Samaranch's offer, I would regret it for most of my life. Our two daughters were nearly sixteen and eighteen respectively and were well educated and never caused any problems.

During the ensuing three months, Samaranch and I never spoke again about our initial conversation. At the end of the third month, it was a Sunday morning, Samaranch called me up at home, saying,

"I assume you know why I am calling?"

My reply was that I thought we could work it out. The next morning, I was in his office, and we agreed the details of my position. He told me that in order to allow me to make the necessary professional adjustments smoothly, my appointment would not be announced until the 1989 IOC Session in San Juan, Puerto Rico, and the decision would remain confidential in the meantime. That gave me the opportunity to attend the 1988 Games in Seoul in order to study the workings of the IOC in minute detail and be ready for my new role.

In Seoul, I was a privileged observer under the cover of my adviser status. As I was still mostly unknown by the Korean organisers, one of my interesting experiences was to attend several competitions as an ordinary spectator and, like everybody else, I enjoyed watching some remarkable performances. It was the Games of Greg Louganis, Steffi Graf and Jackie Joyner-Kersee, and where East Germany's Kristin Otto won six gold medals in the pool and American Matt Biondi won five. The Soviet gymnast, Vladimir Artemov, won four golds and a silver in gymnastics, but, sadly, some of the extraordinary performances in athletics were later tarnished by drug scandals. It was, of course, the Games of Canadian, Ben Johnson, and American, Florence Griffith Joyner. My experiences as a spectator made me realise that at the Olympic Games, there are two worlds: the privileged crowds, thousands of people who are entitled, at various levels, to free access to reserved Olympic transportation on dedicated traffic lanes and free tickets for all events, and the ordinary spectators, local fans or foreign tourists, who have to queue for transportation and to purchase tickets at usually very high prices. Unfortunately for them, over the following years, the situation has not substantially improved. Even so, some creative solutions have been implemented. For instance, at the Youth Olympic Games attendance is generally free of charge, but on the whole, sadly, the chasm between the lucky credentials holders, with free access to the Games, and the ordinary fans has yet to be bridged. It remains a serious issue, even though social networks and new media and applications are changing the odds.

In addition to the above advantages, the members of the so-called Olympic Movement enjoy many other benefits. Some of them get free accommodation and for others the hotel rates are quite favourable. Apart from moving freely throughout the Olympic city and other sites, they are welcome at the various lounges, clubhouses and other hospitality venues operating during the Games, and are fully part of the unique celebration of the Games. The highly privileged crowds include, of course, the IOC members, and for some, their entourage; the higher officials of the National Olympic committees, there are currently 206 of them and often include ministers; senior leaders of all international sports federations; the entire leadership of the organising committee, and many national local politicians; foreign heads of state and governments; key executives of all major sponsors; the senior executives of Olympic broadcast rights holders; commercial partners or suppliers to the Olympic Movement and its constituents parts; representatives of the media; a number of international organisations, and most importantly, all individuals involved in the running and operation of the Games. Finally, last but not least, the ten thousand or so athletes with all their coaches, trainers, officials, medical and other support. It is quite a list and is often referred to, not always positively, as the Olympic circus, jamboree or even bandwagon.

Each category of the Olympic carnival is entitled to a different level of credential, identified on accreditation cards which the fortunate holders must wear at all times. During the Games, the cards are viewed by many as a vital status symbol. The IOC member card, which has the highest level of accreditation, is highly envied. But there are also highly prized levels of accreditation and many ploys and intrigues used to gain VIP status.

During the fourteen years or so of my office as IOC Director General, I witnessed some remarkably creative attempts by mischievous characters who claimed they deserved to be upgraded for various reasons. However, their reasons were never valid. At one point, things went so far that we had to create an accreditation card which carried no privileges at all and granted no access of any kind to its holder, other than to his or her own hotel, to which he or she could gain access without any card!

Such cards meant nothing, but I remember that some people were quite happy to receive them for the status symbol of walking around the host city with a piece of plastic around their neck. I also observed on many occasions that it was often the individuals wearing the lowest rank of credential who were the most arrogant and rude, in particular to the volunteers trying to assist them. Not surprisingly, the Olympic Movement is but a mirror of our world at large, with all its vanities and ills.

It was, and still is, a pity that the higher echelons of the Olympic Family are in fact isolated from the rest of the world during the Games. There is no interaction with the crowds or with the local people at large. Separate accommodation, VIP tribunes at the stadiums, separate hospitality, separate immigration desks at the airports and separate transportation, do not give the members of the Olympic Family any opportunity to share anything with the crowds or local people. Having noticed it particularly during the Seoul Games, during my years as Director General, I made some suggestions to improve the situation so that the IOC and the Olympic Family could mingle with the host people. One of the suggestions was that the athletes' parade, which takes place in the stadium during the Opening Ceremony and lasts for hours, could be transformed into a popular parade in the main street of the host city, which would draw millions of people to a real festival. Samaranch was interested but sceptical. Nevertheless, he allowed me to mention it to the IOC Executive Board, where I was curtly turned down and told that such a suggestion would be regarded as an insult by most athletes and would be impracticable for security reasons.

When I tested my idea on my daughters to get the feel of the younger generation, my older daughter, Maud, suggested the introduction of a moving red carpet, in order to significantly accelerate the athletes' parade during the Opening Ceremony. I thought it a novel idea but, fearing more backlash from the doyens of the Executive Board, I didn't suggest it. The fact remains that the athletes' parade during the Opening Ceremony, albeit important, is a tedious exercise, not only for many spectators and viewers, but also for the athletes, who have to wait for hours before marching into the stadium.

The whole concept was perfectly justified as long as there was no audio-visual media to cover the ceremony and, for the same reason, it was appropriate to build giant stadiums, as only the spectators in the stadium could watch the athletes. Personally, I now consider that both the size of the stadiums and the format of the athletes' parades at the opening and closing of the Games should be revisited to take into account the evolution of the opportunities offered by new media and social networks.

As planned by Samaranch, my appointment as Director General was approved by the IOC Executive Board and announced to the August 1989 IOC Session in San Juan, Puerto Rico. Having watched the dramatic Wagnerian departure of Berlioux at the 1985 Session in East Berlin, I was curious to see, after the Gafner parenthesis, how my appointment as her successor would be received. It was a total non-event.

Samaranch told me to deliver a short speech, which I did. I thought it appropriate to pay tribute to Gafner for his outstanding loyalty and service and imagined that his colleagues would give him a round of applause, but my words fell absolutely flat in silence. There was no hostility from the members towards me, simply a total lack of interest.

Samaranch had other concerns. In fact, I soon realised that he was worried about his re-election as IOC president, which was to take place during the same Session. He'd been elected for a first term in Moscow in 1980 and was a candidate for a second term. There had been some rumours that he might have to face another candidate, the Belgian, Prince Alexandre de Mérode, chairman of the IOC Medical Commission since 1967 and champion of the fight against doping. The prince had acquired recent worldwide media exposure thanks to his determined and clear stance on the Ben Johnson doping scandal at the 1988 Seoul Games.

While various members, including Samaranch, had initially been hesitant at the thought of banning Johnson, the winner of the 100 metres, probably the Games' most prestigious event, Mérode didn't soften, and he acted swiftly. Ben Johnson was sent home in disgrace.

Mérode was a totally independent personality, fully dedicated to the cause of Olympism. A wealthy aristocrat, who lived alone with his mother in a prestigious town house in Brussels, he embodied the traditional values of the gentleman amateur and fair play. His vision of the Olympic Movement was an organisation based on voluntary work. As he could afford it, he gave all his time to his Olympic tasks and represented a conservative vision of a movement free from any outside political or financial pressures. Interestingly, he was regarded as having been close to Monique Berlioux.

The rumours of the possible candidature of Mérode had alarmed Samaranch who, on the eve of the election, nervously awaited the expiry of the deadline for submitting candidates. Personally, I was convinced that the rumours that had reached Samaranch were completely false and that it would have been contrary to Mérode's ethics and loyalty to run against a serving president. In fact, I mentioned the rumours to Mérode, with whom I had established a good relationship. He found the story most amusing and confirmed what I'd thought, that he would never contemplate running against an incumbent president.

When I told Samaranch about my conversation, he was only slightly reassured and still waiting anxiously for the expiry of the deadline. Strangely, even though he was the only candidate, Samaranch remained tense until he was formally re-elected for a second eight-year term. Only then did he relax. I came to understand that, although the IOC was an institution governed by Swiss law, Samaranch had been used to a very different political and legal environment. The concept of an assembly is quite different if you've been used to Spanish politics, especially under the dictatorship of Franco. I saw the dichotomy on a number of other occasions. For instance, whenever Samaranch submitted a matter to a vote by the IOC Session, which was rare, he would never be satisfied if, after some lobbying, I reported to him that I was confident that we had a clear, comfortable majority. He would always send me back to convince the remaining opponents so that he could secure a unanimous vote, which would sometimes lead us to make concessions which, in my opinion, were not necessary.

By and large, Samaranch didn't like democratic votes which, by instinct, he thought risky, and was a man who never liked to take any unnecessary chances. The consequence was that, while he was undoubtedly a great IOC president, his way of chairing meetings could be questionable for those who, like me, had to prepare agendas, put decisions in writing and implement them. He would redraft all minutes of all meetings he chaired in order to eliminate any controversial elements. The most common formula that he liked to use to record decisions was 'Report approved', which could often mean a range of things or even the opposite! His method of proceeding was, in fact, yet another illustration of his determination to exercise full control over all affairs of the IOC. It enabled him to adjust the course of events and, if he felt it necessary, to amend or modify some decisions. And yet, the paradox was that, while his administration was a presidential regime and not a democratic one, he would nevertheless conduct many intense consultations and carefully listen to the advice and opinions of others, which he could often transform into his own proposals.

On the occasion of my debut at the San Juan Session, I had been surprised by the members' lack of gratitude displayed toward Gafner, as well as their indifference regarding my own appointment. It was a good lesson, which I wouldn't forget over the years: most speeches to the Session have no impact whatsoever on the members. Samaranch himself would waste very little time in submitting reports or addresses to his colleagues.

The uniqueness of the IOC's fundamental structure explains why its sessions, or general assemblies, are in no way comparable to the assemblies of other international institutions. As defined by the Olympic Charter, IOC members may not accept instructions or mandates from any organisations when exercising their IOC functions. They are expected to act entirely on their own, to the best of their knowledge and belief. Nobody can take the floor and refer to any form of instructions. In fact, the IOC is a members' club, originally for 'gentleman amateurs' but a club shrewd enough to widen its base to include a global membership, women, professional athletes and people with the skills and wisdom to be influential on the world stage. 'The Club' at work was obvious when the IOC awarded the 1992 Games to Barcelona, the club president's hometown. It was also obvious when, upon Samaranch's retirement in 2001, the

Session co-opted his son, Juan Antonio Samaranch junior, as IOC member for Spain.

By instinct and experience, Samaranch didn't have much confidence in the IOC Session. It took me some time to understand that, for the reasons explained above concerning the uniqueness of the institution, he was probably right. My own Swiss background and experience would have encouraged me to rely more on what, naively, I would have compared to a Swiss assembly. However, it soon became obvious to me that Samaranch knew exactly what he was doing; the Session could be unpredictable, and, as always, he would take no chances. For him, the Session should essentially be a non-assembly. The only exceptions he knew he would have to accept were the elections and, more reluctantly, the choice by the Session of the host cities for the Olympic Games. Samaranch considered that such decisions should be carried out by the Executive Board, the small group of senior members which he chaired, and not by the Session. As far as he was concerned, most members didn't have the competence to assess the qualities and shortcomings of the various candidate cities, and he had a gut feeling that sooner or later, there would be some scandal, as members were courted and lavishly entertained by the various candidates. In late 1998, when a big scandal did occur, he privately admitted that he might have underestimated his actual power and the available range of potential actions he should have taken to prevent it.

While Samaranch did not have much confidence in the collective will of his colleagues, he was very considerate and thoughtful towards all of them individually. He spent a lot of time in conversations or telephone calls with them and was most careful to maintain close personal relationships. The consequence was that his authority was never challenged and that he ruled over the IOC through a shrewd pre-discussed and pre-arranged consensus.

As I took up my new office, the division of tasks had been defined as follows by Samaranch: Gafner would keep the important mission of supervising the Olympic Museum, including its construction, which would eventually cost more than 100 million Swiss francs (about $65 million US); he would also retain responsibility for IOC publications, including the Olympic Review, and would carry out specific missions at Samaranch's request, it being understood that I would be informed of them.

Also, Samaranch asked me if it would be a problem for me if Gafner insisted on keeping his title as 'Administrateur – délégué'. My answer was that I couldn't care less, provided that it was clear to everyone that I would be the person in charge of the IOC's administration. Besides, I'd always considered Gafner's title as a fiction, given that it had been 'borrowed' from the corporate world and did not correspond to the IOC's legal status. As to my own title, Samaranch and I quickly agreed that I would be named Director General. My mission was that of a CEO, with general responsibility over the administration and the carrying out of a number of specific missions as directed by Samaranch. I was also to assume the ultimate responsibility for legal affairs, with the assistance of the IOC Director of Legal Affairs, Howard Stupp. Samaranch never wanted to expand the number of lawyers or paralegals employed in Stupp's department and felt that as I was a practising lawyer, my arrival would reinforce the legal department. I would be allowed to outsource a number of legal matters, including to my own law firm if there were no conflicts of interests. Françoise Zweifel would retain her title of Secretary General, and would assist Gafner with the Museum, where she played a leading role, and would also be in charge of all practical matters relating to the headquarters' operations, including the planning and physical organisation of all meetings and sessions. She would also be in charge of day-to-day affairs and the hospitality of the IOC members. That was a major challenge, which she performed extremely well.

While a few members, usually those active in their professional lives, would not cause any problems, many others expected all kinds of services, including free medical or dental care. Some called on Zweifel for personal problems, while others were excessively demanding and had to be handled diplomatically, which she did perfectly. Occasionally, members who hadn't obtained satisfaction from her would call on me to try and obtain the favours which she'd refused. I remember a particularly amusing episode, when a member came to my office to discuss a pressing matter. To my surprise, he told me that he had a problem with a gold Rolex watch and wondered whether I knew a specialist who could fix it. I told him that in Lausanne, as in many other cities, the Rolex representative was the well-known shop, Bucherer, and gave him the address. The member then asked me whether I could take the watch to the shop myself. I asked him why, and what was the problem with the watch. He then answered that the watch, which was his wife's, had shrunk and become too small. I then realised that his wife's arm had become too thick to wear the watch. The 'problem' was that, free of charge, he expected me to get him a new, larger Rolex for his wife. I pretended not to understand and left him with the address of Bucherer and he was obviously not pleased with my lack of support. However, I must emphasise that as far as my relationship with the members was concerned, it was a most exceptional episode; the vast majority of the members were impeccable in their dealings with me.

On the whole, the division of work between Gafner, Zweifel and me worked smoothly. Gafner never interfered with my areas of competence and we got along very well. With Zweifel, there were some overlapping situations and some moments of tension. I felt she was too protective of her own staff and would never acknowledge any wrongdoing by her or any of her assistants, even when, like anyone does, they had made a mistake. But we never had really serious problems or differences. On one occasion, when I was exasperated by an incident and mentioned it to Samaranch, he told me not to worry and focus on the more important matters which he had assigned to me, adding about Zweifel, "I understand your frustration, but you must never forget that neither you nor I would ever have the patience and aptitude to take care of our members like she does."

He was absolutely right. In a speech that she once delivered to a service club, she described herself as a 'super hostess' or 'governess', which is exactly what she was; a function at which she excelled.

Top: A proud Swiss boy, aged five, 1943

Right: With my father, Jean, looking very fine in his Swiss Army uniform, 1943

Top: Some early jazz at home in 1950. The picture on the wall is of French singer-songwriter Charles Trenet, one of my heroes

Left: 'Pipo', a friend's dog and 'Slim Jim'. Me enjoying the sun in Rimini, 1950

Jessie Caskey

Dudley Carstensen

From 'Hoofbeats' the 1956 Yearbook of John Muir High School, Pasadena, California. I'm listed bottom right by my American name, 'Frank'

Ruth Carpenter

James Carr

Suzanne Carr

Frank Carrard

KHJ-TV California filming the Gene Norman Show, John Muir, 1956. Norman was a very well-known West Coast jazz impresario. Yours truly on piano with the John Muir Band

With two IOC presidents: Irishman Michael Morris, the Lord Killanin (1972-1980) and Spaniard Juan Antonio Samaranch (1980-2010), Courcheval, 1992

A moment of humour with Her Royal Highness, Princess Anne, the Princess Royal, IOC member in Great Britain from 1988 and Adolf Ogi, President of the Confederation of Switzerland, 2000

With German guests. L-R: Thomas Bach, IOC member in Germany and IOC president from 2013; unknown, President Samaranch (1980-2010); Helmut Kohl, Chancellor of Germany (1982-1998); Willi Daume, IOC member in Germany (1956-1991)

Admiring the work of French New Realist sculptor, César (Baldaccini) at the Olympic Museum, Lausanne, circa 1995

Chatting with His Serene Highness Prince Albert of Monaco, IOC member in Monaco since 1985, circa 1995

Walking in the grounds of the Olympic Museum under construction with John Major, Prime Minister of Great Britain 1990-1997 (centre) and President Samaranch, 1992

Her Majesty Queen Elizabeth II of the United Kingdom and her husband Prince Phillip, receiving me in London 1991

The President seems delighted with his gift. President Samaranch, US media mogul Ted Turner, Bibi Samaranch, the President's wife, and film icon Jane Fonda, married to Turner, Lausanne 1992

Where I feel most at ease, 1998

Shaking hands with a president. Bill Clinton, US President 1993-2001, White House, 1996

And receiving the 'Al Merito Civil' (Order of Civil Merit) from a king. Juan Carlos I, King of Spain 1975 – 2014, Madrid, 1986

Welcoming Prince and Princess Takamodo of Japan to the Olympic Museum,
Lausanne, 1996

The Brains Trust. Three great IOC minds. L-R, Dick Pound, IOC member in Canada
from 1978, President Samaranch, Keba Mbaye, IOC member in Senegal until his
death in 2007.

All smiles with tennis legend, Germany's Steffi Graf, the winner of the 'Golden Slam'
– all four majors and Olympic gold (Seoul 1988) in the same year - and the only tennis
player, male or female, to have won each major singles tournament at least four times

It looks like a challenging question at yet another press briefing. With Michael Payne,
IOC Director of Marketing and Dick Pound

The 113th IOC Session, Salt Lake City, February 2002. New president, Belgian Jacques Rogge (2001 – 2013) is in the chair, flanked by his predecessor, Juan Antonio Samaranch. Jacques died in 2021, Juan Antonio in 2010

A typical press onslaught, Lausanne, circa 2001

The 'Bible', the Olympic Charter, the guidebook to all things Olympic, which I helped to re-draft in 1983

A hilarious moment with two giants of the Olympic Movement, and a giant among giants! Keba Mbaye, Juan Antonio Samaranch and Nelson Mandela, IOC HQ, Vidy, 1992

The IOC delegation to South Africa, 1991. South African president F W de Klerk flanked by IOC members, Keba Mbaye, who led the delegation, and Jean-Claude Ganga, IOC member in Congo

A special handshake with a legend. South Africa, 1991

Another thing I had to do all the time. Microphones became a way of life!

Marching ahead with Jacques Rogge at Chateau Vidy. A greying Keba Mbaye keeps us company, circa 2003

With the star of the 2000 Sydney Games, Australia's Cathy Freeman, winner of the 400m in that memorable green bodysuit

Burning the midnight oil to polish one of many important speeches, circa 2002

Another microphone, another day. Vidy, circa 2002

Keeping Samaranch on track! Circa 2000

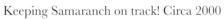

Cuba's leader, Comandante Castro at Vidy, 1999

…and Al Gore, United States Vice President 1993-2001 trying to save the world, 2002

Football legend, Brazil's Pele, comes calling. Vidy, 1998

More smiles with Nelson Mandela, 1992

Monaco's Serene Highness, Prince Rainier (centre), accompanied by his son, Prince Albert, inspects the artworks in the grounds of the Olympic Museum. The artist, Jean-Michel Folon, is to Rainier's right, 1996

With Michelle Verdier, IOC Press Officer at the 104th IOC Session, Budapest, 1995, when Salt Lake City was selected for the XIX Winter Games

All smiles as Atlanta wins the right to host the 1996 Centennial Games with the IOC's Executive Board all in a line. Billy Payne, President of the Atlanta Organising Committee, sits to President Samaranch's left, 1990

Looking pensive with a live microphone at the Salt Lake City Winter Games in 2002. The Games had been preceded by the most difficult period in my time at the IOC.

A new president. German lawyer and Olympic fencing gold medallist from Montreal 1976, Thomas Bach, was elected President of the IOC in 2013

Pleased with our little gifts. Crown Princess Victoria of Sweden Olympic Museum, Lausanne, 1997

Smile for the camera. With George W Bush, President of the United States 2001-2009 Salt Lake City, 2002

Champagne with another president at my home in Cully on the shore of Lake Geneva, six miles east of Lausanne. This time with Richard Nixon in1980 when he was Former President Nixon. He was president from 1969 to 1974 and died in 1994

A very precious family photograph signed by the man himself! L-R my daughters Anne and Maud and my wife Alba

Some advice for President Jacques Rogge, one of the nine presidents of the IOC, four of which I've worked with.

I love toy cars. I started collecting as a boy and never stopped. I have hundreds of them, much to Alba's chagrin!

A more recent guest, French President Emmanuel Macron, arriving at the Beau
Rivage Hotel, Lausanne, where I was Chairman of the Board for many years

With music legend, Quincy Jones, at the Montreux Jazz Festival for which I was proud
to be chairman

17
The Fall of the Soviet Empire

Shortly after I'd begun my new role, I found myself plunged into what was going to be the most important political turmoil of modern history, namely, the fall of the Soviet empire. For me, the story began in the autumn of 1989 in Moscow, where, with Prince de Mérode, I represented the IOC at an international conference on doping hosted by the Soviet government. It was my first important assignment on the international scene as IOC Director General. Many officials from a number of countries were in attendance.

The participants were accommodated in a new and pretentious hotel close to the Kremlin in which the Soviet communist party hosted all its guests. It was luxury at its best by Soviet standards. There were grand marble staircases designed to impress the numerous delegations visiting Moscow. Everything was free of charge, including long distance phone calls, which had to be processed through operators so that, obviously, listening devices could be used. The furniture and equipment in the rooms was ostentatiously tasteless. No tourists or visitors were admitted, and the bookshop offered communist propaganda in many languages and all the daily and weekly papers from the Soviet world, but nothing else.

On 12th October 1989, Ivan Rusak, the Soviet Minister of Sport, hosted a private dinner in honour of the Ministers of Sport of the People's Republic of China and of East Germany, as well as the IOC, represented by Mérode and me. The number of guests was very limited, the food and drinks excellent and the conversation relaxed and informal. During the meal, a guest mentioned the political story of recent weeks, namely, the fact that many East Germans had been leaving the country in their small Trabant cars, headed for Hungary or Czechoslovakia, in what was thought to be a sudden mass exodus. We asked the East German minister whether this meant political troubles for his country. His answer was relaxed. The move, he said, was caused by youngsters who were bored in East Germany because the society was too well organised; they just wanted to see something different and enjoy themselves abroad and would soon return home. He was convinced that it was just a minor incident and that the political situation in East Germany was stable and under control.

While the guests at the dinner might not have fully shared his view, none of us would have foreseen that a couple of weeks later, in early November 1989, the Berlin Wall would fall, a watershed in world history and the beginning of the collapse of the Soviet Empire. If anyone among the guests at the October dinner in Moscow had predicted such a collapse, he would have been considered an idiot.

A few days later, on 18th-19th October, I accompanied Samaranch on a visit to Budapest, where it was obvious that major political changes were under way. Everywhere in the Hungarian capital, all symbols and insignia of the communist regime were being removed by enthusiastic young crowds. The country was undergoing a total political transition, confirmed to us by Pal Schmitt. He was then president of the National Olympic Committee of Hungary and had been an IOC member since 1983. Since then, his political career had culminated in him being elected president of Hungary. Schmitt, a double Olympic gold medallist in fencing, is an interesting example of the political career of an excellent athlete, trained by the communist regime, and who became a sports official in his country. When the communist regime collapsed, he survived remarkably well through the political transition in his country, maintaining his status both on the domestic and international scene. As a former champion, national sport official and IOC member, he had been able to rely on a very strong international network. The only ambition that he could not satisfy was to be elected IOC president in 2001. But he enjoyed many other rewards, including his office as head of state. Before that, with the support of Samaranch, himself a former ambassador, he had successfully conducted a diplomatic career as ambassador in Spain. Schmitt's story is one of the many illustrations of the importance and strength of the worldwide Olympic network, which disregards political as well as other differences of many kinds.

Unfortunately for him, Schmitt's political career nosedived when it was discovered that he'd plagiarised his doctoral thesis, and he was forced to resign as president.

By the end of 1989, there were many signs of fundamental political changes in the communist world. Inevitably, the changes affected the sports communities of all the states involved and it became one of the IOC's top priorities to provide assistance to all the National Olympic Committees impacted by the changes. It turned out to be a major task in which I became substantially involved for four or five years. The recollections which follow are not necessarily expressed in a systematic or chronological way but are vivid in my memory.

One of the striking moments I remember was in 1990 when a joint delegation of sports and political leaders from the three Baltic States, Estonia, Latvia and Lithuania, visited IOC headquarters in Lausanne. The delegation included powerful, determined personalities, who were polite but not overly friendly. Their message to me was simple. "We represent the three National Olympic Committees of the three Baltic States; as you probably know, our countries were invaded by the Soviets during the last world war, which prevented us from carrying out our activities. Now we are back; please tell us when and where we shall attend the next meetings and activities which we were forced to suspend in 1951. Please also note that as of now, we do not recognise any more any of the actions of the USSR's sports authorities."

While I was attempting to tell them that we would indeed have to co-ordinate their return and reconcile it with the National Olympic Committee of the USSR, which was still exercising jurisdiction over sport in the Baltic States, they interrupted to tell me that there was nothing to negotiate because their committees had never received any communication from the IOC indicating that their recognition, which had been granted long before the war, had been suspended or withdrawn. They assumed that the IOC would not have accepted the invasion of their countries by Soviet troops as a legitimate cause for excluding them from the Olympic Movement.

Having done my own due diligence, I knew that they were right and that the IOC had simply ignored the situation and had recognised the political status quo and accepted that the Soviet Olympic Committee had jurisdiction over the entire USSR. I eventually managed to convince the delegation to accept that in order to re-establish their long-standing rights, it was imperative, for practical reasons, to organise a meeting with representatives of the Soviet committee in order to determine a clear plan. The delegation was reluctant at first but eventually acknowledged the importance of such a meeting. I then reported the matter to Samaranch, who immediately called Vitaly Smirnov, a senior IOC member, President of the National Olympic Committee of the USSR and a former minister of sports. Smirnov always had great respect for the IOC and for Samaranch. He immediately accepted the latter's request that he play a leading role in the restructuring of sport in what was rapidly becoming the former Soviet Union.

Thanks to Samaranch's call to Smirnov, I managed to soothe the Baltic delegation which left Lausanne in a pacified mood and with a promise to meet again soon with Smirnov and me. Smirnov's role was difficult. The Soviet state had not yet disintegrated, and there were conflicting political forces in Moscow which made the transition to a new political order fraught with danger. His actions were remarkable, serving the best interests of the Olympic Movement and of the new states which were to replace the USSR. What was even more remarkable was that he managed to steer the process without losing credibility in his own country. Bear in mind that it was a time when many other leaders, in particular political figures like Mikhail Gorbachev, were, and still are, thought of as traitors in the new Russia.

During that entire period, I had to go repeatedly to Moscow, mainly to help Smirnov in his efforts to set up fifteen new Olympic committees, one for each of the new sovereign states of the old Soviet Union. It was fascinating to observe at first hand and to participate in one of the most profound political changes of modern history. It was equally striking to me how warmly I was received by all the sports leaders of the fifteen states. It was a perfect example of the magic of the network of the Olympic Movement.

One of the immediate challenges we faced was that the new states would not agree to participate in the upcoming 1992 Winter and Summer Olympic Games under the Soviet flag. The problem was particularly difficult for team sports. The qualification events were already under way, and it was practically impossible to organise new national teams in time for the 1992 Games. We had to find creative solutions which would protect the athletes without creating political problems.

The situation was complex: the USSR was still more or less in existence; there was the so-called Commonwealth of Independent States (CIS) under creation, which would eventually not include many former Soviet Republics, and there were all the new sovereign States. It was imperative to find a formula which could, for instance, enable the athletes of several different republics to play in the same team. A typical example was ice-hockey: the players had been selected, trained and coached as a single Soviet team, then suddenly, they belonged to several different sovereign states. Together with Smirnov, we found a solution by creating the concept of a special 'Unified Team' which would be recognised as such by the IOC on a temporary basis for the 1992 winter and summer

Games only. Wisely, the sports leaders of all fifteen republics accepted the solution. However, I remember attending some very long meetings in Moscow, watching Smirnov patiently and firmly convincing the leaders. His role was decisive.

There were also some amusing moments. For instance, I remember attending a meeting of the executive body of the newly established Olympic committee in Minsk, Belarus. At the end of the meeting, having dealt with all matters on the agenda, the chairman respectfully asked who he should call in Moscow to endorse the decisions. He seemed not to realise that Belarus had become a sovereign, independent state and that a time-honoured call to the Kremlin was no longer required. Sadly, since then things have changed in Belarus, and its current leadership does not underestimate the importance of sport as a political tool. Indeed, the president of the Belarus Olympic Committee is no less than the head of state in person, whose style of leadership is hardly a model of democracy.

The changes outlined above revealed to me a fascinating aspect of the significance of sport and its extraordinary networks. While those countries were undergoing fundamental political changes, their sports structures were often the first to adjust to the new order, way before their political institutions. A typical example was that of Aleksander Kwaśniewski, who had been a young leader of sport in Poland under the communist regime. I remember him visiting Samaranch in Lausanne, in April 1990. He was very concerned about his future under the new Polish regime. Samaranch strongly encouraged him to remain in office and assured him of the IOC's total support. Over a few years, he became a member of the Polish parliament and was eventually elected president of the Republic of Poland; as such, he played a very important role, not only in his country, but also on the European scene. If it had not been for sport, he would never have had a chance to launch his remarkable political career.

The situation in the USSR was particularly complex. Not only were the fifteen new republics rapidly achieving their independence, but the situation in Russia itself was difficult to handle. The National Olympic Committee of the USSR was facing a most difficult double challenge. On one hand, it had to assist the new countries with the setting up of their Olympic structures, but on the other, it also had to undergo a most delicate transformation from a Soviet organisation into a new, more liberal and exclusively Russian committee. Political tension was very high in Moscow, which affected the Olympic Movement. Once more, Smirnov succeeded, together with a few close friends, in achieving a fundamental change. His focus was the interests of the athletes. Many people forgot that Russia, even without its Soviet satellites, is the largest country in the world and that its role in sport is vital. The challenge was huge.

As a former ambassador to the USSR, Samaranch understood the issue perfectly. He was always highly supportive of Russia, a country in which he was well known and extremely popular. He repeatedly told me to pay special attention to Russia's sport problems, which provided me with an extraordinary opportunity to observe and be involved in a unique political transition. Until early 1992, either alone or with Samaranch or other IOC delegations, I paid a number of visits to Moscow. On each occasion, I noticed an incredible evolution. There was growing uncertainty as to what was ultimately going to happen. Many senior political and sports leaders were wondering more and more what would become of their personal destinies as well as what would be the fate of the political institutions of their country.

In 1990, the political situation in Moscow was particularly confused. Since 1985, Gorbachev had embarked upon programmes known as 'perestroika' (reconstruction) and 'glasnost' (openness) through which the USSR was embarking on major political and economic reforms. Gorbachev was praised in the West for his liberal vision. The cold war was over, and a new era of peace and friendship was in sight. But within the USSR, the reaction was not as enthusiastic. The restructuration he advocated was to be carried out under the sole leadership of the Soviet communist party. Many people, including Boris Yeltsin, had their doubts and believed that while a number of eastern countries were actually implementing true, in-depth reforms, the USSR under the leadership of Gorbachev was stalling. In 1990, Yeltsin was elected president of Russia and until the end of December 1991, there was a sort of coexistence between Gorbachev's weakening USSR and Yeltsin's powerful Russia.

In August 1991, some hard-line communists attempted to restore the old regime by abducting Gorbachev. Although Yeltsin hated Gorbachev, he jumped to his help and resisted the attempted coup, showing great determination, and managed to avoid a bloodbath. In defeating the old communists, Yeltsin acquired a worldwide reputation as Moscow's strong man. By the end of December 1991, Gorbachev had resigned, and the USSR was dismantled.

While Gorbachev has always been hailed as a great democratic icon in the West, it is my deep impression that most Russians have little or no respect for him. He seems to be regarded as a weak personality who betrayed his country, which disappeared as a consequence of his poor governance. Yet, paradoxically, many of those who show him little respect would not want to restore communism, they simply consider that because of him, their country, whatever it was, the USSR or Mother Russia, was being diminished, a feeling that is all too evident in the Kremlin to this day.

During that time, until early 1992 and beyond, it was not surprising that the people I had to deal with in Russia were anxious and confused. What would become of them; who would be their bosses, new faces or familiar ones; would they retain their roles; what would be their salaries, if any; what would be the new laws and regulations? All those and many other questions were haunting them. All of them were extremely cautious, as if the transition would soon end with a sudden return of the old Soviet order. They were not prepared to forget many years of totalitarian rule. In private discussions, most of them were very sceptical. In Moscow, where most of my visits took place, the general atmosphere was bizarre. All the changes were happening with most of the same actors on stage. Yeltsin, the rising political star, had been an active player in the Soviet regime. His background was that of a communist leader, and apart from his obvious courage and independence, he had not been known as a particularly liberal personality.

But newcomers were in their 'starting blocks', eager to take advantage of new opportunities. They were to be the speculators and opportunists, the new oligarchs.

My mandate was about sport, not politics. However, at that time, it was impossible to separate the two. Anyone who tried to help sport had to try and understand how sport would be treated in the new political environment. Under the Soviet regime, the situation had been simple: Soviet sport was entirely controlled by the government. The Soviet sports minister was a highly powerful personality who was implementing Soviet policy which, in short, consisted in training the best possible athletes in order to demonstrate to the world, by collecting a maximum number of medals, that the Soviet system was by far the best.

In June 1991, I attended a meeting with Ivan Rusak, who was still the Soviet Minister of Sport. On that rare occasion, Rusak outlined what seemed to appear as his, or the Soviet government's, new vision of sport. To my astonishment, he quoted conservative economist, Milton Friedman, a total surprise in the mouth of a typically dull communist minister. He insisted on a policy with minimal state control and announced that in sport, state functions would be delegated to volunteer organisations. His ideas suggested a total revolution. He then called on the assistance of western countries and their experience in market economies to provide the financial resources which were badly needed. He ended his presentation by confirming that all the changes would take place in full compliance with the Olympic Charter.

I understood Rusak's unexpectedly blunt message as meaning that the Soviet government, or what was left of it, was dropping sport and leaving it in the hands of local politicians. For a regime which had leaned heavily on sport and youth, it represented a major disruption of its long-standing policy. Incidentally, it was the last time I met Rusak as Soviet minister. The next time I saw him, he had become a modest member of the delegation of the Unified Team at the 1992 Barcelona Games. Sic transit gloria mundi (thus passes worldly glory).

The months and years that followed were quite difficult for the sports leaders of Russia and the other republics. There was an acute shortage of money for sport, and the restructuring of sports organisations that had been dropped by the Soviet regime was a huge challenge. The time had not yet come for major sponsors or broadcasters to step into uncertain markets. Yet, amazingly, in spite of all these obstacles in troubled times, the performances of the athletes remained surprisingly high, as did their contribution to the Olympic Movement.

That was the achievement of major sports leaders like Smirnov and others, who fought relentlessly, often in unfavourable environments, to protect sport and the athletes. The IOC also did its share, although I know that our friends from Russia and the other republics had hoped for more financial support from us. Our task during that period was not always simple, and we had to be very careful to avoid some of the pitfalls prepared for us. One of them had been to celebrate, like many western politicians, the advent of the newly created Community of Independent States (CIS). The CIS was an attempt to re-establish some form of a Soviet empire under a new designation and with new structures. In its early stage, it included twelve of the fifteen former Soviet republics. The three Baltic republics never agreed to join it, and it was soon seen as an attempt by Moscow to regain control over the former USSR. A number of western broadcasters at the 1992 Olympic Games found it easier to refer to a CIS team, which prompted sharp protests from some of the new sovereign states. I remember having to explain to those broadcasters, who had no understanding of the prevailing complex political situation, that any reference to the CIS was causing serious political problems.

One particularly interesting moment during that period in Moscow was a private lunch hosted by Yeltsin at the Kremlin, which Samaranch and I were invited to at the beginning of January 1992. There were five of us, Yeltsin, one of his advisers, Samaranch, Ratner, our interpreter and me. The atmosphere was particularly friendly, the food delicious, the vodka and the wines perfect. We were sitting in Yeltsin's small private dining room. During the lunch, which went on during most of a Saturday afternoon, the snow was falling over the Kremlin, which gave it and Moscow a magical feel.

The conversation was fascinating, lively and spontaneous, in part thanks to the language skills of Ratner, who had the art of interpreting so accurately and sharply that we all forgot that we were not speaking the same language. Yeltsin was relaxed and totally focused on the political situation in his country. He told us that his mission, now that the USSR had just disappeared, was particularly difficult. He had to lead his country towards a new liberal regime; and he had to achieve that with people who had no experience of such drastic change. On the one hand, the Russian people had no idea what was meant by a liberal system. Since 1917, everybody had lived under Soviet rule of varying degrees of oppression. On the other hand, there were many western advisers who were making all sorts of suggestions as if, overnight, Russia could begin to act like a liberal western democracy. Nobody, either in Russia or elsewhere, had any experience of transforming a totalitarian communist structure into a liberal regime.

Yeltsin was very lucid about the challenges and difficulties he would be facing. At the end of the lunch, he went to a small desk where he kept some books and took out a copy of his memoirs in French which he dedicated to me. It was a special moment for me. Samaranch and I left the Kremlin impressed by what we'd heard. Samaranch then told me that contrary to what many people were suggesting, he was convinced that Yeltsin would be a powerful statesman and would not be suddenly ousted like other leaders. I remembered that he was proved right when Yeltsin announced his resignation in a very well-planned way on 31st December 1999. A heavy drinker with serious heart problems, Yeltsin died in April 2007, aged seventy-six.

For Russia, things have substantially changed since then. It is now a major power, along with China and probably soon India, with wealthy Russian entrepreneurs making inroads around the world. The current Russian president's policy is to reinstate the country as a more important power in the world.[1]

I also have several other anecdotes from that fascinating period. For instance, in early April 1992, I was part of an IOC delegation which included Samaranch and Jacques Rogge, then president of the European Olympic Committees and who was to become IOC president in 2001, when we visited the three Baltic Republics. In Lithuania, we were received in Vilnius, the capital, by the president of the Republic, Vytautas Landsbergis, who was quite a personality. He was a highly-thought-of violin player who had acquired international fame as a dedicated fighter for the freedom and independence of his country, which was then under serious threat of a military confrontation with the Russian army.

The situation was very tense when we arrived and Landsbergis was secluded in his presidential compound, surrounded by walls of sandbags, which we had to go around. While we hadn't noticed anything particular during our ride from the airport, his compound was obviously in a state of siege, as if the Russian troops were about to attack. So, our meeting was somewhat bizarre. The president looked much more like a distinguished intellectual, which he was, than a statesman, which he would not remain for long. He appeared to be nervous and rather lonely.

As far as sport was concerned, I was amazed to note that on the walls of his presidential office, he was proudly displaying a framed diploma which had been conferred upon him by Ben Weider, the chairman of an international bodybuilding federation which was then considered to be part of the Olympic community, as a champion of the fight against doping and performance enhancing substances. I didn't know whether the diploma had been placed there just for the occasion of our visit, or whether it was permanently decorating his office. In any event, it was a rather odd distinction, and suggested that the musical president had little knowledge of sport.

---

[1] NB: François' reflections were written before President Putin took a far more belligerent line in foreign affairs and before his hostile attacks on his neighbour in Ukraine.

After an hour of courteous and useless discussion, we left Landsbergis in his fortress. Fortunately for him, the Russian army didn't attack his compound, even though there had been a number of serious clashes. Having left Landsbergis, we met with his prime minister, with whom we had constructive talks concerning the new Lithuanian team for the upcoming Barcelona Games.

In Tallinn, Estonia, we had been invited by the head of state to attend a special dinner in honour of Samaranch. The dinner was hosted in our hotel and the entire delegation, including Samaranch and a number of Estonian protocol officials, was riding in the hotel's elevator when all the lights went out and the elevator suddenly stopped. There was a widespread blackout. We were probably twelve or more, squeezed in the elevator in total darkness. At first, everybody was calm, assuming that we would be quickly assisted, but after a few minutes, the temperature rose sharply, and the air seemed to get thinner. Some of the Estonian officials became very excited and started screaming for help and banging on the elevator's door.

After a few minutes, we heard that someone was using some tools to try and release us. As the attempts were unsuccessful, there was more and more shouting and knocking, while, in a corner of the elevator, the only person who was absolutely still and silent was Samaranch. After some time, still in the dark, someone felt liquid dripping from the ceiling; it turned out to be the blood of a terrified technician who was desperately trying to release us. Finally, the light came back on. The blackout was fixed, and we soon arrived on the ground floor. The Estonians apologised profusely to Samaranch, who looked calmly at his watch and said, "Twenty-seven minutes." He had timed the entire operation. A few minutes later, at the state dinner which had begun half an hour late, Samaranch answered the welcome speech of the Estonian president by saying, "Mr. President, first of all, I would like to apologise for our delay, which is not customary. I hope you will understand that it was due to circumstances beyond our control. And I hope that the young man who shed his blood in his efforts to assist us will not only be bandaged, but also rewarded."

It was typical of Samaranch to remain very calm in circumstances which he could not control himself. It was also typical of him to be mindful of a simple worker. In some other former Soviet countries, bureaucracy had remained incredibly powerful. I experienced that in Kyiv, Ukraine, in April 1992. As commercial flights were still scarce at that time, I'd arrived with Samaranch and others in a private jet, to pay a visit to the president of the Republic. Upon arrival, spared of all immigration and customs formalities, we were picked up on the runway by a fleet of official cars which proceeded at speed to the presidential palace, where we attended an official reception. As Samaranch had another onward journey the next morning, I had to fly back to Switzerland alone. In those days, there was only one commercial flight to Geneva via Frankfurt. So, I was driven to the airport in a presidential car escorted by an officer of the president's office whose mission was to ensure that my departure went smoothly. He was a young security officer, dressed in plain clothes, fluent in languages and quite friendly.

At the airport, he escorted me to the VIP lounge, where he sat with me while I waited to board my flight. Then, an officer in uniform, who seemed to be of high rank, went through the lounge to inspect the passengers' passports. When he came to me, he gave me a polite military salute and took my passport, which he examined at length, flipping back and forth through all pages. My passport was perfectly valid, and I didn't know what to make of his special interest. He then spoke to me in very approximate English and told me that I couldn't be allowed to leave Ukraine. My security officer immediately intervened to clear up what was clearly a misunderstanding.

It turned out that the passport officer insisted that I couldn't leave Ukraine because I hadn't entered it legally, as I had no visa. The tone of the discussion between both gentlemen became more and more heated, until my escort displayed his own presidential credentials and explained to his colleague the circumstances of my arrival and the pickup by order of the President. This was beyond the officer's logic, which was simple: this man can only be authorised to leave Ukraine if he was legally authorised to enter it!

By then, all the other passengers were boarding the flight, and I was seriously concerned that I would miss it. My escort told me that I shouldn't worry, because he'd given an order to the airport to block the flight! Meanwhile, the dispute over my status was still going on. Then, I was told that a solution had been found. The immigration officer would issue an entry visa to me, which would enable me to enter Ukraine and then immediately leave on the waiting plane. So, the officer disappeared with my passport and, after twenty minutes, came back. I had my visa. But that wasn't the end of the story. There was a charge, the equivalent of $20 dollars in local currency, to pay for my visa. My plane was still on the runway with its full load of passengers but was clearly of no concern at all to both officers. My escort became furious at the immigration officer and told him that there couldn't be a charge as I was on an official visit. Of course, I offered to pay for my visa, but by now it was a point of principle between them. Finally, they reached a new settlement. The immigration officer would cancel the first visa and would issue a new one, free of charge. He disappeared once more with my passport and ten minutes later came back again. At long last, I was legally admitted to Ukraine which I left immediately.

The security officer apologised to me and expressed his hope that I would remember this unfortunate incident as evidence that the situation in former Soviet states was still rather confused. The immigration officer called two armed guards, who drove me in a military vehicle to the aircraft, which had been waiting for over an hour. Both guards then escorted me to my seat, which was on the front row of the plane. As they left, I looked behind and saw a sea of unfriendly faces. They probably thought that they'd been delayed because of the extradition of a criminal which, of course, I nearly became. Once in Frankfurt, as you would imagine, I quickly left the plane without looking back.

The whole period of transition from communist to liberal economy in the former USSR and its satellites was a fabulous lesson in human behaviour. There were those, like Ivan Rusak, who practically disappeared into mediocrity; there were others, like Smirnov, who managed to stay in prominence, and there were those who managed to achieve impressive promotions. One notable example was Alexander 'Sacha' Kozlovsky. I first met him in the late eighties, when he was a deputy Soviet minister of sport. Kozlovsky is a highly intelligent personality, well educated, speaks several languages and is very charming. He went through difficult times during the transition but succeeded, with Smirnov's and Samaranch's support, to stay afloat. As vice president of the Russian National Olympic Committee, he was elected to the board of the European Olympic Committees and carefully cultivated all his contacts. After ten years of modest offices, he entered politics and became an influential member of the Duma, the Russian parliament, with an important office in charge of foreign affairs.

I remember that during the transition in the early nineties, he had acquired two or three dogs and his friends made fun of his acquisitions, saying that with his small salary, he would never be able to feed his dogs. His answer was that during more than thirty years, he'd tried to be a good communist and apparently failed, so he should now be left in peace while trying to become a good capitalist.

Since those days, I have been back to Russia many times. The consequences of the turnover have been very harsh for many people, in particular senior citizens who are still enduring financial difficulties. On the other hand, a number of younger entrepreneurs and speculators have quickly made colossal fortunes by taking over industries and businesses formerly owned by the Soviet state. The circumstances of many of those deals are often quite opaque, as are the relationships of their beneficiaries with the politicians in charge of the new Russia. It is clear that Putin appears to be in full control of the country. While Russian society has totally dismissed communism, many aspects of Putin's governance are reminiscent of the Soviet rule. Old habits die hard. And many people are still nostalgic about Soviet times. For instance, that's illustrated by the fact that Yeltsin replaced the old Soviet anthem with a Russian hymn, which was unpopular. However, Putin quickly restored the Soviet national anthem, which is beautiful, to the great satisfaction of the people.

Sport and politics are closely linked in Russia, which illustrates the survival of Soviet culture and explains the systematic creation of methods to help Russian athletes avoid sanctions for doping offences. That was particularly true during the 2014 Sochi Winter Games. The discovery in 2016 of how the Russian testing laboratory manipulated its samples created a worldwide doping scandal of epic proportions with far-reaching consequences for the entire sports community around the world. On 5th December 2017, the IOC, believing that there was, 'a systemic manipulation of the anti-doping rules in Russia', suspended the Russian Olympic Committee with immediate effect and excluded former Minister of Sport, Vitaly Mutko, then a Russian deputy prime minister, from any participation in all future Olympic Games. Also, there would be no official Russian participation at the 2018 Olympic Winter Games in PyeongChang, Korea. Some individual Russian athletes were invited but could not represent their country. While the sanctions were fully justified, they caused deep humiliation and I am convinced that the vast majority of Russians, including in particular its young athletes, want clean sport.

The whole sorry episode of Sochi illustrates the paradox which has prevailed since the days of Pierre de Coubertin, the founder of the Modern Games. According to his noble principles, the Games are supposed to be competitions between athletes and not between countries. Sadly, the principle is widely ignored by the media, governments and people at large whose national pride is clearly linked to the success of their athletes. And the IOC would look naïve if it pretended to dismiss national pride by not adding medal counts by countries.

In spite of everything I've described above, I remain confident that a great nation like Russia, with its exceptional human resources, will eventually resolve its problems.

As for the long-term consequences of the 2016 doping scandal and the sanctions against Russia, they are difficult to predict in as much as, regrettably, they must be evaluated by taking into account the broader political framework to which they belong. The repeated escalation of economic sanctions and other threats against Russia does not seem to achieve its expected result. The more the sanctions are applied, the more Russia's resolve stiffens. Without approving Putin's aggressive behaviour, it must be said that most westerners have a poor understanding of Russia and the Russian people. The vast majority of Russian people feel, rightly or wrongly, that once more, as it has throughout history, Russia is being threatened by the West, and, at least for the time being, they rally behind their leader.

As too often in too many parts of the world, borders are the cause of conflicts and wars. Borders are a relatively recent creation of politicians eager to defend and safeguard their privileges. One of the most horrible illustrations of that is the plight of desperate migrants from Africa and the Middle East who try to enter Europe through Greece, Italy or Spain. Sooner or later, in the new developing global order, borders will eventually disappear. Unfortunately, until they do, borders will remain the source of dramatic confrontations, which brings me back to Coubertin's principle that competitions should be between athletes and not between countries. The issues of migrations, borders, autonomy and sovereignty will have an impact not only on geopolitics, but also on international sport and may, in a spirit of reconciliation, provide an opportunity to reflect on the issues of nationhood and nationalism in the future.

18
Yugoslavia

While the Soviet regime disappeared without substantial bloodshed[1], the changes which took place in the former Yugoslavia during the same period and thereafter were far more distasteful. Unfortunately, there, the disintegration of communism was accompanied by rebellions, civil wars and genocides which have left deep scars.

In the early nineties, the most powerful nation within Yugoslavia was Serbia, and its strongman was Slobodan Milosevic, who was later to end his life in a Dutch jail, under the authority of the International Criminal Court. Milosevic was president of Serbia in what was known as the Socialist Republic of Yugoslavia, a totalitarian state of many nationalities formed after World War II by resistance fighter, Josip Broz, known as Tito. I had the dubious honour of being introduced to Milosevic at a dinner which he hosted in Belgrade for a few international sports leaders in the spring of 1990. My recollection is of a rather unpleasant, rough personality, lacking any charisma, and of an uninteresting meal.

While armed conflicts were erupting all over Yugoslavia, in particular between Serbia, Croatia and Bosnia, the United Nations was attempting to restore peace. As Milosevic was ignoring and disregarding several UN resolutions, the UN Security Council decided, for the first time in the history of the UN, to directly hit sport by imposing sanctions preventing Yugoslavian athletes and teams from representing their country in all major competitions. The rationale behind the Security Council's decision was that while other political or economic sanctions appeared ineffective, the importance of sport in Yugoslavia was such that sporting sanctions might have more effect. The sanctions were embodied in resolution 757 (1992) in what the Security Council characterised as, 'the very complex context of events in the former Socialist Republic of Yugoslavia'.

The very concept of sanctions against sport was blatant evidence of the UN's inability to take any adequate political measures. As far as the IOC was concerned, it was an outrageous affront to those who were among the most innocent of people, the Yugoslavian athletes. Resolution 757 was, in fact, particularly aimed at preventing the

---

[1] As stated earlier this was written before the Russian invasion of Ukraine.

participation of any Yugoslavian athletes at the upcoming Barcelona Olympic Games to be held two months later, in July 1992.

It was a bad decision in many aspects: first, as far as its impact on the Yugoslavian population and sports movement was concerned, it missed its target. If anything, the reaction was to rally and unite many Yugoslavs behind their athletes, thus arousing sympathy for young men and women who had no responsibility for the political disaster in their country. As for the international Olympic and sports movement, it couldn't accept a political decision directly hitting the Olympic Games and their athletes. We had to react.

Legally, the IOC, as a nongovernmental organisation, was not bound by a UN resolution, the enforcement of which was to be carried out by the UN member states. Of course, Spain was first in line and keen to find a solution protecting the Games while complying with the resolution. As a former Spanish ambassador, Samaranch was particularly well prepared to negotiate with his peers. As the IOC was not a party to the UN procedure, I was instructed to meet informally with the chairman of the Security Council, who was then the representative for Brazil. He received me and one of my colleagues in his New York office at the UN. The purpose of the meeting was to determine whether a solution, prepared by the IOC together with the Spanish government, could be acceptable to the Council. The solution proposed was that the IOC would establish a special category of athletes, named the 'Independent Athletes' which would include all eligible Yugoslavian athletes. They would take part under the direct supervision of the IOC and compete in white uniforms under the Olympic flag.

Formally, there would be no Yugoslavian team, but the athletes would not be deprived of their right to compete. The negotiations were complex as they involved Spain as a state, the UN Security Council, the Barcelona Organising Committee, the IOC and the National Olympic Committee of Yugoslavia which was itself then closely linked to the Yugoslav authorities. Understandably, the latter did not like the proposed solution under which their country would not be represented at the Games. But there was no other option and finally, reluctantly, they gave in and the plan was unofficially approved in New York, thus allowing Barcelona and the Games to welcome the 'Independent Athletes'.

During the course of the negotiations, it became clear that the UN diplomats and officials had no idea about sporting competition. For instance, they thought that there was no need for the competing athletes to be supported by coaches, physicians and other staff. It was believed that the athletes could participate without any entourage. These and other facts had to be explained to the UN representatives, who were totally unaware of the practical consequences of the adoption of the resolution. In fact, my impression was that they couldn't have cared less. They probably realised that the whole political exercise had been a flop.

Several months later, during the Barcelona Games, I was to experience one of the amusing consequences of the UN's decision. The Yugoslavian sports minister, who would have led the Yugoslavian delegation at the Games, announced his arrival in Madrid, without mentioning the Games. As the diplomatic ties between Spain and Yugoslavia were not broken, Spain could not refuse entry to the minister of a recognised government. From Madrid, he proceeded to Barcelona, on a 'private' visit. There, he wanted to visit 'his' athletes in the Olympic Village.

He was informed officially that he couldn't attend the Games as a representative of Yugoslavia. However, he was eventually granted temporary day passes like any other authorised visitor in a purely private capacity, provided he kept a very low profile, which he did. Diplomacy and wisdom had prevailed over stupidity and bureaucracy. The fact that the Security Council had been chaired by an intelligent, sophisticated Brazilian diplomat had been of great help in finding a solution to protect athletes' rights. Since then, I haven't heard of any new UN sanctions directed at sport. To the contrary, the relationship between the IOC and the UN has turned into a very positive and constructive form of co-operation. The IOC now enjoys the status of observer at the UN General Assembly, and there are regular meetings between the IOC president and the UN secretary general.

Quite apart from international politics and diplomatic wranglings, the Barcelona Games were also an amazing gathering of humanity. Of course, the Ancient Games were a Mediterranean celebration within the Greek diaspora and Spain and the Catalans managed to capture the artistic and cultural ambiance of that very special environment. The Opening and Closing Ceremonies were truly memorable and who will ever forget Montserrat Caballé and Freddie Mercury's duet, 'Barcelona', the fountains on the Ramblas, or the wonderful Estadi Olimpic de Montjuic, where the flaming arrow of Paralympic archer, Antonio Rebollo, lit the Cauldron. By the way,

Rebollo was one of two hundred archers considered for the role and after months of gruelling practice, he was chosen only two hours before the Ceremony.

In the sporting arena, it was the Games of US basketball's Dream Team and of Germany's Unified Team, and featured the marvels of America's Evelyn Ashford and Algeria's Hassiba Boulmerka on the track and of Hungary's Krisztina Egerszegi in the pool. There was also that famous moment of triumph in defeat as Britain's Derek Redmond, after pulling his hamstring on the third bend of the 400-metres semi-final, got up and with the help of his father, who jumped from the crowd, limped to the finish in tears of pain.

19
South Africa and Mandela

A fundamental principle of Olympism, enshrined in the Olympic Charter, is the fight against all forms of discrimination. In South Africa, since the beginning of the twentieth century, a policy of apartheid, an Afrikaans word which means 'separateness', gradually established a constitutional and legal system which institutionalised social discrimination based on the supremacy of the minority white race.

A crucial part of apartheid included how sport was played. South Africa's different races were required to play sport separately, and multiracial teams were prohibited. This was contrary to the most fundamental Olympic principles and values and could not be tolerated by those of us who upheld those principles.

Apartheid's impact on sport began to become a major international issue during the 1950s and 1960s. The traditional British sports of cricket and rugby maintained sporting ties with South Africa, much to the annoyance of international anti-apartheid groups who protested against the contacts. Other sports, like table tennis refused to play South African teams chosen on racial grounds. Apartheid in sport became a major international political issue.

The IOC first intervened in 1962, when it barred South Africa from competing in the 1964 Tokyo Games, then did so again for the Mexico City Games of 1968. However, South Africa remained affiliated to the IOC, but a crucial decision was taken at the 1970 IOC Session in Amsterdam. By thirty-five in favour, twenty-eight against and three abstentions, the IOC decided to withdraw its recognition of SANOC, the South African National Olympic Committee. It was a result achieved after a long period of tough deliberations and much hesitation, the narrow margin illustrating how conservative the IOC was at the time. These days, such a close result would definitely be considered shockingly unacceptable.

As soon as Samaranch took over the IOC presidency in 1980, he realised that the case of South African sport was a particularly delicate and sensitive issue which he considered as a major priority. His line was clear: as long as apartheid controlled sport in South Africa, there would be no compromise. On the other hand, he watched closely the evolution of the situation as the international condemnation of apartheid gathered pace, and prepared the IOC for an immediate response as soon as apartheid came to an end. However, Mandela was still in jail and the Afrikaner Nationalist regime was still in power.

Samaranch wanted the issue to be solved by Africans, and to that end relied on the exceptional personality who was probably his closest and most loyal confidante and friend, Judge Kéba Mbaye, the IOC member in Senegal. Mbaye was a legal scholar of the highest order and a man of charm and distinction.

In 1988, Samaranch appointed Mbaye as chairman of the newly created Commission on Apartheid and Olympism. Its mission was to closely monitor the development of the situation in South Africa. Samaranch, ever astute, had sensed that there would soon be drastic political changes in the country and he wanted the Olympic Movement to be prepared and to take a leading role in the process of change.

Under Mbaye's chairmanship, a number of important meetings were held in 1988 and 1989, which confirmed the Samaranch 'Africa Solution' doctrine where the IOC would not rehabilitate South African sport unless the African sports movement so recommended.

Two major events occurred in February 1990. On 2nd February 1990, F. W. de Klerk, the president of the South African Republic, delivered a memorable speech which is considered as a major turning point in the history of South African politics and the beginning of the end of apartheid. A few days later, on 11th February 1990, Nelson Mandela was freed after having spent twenty-seven years in jail.

His release was broadcast live across the world. At the time, I was attending meetings with the US Olympic Committee in Arizona, and I remember very clearly a telephone conversation with Samaranch, in which he said that we would soon have to move towards the rehabilitation of South African sport. I knew he had in mind the 1992 Barcelona Games. But, in accordance with his own doctrine, he had to defer to the Africans who were extremely cautious and considered that as long as apartheid had not been formally and effectively abolished, South Africa could not be welcomed back into world sport.

Many more meetings took place during 1990. On 1st February 1991, de Klerk confirmed his commitment to move towards the abolition of apartheid. By then, Samaranch was afraid that the

Olympic Movement would be left behind by the rapidly evolving situation. He managed to convince a reluctant Mbaye, who was extremely cautious by nature, that the time had come to act and send an IOC delegation to South Africa.

Of course, the delegation would be led by Mbaye and be composed of a majority of senior African IOC members. It would also include the African American Olympic champion and athletics icon, Edwin Moses, as well as Kevan Gosper, a senior IOC member from Australia. He and I, who oversaw the co-ordination of the delegation, were the only white delegates.

The delegation left Geneva on 23rd March 1991 for Johannesburg and returned on 28th March after a hectic itinerary which took us to Cape Town, Ulundi and Nelspruit. In Johannesburg, we met with representatives of all political parties and movements, including the most radical as well as conservative ones. In Cape Town, we were received by President de Klerk, who clearly confirmed his commitment to the dismantling of apartheid.

We then flew to Ulundi, capital of KwaZulu-Natal, to meet Chief Buthelezi, a major political figure as leader of the Zulu Nation and later founder of the Inkatha Freedom Party. The climax of our visit was our meeting with Nelson Mandela at the small local airport of Nelspruit, where he joined us by helicopter. The meeting, which was entirely informal, took place in the modest pilots' lounge of what was a very small airport with a short grass runway.

Mandela greeted each of us warmly, as if we were old friends. I was immediately impressed and fascinated by his extraordinary personality. Here was one of the most important people in the world, a man who had dedicated all his life to the fight against discrimination and for human rights, who was admired by the whole world, sitting among us and drinking a cup of tea while discussing our plans for the reintegration of his country into the international sporting community.

He was quiet, relaxed and direct. His manners were those of a wise, elderly African leader who gave the impression that his entire life had been spent peacefully as a senior magistrate. It was impossible to imagine that he had spent twenty-seven years in jail. At the end of our meeting, it was clear that Mandela would support our plan for reintegration. The objective was to welcome a new South African team at the 1992 Barcelona Olympic Games.

This was my first opportunity to meet Mandela and I immediately realised that he was, by some distance, the most impressive personality I had ever met. This first impression was reinforced during several later meetings, when I had the privilege to get to know him more informally. I must confess that until then, I had admired him from a distance for his courage and determination but had not appreciated the exceptionally profound and charismatic nature of his personality.

There was still a lot of work to be done in South Africa to achieve our objectives. While Mandela was indeed a major political figure, he was not yet President of South Africa. A number of sports organisations still had to be convinced. A second delegation, chaired by Mbaye, went to South Africa in March 1992. This was the opportunity for a second meeting with Mandela. He, in turn, visited the IOC headquarters in Lausanne in May 1992.

While preparations for the Barcelona Games progressed, we ran into a practical difficulty. Under most international eligibility standards, the South African athletes who were eligible for the 1992 Games were white. This was no surprise, as most young black athletes had not yet had a chance to train at the same level as their white counterparts. At that point, based on the eligibility standards of the governing bodies of the various international federations, it appeared that the South African Olympic team for the Barcelona Games of 1992 would have been nearly all white; hardly the outcome we wanted.

As often, Samaranch had the solution: it was decided that for its first reappearance on the world stage in Barcelona, the South African team parading at the Games would, regardless of eligibility standards, include a substantial number of deserving, young black athletes. Thus, with Mandela sitting next to Samaranch in the royal box, together with many other heads of state, the entire world could witness the profound symbolism of a multiracial South African team parading at the Barcelona Opening Ceremony.

After Barcelona, there was still much to do to reinforce the new South African Olympic organisation. This gave me the unique opportunity to meet Mandela on a more personal basis on several occasions in both Spain and Switzerland. In May 1992, I was particularly pleased to be asked, together with Mbaye and Fekrou Kidane, one of my IOC colleagues, to accompany and entertain Mandela during the few days of a visit he paid to the IOC in

Lausanne and to Montreux, where he had been invited by Samaranch.

I had the honour to escort him on a long mountain excursion and to visit the famous Castle of Chillon, near Montreux. There, to the astonishment of visiting tourists, he carefully inspected the underground cell of the famous 'Prisoner of Chillon', the Genovois monk, François Bonivard who was chained in his dank and cold dungeon for six years. The scene must have been a very poignant one for Mandela. He was very informally dressed in a sports jumpsuit, and a baseball cap, which did not stop the tourists from recognising him and taking pictures, to which he submitted graciously and with remarkable humility.

I also arranged a private boat tour of Lake Geneva, which he thoroughly enjoyed. We ended up at my village, Cully, and at my home, where, with a couple of our close local friends, he met my wife and two daughters and shared some bottles of local white wine.

We ended up having dinner at Hotel du Raisin, a well-known local inn around the corner. Cully is a small village by the lake, surrounded by beautiful vineyards. So personable and humble was his demeanour, we felt we were in the company of an old friend. He was curious about all aspects of our lives, our customs and interests, and asked all sorts of questions about Switzerland, its politics and traditions. During all that time, his extraordinary persona radiated the warmth of his humanity. They were, without doubt, the most memorable days of my life.

During Mandela's visit, I noticed that while he was wonderfully kind to us as his hosts and to all the people he met, he had certain reservations about official and political Switzerland. He was keenly aware of the fact that during the apartheid period, the official Swiss and business establishment had been very supportive of the previous South African regime. He had mentioned this to me privately, and when representatives of the Swiss government seized the opportunity of his private visit to Switzerland to hastily organise a meeting for him in our capital in Bern, he was quite reluctant to oblige.

We did not want to interfere, as the IOC had no official role to play in Swiss-South African relations. The meeting eventually took place but, of course, we did not attend. It is hard to know what transpired, but I am sure Mandela would have quizzed them at length on their thoughts about his country, past, present and future. During Mandela's stay, my feeling at all times was that while most kind to the Swiss individuals he met, he remained aloof from 'official' Switzerland. This was quite understandable as my country's government was engaged in an uncomfortable political re-evaluation of its relationship with South Africa.

During the following years, I had several more opportunities to meet Mandela, albeit more briefly and more formally, as he became president of South Africa. On each occasion, before even greeting me, his first words to me were, "How is the family back home?" As I write these lines, reflecting on many episodes in my life, which allowed me to meet or run into many powerful and fascinating individuals, Nelson Mandela remains by far the most impressive personality I ever met in my entire life.

It is a pity for South Africa and the world that his advanced age did not allow him to remain for much longer as South Africa's head of state and the leader of his nation and its people. Now that he has gone forever, we should all fervently hope that his legacy will last, not only in South Africa, but as a model for the world, a model of tolerance, simplicity, integrity and directness, to which all leaders should aspire.

Unfortunately, I'm afraid that most of the resounding tributes seen and heard around the world at the time of Mandela's death were well-meant but have proved to be hollow.

20
The Magic of Lillehammer 1994

In mid-September 1988, the IOC held its Session in Seoul shortly before the beginning of the Summer Games. The most important item on the agenda was the election of the host city for the 1994 Winter Games. By then, the main contenders were Falun, Sweden, and Lillehammer, Norway. The vote was to take place at what was then the very best hotel in Seoul, the Shilla. The announcement ceremony was going to be held in a luxurious green theatre in an exotic park adjacent to the hotel. There were plush armchairs for the many distinguished guests waiting for the outcome of the vote. In the front row, right in the middle, was the King of Sweden, surrounded by the Swedish delegation, impeccably dressed in their blue and gold uniforms.

The Norwegians were seated to the side. The seating arrangement had been decided with the approval of Samaranch, who would deliver the announcement from the stage, exactly across from the King of Sweden. While Samaranch, as always, had not given any indication as to his own preference, he never voted. Most insiders assumed that Falun would be the winning city. When Samaranch arrived on stage, followed by the eighty-seven IOC members, he looked directly at the Swedish monarch with what seemed to be a smile, which many in the audience interpreted as an indication of a Swedish victory. However, contrary to common belief, Samaranch never knew the name of the winner until he opened the envelope in front of the world's media. So, when he opened the envelope, he looked towards the Swedish delegation and read, "The 1994 Winter Games is awarded to the city of Lillehammer, Norway."

The Swedes were stunned and hugely disappointed, while the Norwegians immediately began to celebrate their victory very loudly. Their lobbying had been far more effective than the Swedes, who, by the way, despite their repeated efforts and dedication to the Olympic Movement, have never succeeded in being awarded any Winter or Summer Olympic Games since 1912.

Samaranch never openly expressed his disappointment. However, I'm convinced that he didn't feel comfortable with the Norwegians and that he would have preferred Sweden. Subsequently, the relationship between Samaranch and the Norwegian media turned out to be very difficult throughout the following years until the end of the Lillehammer Games and beyond. The Scandinavian media in general is very critical, fiercely independent and politically mainly left leaning. They didn't like Samaranch's political past in Spain under Franco and had little time for the IOC in general.

Lillehammer is a small community located more than a hundred miles north of Oslo and in 1994, numbered less than 25,000 inhabitants. Indeed, at first sight, it looked like a rather improbable candidate. But its bid did have a major advantage in that it was endorsed by the entire nation and, in particular, by the Norwegian government. The concept was original and bold. It turned out to be a stunning success. Under the leadership of Gerhard Heiberg, now a senior IOC member, the organisers delivered an extraordinary Games. They created many innovations. For example, they developed a unique integrated design, blending elements of advanced contemporary style with ancient pictograms, so one could instantly identify any venue, any product, any correspondence or any logo as related to the Lillehammer Games. In terms of planning and organisation, the Lillehammer team also proved to be exceptionally remarkable. There was only one hotel in Lillehammer, so a plan for modern temporary accommodation was quickly implemented.

The Norwegians were also quite advanced in terms of environment protection. In fact, one amusing example of their creativity involved food plates. In all lounges at all Games venues, simple hot food was available on plates made of potatoes. So, when the guests finished their meal, they would just eat their plates! Apart from their skills and ideas, the Lillehammer organisers were also blessed with great good fortune. In 1993, exactly one year before the opening of the Games, I was in Lillehammer with Samaranch. There was not even an inch of snow, it was raining, the little town was dead and the atmosphere distinctly gloomy. Understandably, we began wondering if Lillehammer had been a good choice.

One year later, when we arrived for the Games, we found at least three feet of fresh, crisp snow. The Opening Ceremony, anchored by the famous Norwegian actress, Liv Ullmann, was perfect, with a sky that reminded me of the winter snow scene in David Lean's classic 1965 film Doctor Zhivago. The next morning, and for the entire duration of the Games, the sky was crystal clear blue, and the sun shone all day. The small city was decorated tastefully, and thousands of visitors walked its main street in perfect harmony. The Norwegians were enthusiastic spectators and many of them spent their nights under canvas in sub-zero temperatures, but they didn't seem to mind.

There were also some remarkable sporting highlights. Local hero, Johann Olav Koss, won three speed skating events and set a world record in each one. Vreni Schneider of Switzerland won a complete set of medals in alpine skiing, and Manuela Di Centa of Italy won medals in all five cross-country events. The women's biathlon was dominated by Myriam Bédard of Canada, who won both individual races.

Swiss pair, Gustav Weder and Donat Acklin, became the first repeat winners of the two-man bobsleigh. Russian pairs skaters, Ekaterina Gordeeva and Sergei Grinkov, returned to repeat their Olympic victory of 1988. American Bonnie Blair made history by becoming the first woman to win three consecutive speed-skating titles in the 500m and to win a second 500m/1000m double. All in all, they really were the best Olympic Winter Games ever.

While we were in Lillehammer, an IOC delegation led by Samaranch, including, among others, Jacques Rogge, then president of the European National Olympic Committees, flew from Oslo to Sarajevo, to commemorate the tenth anniversary of the Sarajevo Winter Games and to express the IOC's support for the Bosnian Olympic Committee. We were suddenly plunged into another world, a world of war, ruin, terror, desolation and misery. Sarajevo was under siege during the Bosnian War as part of the collapse of Yugoslavia, and the United Nations had sent in a multi-nation peacekeeping force.

There were no civilian flights to Sarajevo. So, from Split, in Croatia, we had to board a French military Hercules to Sarajevo. We had been instructed to wear helmets and bulletproof vests. During the flight, I noticed that the French military personnel were standing by the doors and staring at the bleak winter landscape. After one of them had been looking for some time, I asked him if he'd seen enough of the sombre landscape. His answer was somewhat disconcerting, "I'm not looking at the landscape, I'm checking for ground-to-air missiles."

Once we landed, we were ordered to walk across the tarmac under the protection of an armoured vehicle because of the threat of snipers from the rooftops. From the airport, we were driven in a UN military convoy to the city, where we had three meetings, one in the offices of the Bosnian Olympic Committee, a second one in a hotel and thirdly, a lunch offered by the president of the Republic of Bosnia-Herzegovina. Sarajevo was still in a state of war. While there was no more bombing, snipers were still active. There was practically no electricity and no heating. The people looked poor, sad and exhausted.

During our meetings, everybody was extraordinarily kind to us, expressing their gratitude for our presence. The IOC visit to Sarajevo was purely symbolic, we wanted the people to know that while the Games were being celebrated in Lillehammer, the IOC had not forgotten Sarajevo and its people. The gesture was very well received, in particular because Samaranch himself was there. Of course, the IOC and the entire Olympic Movement were also providing substantial material and financial assistance to the Bosnian Olympic Committee. But our physical presence, under very difficult circumstances, was appreciated.

The lunch offered by the president of the Republic in his 'palace' was surreal. There were recent bullet holes in the dining room, the menu was frugal, but the waiters, in full military uniform, wore impeccable white gloves. The president apologised for not offering us wine, but only champagne. He explained that the wine reserves of the presidency were totally exhausted and that by then, the cellar only contained a few bottles of champagne! I remember that during the lunch, we could hear the sound of sporadic snipers' fire. At the end of the day, we were driven back to the airport, from where we flew back to Split and Oslo. The return to the warmth, peace and joy of Lillehammer was a relief. We had seen the best and the worst of our world in just a few hours.

That trip to Sarajevo left me with a touching personal memory. When we arrived at the airport, we were welcomed not only by a number of officials, but also by a small crowd of Bosnians, mostly elderly people carrying welcome posters made up of old cardboard. The weather was cold, they were poorly dressed and looked exhausted. On the other hand, we were warmly dressed in our fashionable winter sports overcoats, which could have been viewed as a provocation by the poor Bosnians. But their attitude was totally different. They were delighted to see us and waved Olympic flags as we boarded the heavily armoured UN vehicles. Then I noticed that a few elderly ladies were offering us pullovers bearing the Olympic rings which had obviously been knitted by them. I was handed one of them and was deeply touched by the old woman's gesture. But, as I was trying to thank her, I was pushed towards the vehicle by a soldier, which caused me to slip on the icy ground and I let the gift fall. The poor woman looked so forlorn as her hard work fell into the mud. The soldier picked me up and with a heave, loaded me into the vehicle, which immediately backed away, crushing the pullover under its wheels.

I have never forgotten the devastated look in the poor woman's eyes. There she was, in a city devastated by war, not asking for anything but, on the contrary, offering something precious to a stranger to keep me warm. It was a wonderful example of generosity and dignity, and, albeit involuntarily, I had ruined the impact of her gesture. I never had the chance to see her again and, to this day, feel sad about the incident.

21
Are the Olympic Winter Games Still Viable?

Taking into account the great success of recent Olympic Winter Games, one might take for granted that their future is secure. Yet, in my opinion, this is not the case. Since Lillehammer, the Winter Olympics have gradually evolved towards a new business model which may be described as a division between the major sports on ice like ice hockey, skating and curling on the one hand, and, on the other hand, those sports competed for on snow, like skiing, snowboarding, and biathlon. While the former requires large indoor venues, which are normally found or built in large cities, the latter events take place at or near resorts which are usually located away from major cities.

Apart from large indoor venues, cities offer significant facilities for accommodating officials, sponsors, media and spectators. The apparently unavoidable consequence of that is that the Winter Olympics have to take place in a city for their large venue events and in a mountain resort for the snow sports, often located a long distance away. That means at least two very different environments and people behave differently in a city as opposed to a resort. It is also likely that the weather will be very different, snow in the resort and rain in the city, as was the case in Vancouver in 2010. The distances and transportation times lead many people to avoid travelling between the city and the resort and vice versa. The logical outcome of that is, in spite of all the Olympic pageantry displayed everywhere, the prevailing spirit at the Olympics is more and more that of each individual sport rather than a unified Olympic experience. In the cities, the major venues are controlled by the individual international federations rather than by the IOC or the Games' organising committee. Each sport has its own lounge where the sport's leaders entertain their own athletes, friends and sponsors, so that the atmosphere is more like that of separate world championships rather than the unique experience of the Olympic Games. The same can be said of the sports located in mountain resorts.

That situation of a clear division between the winter sports is further reinforced by the fact that the athletes themselves are separated so that they can be closer to their competition venues. For athletes, the original feature of the Olympic Games experience was that, in order to promote international harmony and understanding, they stayed together in an Olympic village rather than in hotels. Now, the concept of a single village for all athletes, in accordance with the ideals of the Olympic Movement, has been seriously eroded. For example, to my knowledge, the International Ski Federation has never accepted that its athletes stay in the Olympic Village, even when the village was near to the skiing venues. The position of the FIS, as expressed by its late president, Marc Hodler, also a senior IOC member, who ruled as president for forty-six years, was categorical: the skiers must sleep nearby to their competition venue.

Hodler's influence over the Winter Olympics was such that nobody dared challenge him. In fact, Samaranch let Hodler become the most influential IOC member regarding any matter concerning the Winter Games and winter sports. In my view, such a division of powers between Hodler and Samaranch, who was not a fan of winter sports, was not healthy. Samaranch's 'understanding' with Hodler had been arranged in 1980, at the time of the IOC presidential election. Hodler had been a candidate against Samaranch but he withdrew and since then Hodler reigned supreme over the Winter Olympics until 2002. While he was praised as a truly great Olympic leader, his first loyalty was always towards his own sport, skiing, and his priority was the wellbeing of 'his' athletes, the skiers, and their technical entourages. I suspect that he considered that the true spirit of sport was to be found in skiing and that all other sports should be regarded as less true. I also suspect that, while he didn't say so, the concept of an Olympic village didn't appeal to him. As far as he was concerned, the athletes should be close to their venues and if that meant separate accommodation sport by sport, so be it. His vision was very helpful for the autonomy of the various international federations, but not helpful to the promotion of the Olympic ideal. The problem was made more acute by the fact that Hodler was systematically appointed by Samaranch as chairman of the successive co-ordination commissions for the Winter Olympics, which empowered him with vast authority.

Hodler's stance, combined with the ambitions of other leaders of international federations, has contributed to the current weakened status of the Winter Games. While Lillehammer delivered the best Winter Olympics, the evolution since then should cause the IOC to seriously review the situation, not only in terms of practical solutions for venues and accommodation, but also in terms of their compatibility with the fundamental values of Olympism.

I am neither a theoretician nor a dreamer but am convinced that if the IOC does not determine more clearly where it wants to go with the Winter Games, the time might soon come when the Winter Olympics will be nothing more than a temporarily prestigious, momentarily commercially valuable brand that is no more than a set of additional world championships. Also, when considering the concept of a Winter Games, we should remember that Coubertin, our founder, had not foreseen a Winter Olympics. It might therefore be that the IOC should revisit the concept with a creative and original approach. For instance, is it really necessary to kindle the Olympic flame for the Winter Olympics in Olympia and have Greek actresses invoking ancient Greek gods in honour of a Games invented in 1924 in Chamonix, a French tourist resort?

Let me be clear, I am not advocating the removal of the Winter Games, I am simply suggesting that the whole concept should be revisited. Indeed, the following episode illustrates some of the issues I am referring to. During the preparations for the Lillehammer Games, the Norwegian organisers considered that the kindling of the Olympic flame in Olympia was totally absurd for a winter festival. Considering that Norway claims to be the cradle of skiing, which might well be true, they proposed that for their Games, the Olympic flame should be kindled not in Greece, but in Norway. The idea was creative and made a lot of sense. Hodler, who was particularly fond of Norway, was prepared to endorse it, but there was a difficulty.

According to the Olympic Charter, while the Olympic flame is defined as belonging to the IOC, it is further specifically defined as, 'the flame which is kindled in Olympia under the authority of the IOC', language that was the result of a compromise between the IOC and the Greek Olympic Committee. The Greeks, with some justification, consider that in reality, the Olympic flame, which is sacred, belongs to Greece and its people, and that its guardian is the Greek Olympic Committee. When the Greeks found out about the Norwegian initiative, there was an uproar which developed into a crisis. The Greeks complained vehemently to the IOC, demanding that the IOC exercise its authority and that the Norwegian plans be cancelled. The Norwegians can also be tough and believed that they had received at least a tacit endorsement from the IOC through Hodler. Sensing that the incident was about to turn into a Greek tragedy, Samaranch decided that I should fly to Athens with

Gerhard Heiberg, the chairman of the Lillehammer Games, to find a solution to the problem.

So began a negotiation with the Greek sports and political leadership, which were like talks to create a tripartite peace treaty in times of war! Fortunately, Heiberg and I got the intelligent support of Lambis Nicolaou, then one of the two IOC members for Greece. After many hours of heated discussions, we reached a compromise which may appear derisory, but which restored peace with the Greeks. The settlement was that the Olympic flame would indeed be kindled in Olympia, according to the Charter. Simultaneously, the Norwegians would kindle their flame in Norway and with it hold a national torch relay to Oslo, where the Olympic flame would arrive by plane from Greece. At that point, the Norwegian flame would be ceremonially melded with the Olympic flame. Then, from Oslo onwards, there would be a single torch relay, ending in Lillehammer, where the Olympic torch would light the Cauldron during the Opening Ceremony of the Games. An Olympic truce had been reached, and the honour of both Norway and Greece had been saved.

The episode illustrates the extent to which sport and the Olympic Movement are a mirror of international society. It also demonstrates how, sometimes, sports leaders can be unaware of the real needs and aspirations of the athletes. Considering that the concept of an Olympic flame began at the Amsterdam Games of 1928 and, with little substance in Greek history, developed as a torch relay from Greece for the Berlin Games of 1936, if any competitor in Lillehammer had known about the 'peace treaty' negotiations that had to be held in order to ensure the flame's arrival at the Games, they would have thought it patently ridiculous. And they would've been right.

Revisiting the format of the Winter Olympics, which should not only be a commercially viable model but also a truly Olympic concept, is a very serious challenge. Most former Olympians recall the unique experience offered by the Olympic village, which should be a singular phenomenon, not a multiple one. In Lillehammer, the Olympic spirit prevailed, not only thanks to the extraordinary enthusiasm of the organisers, the Norwegian people and their authorities, but also thanks to the unique special atmosphere created by the fact that Lillehammer was a tiny, compact community, where its short main street became the sporting capital of the world for seventeen magical days.

Such magic can't be conjured up in a major city. Interestingly, the Winter Olympics were also successful in terms of Olympic spirit in those cities which were small enough to offer the intimacy of a global party, like Calgary (1988), Nagano (1998), Salt Lake City (2002) and even Sochi (2014). There are lessons to be drawn, therefore, for the future. Sochi's Games were a great success for everyone, in particular the athletes. All the venues were excellent and so were the Olympic villages. The staff were well trained and enthusiastic, and Russia delivered Games that were technically outstanding. Thanks to the concentration of important clusters, the atmosphere was a truly sporting one. Of course, that assessment does not take into account any cost factors, which cost President Putin's government and various oligarchs many billions of dollars, nor can we evaluate the actual sporting legacy of the Games, which may not bear much scrutiny.

However, as a template for compact Winter Games, the Sochi model should be regarded as an important contribution to the search for a definition of future Winter Games. Its format was totally distinct from those of previous Games in that there was no real metropolitan city directly involved for the participants, and all the events were concentrated in two different clusters, one, the Olympic Park, on the seashore near Adler, a rather small community, and the other in the mountains, less than an hour's easy drive away. The athletes were housed in the Olympic Park, while all Olympic officials stayed in adjacent hotels. There was no time wasted in excessive travel, as had been the case for all previous Games, and the airport was a few minutes' drive away from the park.

So, on the whole, the Sochi concept was excellent. However, I haven't forgotten the intolerable behaviour of the Russians at many levels which caused the worst doping scandal in the history of sport and will leave a scar on sport for generations to come. Even so, the key question remains, could a Sochi model be reproduced elsewhere in the future? Taking into account significant opposition groups and the extraordinary costs issues, the answer is that it's probably unrealistic to think that it could happen in a democratic country. However, there are some voices which suggest that the IOC should consider adopting a permanent site for the Winter Games, a solution which has, by the way, also been suggested several times for the Summer Olympics.

This is a major challenge that the Olympic Movement cannot ignore, and must address in a creative way, and requires closer than ever co-operation between all concerned. The decision taken by the

IOC Session in Kuala Lumpur on 3rd July 2015, to award the organisation of the 2022 Olympic Winter Games to the city of Beijing, China, illustrates the seriousness of the problem. The IOC members had a difficult choice to make. The only two remaining candidate cities were Almaty, Kazakhstan, and Beijing, People's Republic of China. Beijing had successfully organised impressive Summer Games in 2008. Even so, the world at large asked the obvious question, why, just seven years later, would the IOC decide to return to Beijing, this time for a Winter Games?

Beijing's hugely polluted metropolis is probably one of the last places in the world suitable for a winter sports resort. Almaty's bid was much closer to a real winter sports model, yet the IOC chose Beijing. Whatever the motivation of the deciding majority, the decision shows that the IOC doesn't have a clear policy in terms of what it expects. In any event, the current IOC president, Thomas Bach, who was not in charge when the bidding process for 2022 was launched in 2011, has launched a very ambitious project called 'Olympic Agenda 2020' which, in particular, offers new opportunities and facilities to those cities interested in hosting the Olympic Games.

Having attended all Winter Games since 1988, I have had a unique opportunity to observe their evolution and the problems they are facing. The challenges are diverse. First, as already mentioned, it is a fact that in most countries of Western Europe, the cradle of Winter Olympics, many people are hostile to the very concept of hosting such events. The most frequent argument advanced by opponents is of a financial nature: the Games cost too much to the taxpayer; the budgets submitted are never respected and much money is wasted without significant benefit for the future of the region or country.

Apart from such financial issues, environmental concerns are raised: the impact of Winter Games on nature is unnecessary and negative. Another difficulty that affects the Winter Games lies in global climate change with the progressive and spectacular reduction of natural snow. For all those and other reasons, there are currently fewer and fewer candidates to host the Winter Olympics.

Having analysed and reflected on the problem, I have reached the conclusion that the IOC, in the wake of its new doctrine of Agenda 2020, should acknowledge the de facto split between snow and ice, and should replace the Winter Olympic Games by the Snow Olympic Games, which should attract many bids from ski resorts, and the Ice Olympic Games which would interest large cities. In order to maintain a four-year cycle for the participants, the two Games could be held alternately every two years and, crucially, would create the unique Olympic spirit and party atmosphere that is central to a successful host city.

The Olympic Winter Games were not part of Coubertin's original vision when they were first held in Chamonix in 1924. They were staged outdoors, there was no television then. Times have changed; the IOC has changed. Let's hope that it will now adapt to the many challenges the Winter Olympic Games are facing. In fact, the same challenges also face the Summer Games and, more generally, all sport. I will return to those challenges later.

22
The World's Most Exclusive Gentleman's Club

Every other odd-numbered year, the IOC Session chooses the host city for the Olympic Games to be held seven years later. The Session, the IOC's annual general assembly, includes all its members, currently one hundred and five active and forty-five honorary individuals from all over the world. IOC members are co-opted, supposedly to ensure that they are independent and represent the sole interests of the IOC in their countries and in the sports organisations in which they serve, not the other way around. Officially, members are required to, 'represent and promote the interests of the IOC and of the Olympic Movement in their countries and in the organisations of the Olympic Movement in which they serve'.

Sadly, that is not true for several members who, in fact, represent various conflicting private or public interest groups. The members are co-opted from very different personal, professional and political backgrounds, and from diverse cultures across the world. Apart from many people of great distinction, the membership includes three heads of state: Luxemburg, Monaco and Qatar; and several other royals: the United Kingdom, Denmark, Liechtenstein, Malaysia, Saudi Arabia, Kuwait, United Arab Emirates and Jordan. Members are expected to share a common ideal, Olympism, that important, if somewhat vague, set of philosophical principles that lie at the heart of what sport is thought to be about, and here I must quote the IOC itself.

'Olympism is a philosophy of life, exalting and combining in a balanced whole the qualities of body, will and mind. Blending sport with culture and education, Olympism seeks to create a way of life based on the joy of effort, the educational value of good example, social responsibility and respect for universal fundamental ethical principles.

The goal of Olympism is to place sport at the service of the harmonious development of humankind, with a view to promoting a peaceful society concerned with the preservation of human dignity.'

Also, although defined in various different ways, 'the *fundamental ethical principles*' referred to in the IOC's outline above, are, as the IOC puts it:

Excellence, *doing the best you can, in sport and in life by taking part and striving for improvement, not just by winning.*

Friendship, *using sport to develop tolerance and understanding between all people, performers, spectators and citizens.*

Respect, *having consideration for oneself, others and the global environment.*

Some IOC members are wealthy, but not all, and are expected to serve on a volunteer basis, without compensation for their commitment. They include   former and current athletes, entrepreneurs, industrialists, bankers, sports administrators, ministers, heads of state and royals. While it encourages the inclusion of women, and indeed in increasing numbers, it still has the aura of a private gentlemen's club. Not only that, its membership is such that it could easily be defined as the most exclusive in the world.

Perhaps another less critical comparison would describe it as a volunteer parliament of international sport dedicated to the promotion of Olympism and its values, using a self-appointed mandate to celebrate the Olympic rings, one of the most famous and valuable brands in the world. In truth, the IOC is a unique institution and a mirror of our world, with some exceptional personalities at the highest level, as well as some far more mediocre individuals. Unfortunately, some IOC members use their position to improve their own status in their home countries and expect to be compared to and treated like ambassadors or ministers. Indeed, all of them enjoy various degrees of VIP treatment, to which they have become accustomed and often take for granted. Although it's true that the IOC has a very important mission for the sake of international sport and the world's athletes, that comes with the risk of being seen as isolated in an ivory tower, far removed from the real world.

The main remit of the IOC is to select the host cities for the Games and define the sports programme for their celebration. Until 2016, the selection of the host cities was achieved through an election procedure providing for the successive elimination of several candidates through one or several secret ballots until a city obtained a majority. The outcome of the vote was publicly proclaimed by the IOC president at a somewhat dull announcement ceremony which was supposed to be broadcast live to the world, but, in fact, was only of interest to the media of the countries of the bidding cities.

In my view the announcement ceremony invariably followed a rather archaic protocol, more reminiscent of the election of the pope than the celebration of the most important, joyful and multisport event in the world. All the members of the IOC would walk onto an elevated stage on which, with pompous gravitas, they would stand in sombre ranks as if they were Gods on Mount Olympus. A better analogy was offered by Samaranch every time he witnessed it. He suggested that as the members trudged onto the stage, it was like watching old elephants plodding off to the Elephants' Graveyard. As only one city could be the winner, the contrived tension was accentuated by the fact that everybody knew that the vast majority of the audience would be disappointed. After a wait of several long minutes, the IOC president would arrive at centre stage, where an innocent child would present him with a sealed envelope containing the name of the winner. The president would then thank all the candidate cities for their excellent work before, just like at the Oscars ceremony, solemnly opening the envelope, and after a very pregnant pause, announcing the name of the winning city.

An eruption of utter delight by the winners and tearful distress by the losers would explode from the audience. The IOC members would then, just as solemnly, exit the stage amidst the uproar, so that the parties and the wakes could begin. I attended at least fifteen such announcements, nine of which were presided over by Samaranch. Nowadays, thanks to the IOC's renewal and to the appointment of younger members, I should say the process is far less portentous. In fact, on several occasions when I was Director General, I suggested changes to the ceremony that I thought projected a negative image of the IOC which looked more like a gathering of the ageing senior citizens of an old people's home than the leadership of a movement dedicated to the youth of the world.

At the time, the average age of the members was well over sixty, but although Samaranch shared my views, he suggested that I should refrain from any attempt to update the ceremony. My thoughts had been leaked and some members had strongly cautioned Samaranch against change. The ceremonial didn't change under the Jacques Rogge presidency, which followed Samaranch, and the byzantine ritual was only abandoned in Lima, in 2016, with the IOC Session by consensus simultaneously awarding the 2024 and 2028 Games to Paris and Los Angeles respectively. The fact that the announcement ceremony has been entirely revamped is a positive sign and thankfully different from the pitiful sight of the world's leaders jockeying for position as they have their photograph taken at frivolous world summits.

The IOC elephants may have looked old and obsolete in the past but they were certainly less harmful and possibly more useful than most politicians of today. Of course, unlike their political counterparts they don't have to campaign for re-election. They are re-elected every eight years by their peers, who, in turn are also re-elected! While this form of co-option is certainly undemocratic, it has distinct advantages, which are best understood if I offer an outline of the Olympic Movement, its objectives, constituents and structures.

The Olympic Movement is defined in the Olympic Charter as the, *'concerted, organised, universal and permanent action, carried out under the supreme authority of the IOC, of all individuals and entities inspired by the values of Olympism'*. It covers all five continents and reaches its zenith with the gathering of the 'Youth of the World' at the Olympic Games. Belonging to the Olympic Movement requires compliance with the Olympic Charter and recognition by the IOC. The three main constituents of the Olympic Movement are the IOC, scores of International Sports Federations (IFs) and currently 206 National Olympic Committees (NOCs) across the world and includes in those countries everyone who cherishes the Olympic Games and Olympism. Thus, the Olympic Movement is indeed a major global organisation which numbers hundreds of millions of individuals throughout the world. Its main component, the IOC, was founded in Paris by Coubertin in 1894. In 1915, during World War One, its headquarters was transferred to Lausanne, Switzerland, where it still is today.

The status of the IOC has often been questioned. There have been many proposals, even pressures, that it be modified or even transformed. Several politicians have insisted that the IOC become an intergovernmental organisation to which IOC members would be appointed by their governments. Not surprisingly, the IOC has firmly resisted such proposals. In support of its position of governmental independence, the IOC can claim that since its foundation in 1894, it has successfully survived two world wars and many other major political or economic crises. Indeed, the cornerstone of that achievement is the IOC's complete institutional independence from all political pressures, which derives directly from its undemocratic co-option practice.

The IOC is not a corporation and has no owners other than its own members. There is no 'entitlement' to become a member of the IOC; it's not a foundation, but simply an 'association', a legal structure commonly used under Swiss law for clubs. The actual power of the IOC derives from the fact that it selects the host cities for the Olympic Games, which, as the most important global multisport competition, have become the world's greatest celebratory gathering of any kind. The IOC's ownership of the Games and of its symbolic five rings has allowed it to negotiate very lucrative agreements, in particular with exclusive sponsors and worldwide broadcasters. That means that, not only does it enjoy unique political independence, it also has powerful financial independence in significant measure.

That independence is the result of the work of a small team of dedicated IOC members and a competent staff of senior professionals. Most IOC members are not involved in the actual management and governance of the IOC, but some sit on commissions to oversee specific parts of its organisation. IOC members are required to attend the annual Session which is held each year in a different country around the world. Apart from electing the president and the members of the IOC Executive Board, their real power lies in the votes they cast to designate the host cities. That leads to candidate cities' representatives, ministers, ambassadors, sponsors and consultants lobbying IOC members in the hope of obtaining their vote. Thus, IOC members are usually treated like VIPs or even ministers of state, and in the case of the president, like a head of state. Most of them quickly become accustomed to such privileges: no queues at airports, simplified immigration procedures, special lounges, limousines flanked by motorcyclists, sumptuous champagne receptions and extravagant official banquets with haute cuisine and fine wines.

Until recently, the IOC Session rarely produced anything of significance, and serious debate was rare. As a body, there was little consistency or coherence. The multicultural structure of the Session was such that it's best compared to an international organisation like the United Nations or UNESCO. While the IOC as an institution is far from perfect, it has nevertheless succeeded so far, and has, on the whole, taken mostly appropriate decisions for the development of the Olympic Movement and for the promotion of Olympism in the world. The few surviving elephants may still look ponderous and dull but things are changing quite quickly, thanks to the arrival of many younger and less sober members. Times are changing, and the more recently co-opted members are far less pompous and conservative than their predecessors. Of course, only time will tell if the IOC and the Olympic Movement will be able to meet successfully the challenges it will face.

23
The Olympic Movement - Family, Sect or Network

So, what exactly is this thing we call the Olympic Movement, a phenomenon that is supported by hundreds of millions of people around the world? Until about thirty years ago, the Olympic Charter defined the adherents to the Olympic Movement as 'the Olympic Family', which was a concept that would have been understood by Coubertin in the early days of the Olympic journey. However, such a paternalistic definition is surely now obsolete and doesn't correspond to the norms of modern society. Today, the concept of the Olympic Family has essentially disappeared from the Olympic Charter, largely because it implies an artificial elite or caste quite different from the universal inference in the word 'movement'.

Some people have attempted to describe the Olympic Movement as a sort of sect. They cite its rituals and protocols in things like the kindling of the Olympic flame in Olympia, replete with its pagan and mythological symbolism. It is certainly true, for instance, that anyone who is witness to the final of an Olympic ice-hockey tournament would find it difficult to see any kind of link, whether intellectual, emotional or philosophical between the drama on ice that is hockey and the ritual symbolism of the ancient Greek flame, let alone the elegant writings of Coubertin. Yet such links are supposed to be apparent to all participants and acknowledged by all as essential ingredients of Olympism and the Olympic Games.

Indeed, the tenuous nature of that link is why the IOC should be extremely careful and give serious thought to some elements of Olympism of which the IOC is the trustee and guardian. For example, I am convinced that the Olympic flame's rituals and the Olympic torch relay are at risk. This is particularly true for the torch relay since, with the considerable encouragement of Coca Cola, a major IOC sponsor, it has become far bigger than a relatively simple and symbolic event for the host country of the Games. For most people, their perception of the Olympic torch relay as a true Olympic symbol is illustrated by carrying the flame lit in Olympia. The torch is held aloft throughout the host country until it ignites the Cauldron in the Olympic Stadium during the Opening Ceremony of the Games. It then burns brightly until its nostalgic extinction at the end of the Closing Ceremony. However, the IOC has twice accepted that the torch relay should step back from its traditional national concept and become an international event.

The first exception was granted to the charismatic and intelligent leader of the 2004 Athens Organising Committee, Gianna Angelopoulos. One of her main arguments was that a torch relay limited to Greece would, to a certain extent, be a non-event inasmuch as Greece would see no point in waiting for the arrival of its own flame. In addition, she convinced the IOC that transforming the torch relay into a major global event would promote Greece and the Olympic Movement and give it a global dimension compatible with the twenty-first century. The marketing gurus who, more and more, consider themselves as the true guardians of the Olympic values, another danger, endorsed the new concept enthusiastically. I tried to convince both Jacques Rogge, then in charge of the co-ordination of the 2004 Games, and Samaranch to keep the torch relay within Greece, but in vain. They said it was the Greeks' call, not mine. In fact, Athens' international torch relay turned out to be a success.

Not surprisingly, the success led the 2008 Beijing organisers to announce their intention to also organise an international torch relay. One might have thought that the size of China and its vast population, would persuade the organisers that a national relay would have been a major event in itself, without any need to expand it internationally. But Athens had created a precedent and it was then a matter of principle and prestige for the Chinese. The marketing gurus applauded once more and the Chinese request was approved. At that stage, nobody had envisaged that by going international, the torch relay would offer a unique platform for demonstrators and supporters of many causes, including opponents to the Chinese government. The Beijing torch relay became a disaster in most major cities of the world. Instead of promoting the values of Olympism as such, it became a major anti-Chinese flashpoint, as well as instigating a wave of criticism of the IOC, which was pilloried by many human-rights activists, and a host of media for not supporting the cause of Tibet.

The Beijing torch relay was a costly but useful lesson for the IOC. It confirmed the need, from time to time, to review Olympic institutions in the context of modern society. I'm not advocating the cancellation of the flame or the relay, but I am saying that as the world evolves, the IOC should be more proactive and reflect on its important institutions. Such reflections should be conducted at the highest level and not left to the marketing gurus. If that had happened, the Beijing relay disaster may have been avoided. While it was obvious that Greece would not attract any opposition on the international scene, it was equally obvious that China and its Tibet policy would be perfect targets for many groups with axes to grind.

Fortunately, the 2010, Vancouver, and 2012, London torch relays were spared any significant incidents and took place in the best Olympic spirit. However, in my opinion, that was due to the fact that the people of Canada and Great Britain, like the Australians and the Americans, are inspired by a true spirit of sportsmanship, as was also evidenced by the atmosphere and ambiance in all the venues during their Games. On the other hand, the 2014 Sochi torch relay was captured by Russia as an instrument of propaganda to demonstrate the Russian technological achievements. For instance, it sent a torch into space and under the sea. Until then, it had been an important principle that once kindled in Olympia, the Olympic flame should never go out before the Closing Ceremony of the Games. The Russians didn't seem to be overly concerned by principles, as the flame went out on several occasions and was lit again with cigarette lighters! This shows that the only way to avoid deviations from the original spirit of the Olympic torch relay is for the IOC to keep tight control over such an important event.

Another important issue for the Olympic Movement and the IOC is their current relationship with the heritage of Coubertin. The preamble of the Olympic Charter recalls that 'Modern Olympism was conceived by Pierre de Coubertin…', which is correct. He deserves and enjoys wide recognition for his original ideas. However, times have changed since 1894; our society is different, and sport has evolved. Some of Coubertin's attitudes, such as his prejudices about women and his aristocratic elitism, are anathema today. In that context, one issue which the Olympic Movement is facing is what I would suggest is an excessive, almost religious cult of personality around Coubertin. Within the Olympic Movement, there are many scholars who are engaged in endless so-called academic debates to dissect his writings.

While Coubertin deserves everybody's respect, he is no god. Nobody knows what he would say or write today and frankly, it doesn't matter. His writings, which are not universally profound, are no bible and, in the twenty-first century, what matters is to promote good values and simple principles, without having to constantly refer back to Coubertin. The Olympic Movement should have the strength to stand on its own feet and to convey a modern vision of Olympism. Such a vision can be very simple: Olympism seeks to convey three forms of respect through education in sport: self-respect, which implies keeping a sound mind in a healthy body; respect for others, which implies tolerance and understanding, and respect of the rules, which leads to social integration.

Those very simple values should be taught in all schools around the world through an 'Olympic' approach to sport using a modern form of Olympism compatible with our times, rather than Coubertin's frozen definition from 1894. Of course Coubertin should be honoured, but the time has come for the IOC and the Olympic Movement to move on, which the current president, Thomas Bach, has clearly realised, and by doing so, avoid the risk of being dismissed as a sect rooted in Greek mythology and French Belle Époque elitism.

The Olympic Movement is neither a family, nor a sect, but it is a unique and formidable international network. Sport allows for the establishment of a worldwide web of relationships essentially based on friendship, understanding and tolerance, and that's where the Olympic Movement, including, of course, the IOC, is strongest and at its best. During my years at the IOC, I had the opportunity to meet countless impressive people around the world. Some were great active or retired athletes, others were major corporate or media leaders, and there were notable statesmen and stateswomen, heads of governments, ministers, senior civil servants and intellectuals. On every occasion, including during some delicate negotiations, being an IOC representative always made the contact easy and relaxed. The reason for that was very simple: the Olympic agenda is almost always positive; we are usually bringing good news and the Olympic Movement has no hidden political agenda. Not only that, many of those I've mentioned above are also part of the Olympic Movement and share the values of Olympism.

As the self-proclaimed 'supreme authority' of the Olympic Movement, apart from its main responsibility to oversee the Olympic Games, the IOC is essentially the co-ordinator of the activities of the Olympic Movement. The actual power within the IOC is held by a president and the Executive Board, all elected by the Session. The president serves for an eight-year term, renewable only once for four years, and the Executive Board for four-year terms. The Session is a rather unpredictable body but is usually inclined to follow the proposals of the president and the Executive Board. Interestingly and importantly, a review of the IOC Session's main decisions over recent decades, including, of course, the choice of the host cities of the Olympic Games, reveals that they were generally both thoughtful and considered.

24
Atlanta 1996, The Centennial Games

The 1996 Atlanta Olympic Games produced great sporting moments in front of enthusiastic crowds, and the athletes were well taken care of in the Olympic village, located on the campus of the Georgia Institute of Technology, better known as Georgia Tech. On the other hand, there were many operational problems in several key areas like information technology and transportation issues which caused an uproar from the media. The training of volunteers, whose motivation was generally wonderful, had been minimal and incomplete. Also, the organisers had failed to control the presence of hordes of street vendors, which made some of the city's main streets close to venues look like cheap flea-markets.

After a few days, Samaranch was working on the wording of his comments during the Closing Ceremony, which is broadcast live to the world. At all Games, the formula used by the IOC president to describe the quality of the Games was eagerly awaited by the local organisers and spectators. Until 1996, he had consistently proclaimed the Games as 'The best Games ever', which was particularly pleasing for him in 1992 in Barcelona, his home city. Because of vital shortcomings, such an accolade could not be said of Atlanta. Samaranch was looking for another formula which could use different superlatives without offending the Atlanta organisers.

The Games had begun on 19th July and by the end of the first week, the mood was one of mixed feelings. On the evening of 26th July, I went to bed early at the IOC official hotel, the Marriott Marquis. I had taken some medication given me by the IOC physician, Patrick Schamasch, to cure a fever I'd caught from the difference between an excessively low room temperature from its air-conditioning and the outdoor heat of the US South. I'd told the hotel operators to refuse any phone calls. I was deeply asleep and sweating when my phone rang. I picked up the receiver and heard an unknown female voice saying, 'Mr. Carrard?' and saw that the time was 1:40 am. Furious, and thinking the voice belonged to a journalist, I hung up. One minute later, the phone rang again. I lifted the receiver again and while I was trying to prepare some really rude reply, the same voice hurriedly said that she apologised, that she was assistant to Billy Payne, the CEO of the Games, and that we had a serious problem because a bomb had just exploded in the Olympic Park, and that she had been instructed to call me so that the IOC knew about the incident. As you might imagine, I was suddenly wide awake!

I thanked her and asked her to tell her boss that we would call him as soon as I'd told Samaranch. I jumped from my bed and saw through my windows that the centre of Atlanta, twenty or so floors below, was illuminated by the flashing lights of a sea of police, fire and ambulance vehicles. I immediately turned on the four or five TV sets in my room and saw the startling reports and began to think of a possible terrorist attack. There were reports of casualties and even deaths. The information was contradictory but the situation was obviously serious.

I shaved, took a quick shower, got dressed and rushed to the upper floor to wake up Samaranch. I dashed through his security people, who knew me, knocked at Samaranch's assistant's bedroom and went straight to wake him up in his room. He was deeply asleep and totally surprised to see me sitting on his bed. I briefly told him about the news, to which he listened calmly. He then stood up, walked to his desk in his sitting room and turned on the wall of TV screens which gave him simultaneous views of twenty-four channels and feeds from the competition venues. The room was instantly transformed into a surreal multiple screening room. All the screens were showing images of rescue operations from the Olympic Park. The Park, a great concept in the middle of Atlanta, had been created as a place where the thousands of visitors to the Games could meet. As a public space where people could gather without tickets or accreditation, it had also become a soft target for anyone with evil intent, and at the time would have been packed with thousands of people enjoying themselves, which was a terrifying thought for us. Indeed, the images were reminiscent of a war zone. We were then joined by Annie Inchauspé, Samaranch's Basque assistant, and knowing it was going to be a very long day, he asked her to make some strong coffee. Annie made the coffee, then began to wake up all available members of the Executive Board, asking them to join us.

By then, it was past 2:00 am. The news was contradictory about the number of casualties. There were reports of two to four deaths, possibly more. Billy Payne called back to inform us that an emergency meeting was being planned for 3:00 am, chaired by Georgia's State Governor, Zell Miller. Samaranch immediately responded, saying that any decision would require the IOC's approval and that his attendance in person was essential. After further discussions over the phone, the format of the meeting was changed into a circular conference call to be held at 3:45 am for all institutions and agencies involved in the staging and security of the Games. Samaranch appointed me to be the IOC spokesperson for that call.

As time passed, it was obvious that the key issue was to determine whether the bombing was an isolated criminal act or part of a possible terrorist conspiracy. Everybody was wondering whether there could be a link to the crash of TWA flight 800, which exploded and plunged into the Atlantic Ocean, shortly after taking off from New York, just two days before the Opening Ceremony. All kinds of speculations and rumours spread around the world, and there was massive pressure from all media to find out whether the Games would be suspended or cancelled. By around 3:30 am, about two hours after the explosion, we knew that there were no other bombs in Atlanta and that at that point, nobody had claimed responsibility. Together with the Atlanta organisers, we made up our minds that the Games should continue. It was agreed that we would inform the officials at the beginning of the conference call and that a press conference should be held immediately thereafter.

The conference call quickly turned into one of those endless and mostly useless surreal conversations. All possible federal, state and city authorities and agencies involved in any aspect of security and law enforcement had been invited to participate, together with ACOG (the Atlanta Centennial Olympic Games Organising Committee) and the IOC. The conference began with a long roll call, during which a host of people introduced themselves and outlined their mission relating to the consequences of the bombing. It quickly became obvious to me that the priority of the speakers was to ascertain which agency held jurisdiction to lead the investigation and make the appropriate decisions.

Nobody seemed to be in command, and we had to listen to lengthy arguments between the representatives. Together with ACOG, we repeatedly insisted that in view of the fact that the explosion appeared to be an isolated crime, which had caused one death, we had decided that the Games should continue that very morning without any change to the schedule. We also insisted on the necessity to make an immediate announcement. However, we were repeatedly told that while our decision was not challenged in principle, any announcement should be postponed until more clues had been investigated, but nobody dared to suggest a time-frame.

More than an hour passed without any decisions, at which point, we told everyone on the call that we couldn't wait any longer and that the IOC and ACOG were going to announce in a press conference that the Games would go on, that a minute's silence would be observed at all venues, that all flags would be lowered to half-mast and that the Centennial Park would be closed temporarily for investigation purposes. While no one openly objected, we felt uncertainty and even reluctance from several agencies that wanted us to wait, but without proposing an alternative plan. We eventually moved to the Press Centre, where, after a few last-minute delaying tactics by some agencies, a press conference finally took place at approximately 5:20 am, when I announced to the hundreds of media representatives that the Games would go on. By then, it was nearly noon in Europe, where rumours about a possible cancellation of the Games were rife. In Atlanta, for everyone involved in competition, including the athletes, the announcement came only just in time.

Sadly, the saga of the bombing dragged on for several years. No link was established to the TWA plane crash, which turned out to be an unfortunate accident. In Atlanta, the FBI took up the case and soon turned its attention to Richard Jewell, a security guard, who had originally alerted police to the presence of a knapsack before it exploded. Although the FBI had no evidence linking Jewell to the crime, he matched the personality profile the FBI had drawn up of the bomber. The FBI subjected Jewell to hours of intensive questioning, which turned up nothing. Frustrated by their lack of progress, the FBI attempted to put pressure on Jewell by leaking to the press that he was a suspect. A media circus developed and Jewell was under around-the-clock scrutiny by journalists. He still refused to admit any wrongdoing, and after three months in the spotlight, the FBI realised that he was innocent, by which time they had no more leads. Jewell got several undisclosed sums in compensation, most of which he said was used to pay his lawyers. He died of a heart attack in 2007 at the age of forty-four.

In 1998, Eric Rudolph, a vociferous opponent of abortion, was identified as a suspect in the bombing of an abortion clinic in Birmingham, Alabama and the 1997 bombings of a gay nightclub and an abortion clinic in Atlanta. He was then charged with the Atlanta Olympic Park bombing, and after a manhunt that lasted more than five years, Rudolph, who had vanished into the Appalachian Mountains, was arrested by police in North Carolina. He confessed to all four bombings and was sentenced to multiple terms of life imprisonment in 2005.

The Atlanta bombing taught me a lesson about how power and resources are determined in America. There is a constant struggle for power: at the federal level, between the various federal agencies; between federal government and state authorities, and between state and city bodies; and the costs involved are huge. Those conflicts can become bitter feuds and can seriously impair the efficiency of governmental action. As far as the Olympic Games are concerned, the IOC vigorously recommends that security is placed under the authority of a single commanding officer. The recommendation is usually accepted without difficulty, except in the USA, where the various levels of authority are fiercely guarded.

Another anecdote illustrates that US insularity. At the end of 2001, before the 2002 Salt Lake City Winter Games, I was invited to attend a meeting, during which some important new security measures would be explained. For obvious reasons, anxieties about the security of the Games had increased dramatically after the appalling 11th September attacks on the World Trade Center in 2001, which had caused President George W. Bush to allocate additional funds to the security of the Games. One of the main measures announced at the meeting represented substantial progress. All the various security forces used for the Games would be able to communicate through a single radio channel. Although I was pleased to hear about the plan, I was horrified to realise that up to that point, the security forces used their own separate channels, hardly conducive to co-ordinated responses in a crisis!

Another lesson to be learned from Atlanta was the absence of a single security chief to respond to the bombing. The multiple agencies involved meant that nobody was able to assume any responsibility for any decision that entailed risk of any kind. So, I am convinced that without the determination of ACOG and the IOC, the prevailing opinion of the agencies involved would have been to suspend the Games and possibly even to cancel them.

On an entirely different and much lighter note, the Atlanta Games provided some of us with an unexpectedly negative reaction from the Atlanta organisers to what the IOC thought was a straightforward suggestion about the dress code for officials during the Games. As the climate was particularly hot and humid at the end of July, and as the dress code for many Americans at that time of year is usually very informal, particularly when attending sporting events, we suggested that the IOC dress code should be casual at all the venues. It turned out that we couldn't have been more wrong. Our friends in Atlanta replied, somewhat curtly, that although they wouldn't prevent foreign officials adopting a casual dress code, they would wear suits and ties out of respect for the athletes and the dignity of the event. A little shamefaced, we, of course, did the same.

For the Closing Ceremony of the Atlanta Games, after consulting several of his closest advisers, including me, Samaranch eventually decided to declare the Atlanta Games as, 'most exceptional' and not the 'best Games ever'. I thought it was a good compromise for what had been, besides a few bumps on the road, an extraordinary experience. However, ACOG was not best pleased.

I still have fond memories of the Games. Michael Johnson won both the 200 and 400 metres on the track, the first man to do so, and both in stunning world record times. Carl Lewis won his ninth gold medal, an astonishing haul, by winning the long jump, while the 4'10" 'pocket Hercules', Turkey's Naim Suleymanoglu, won a weightlifting gold and became the first lifter to clean and jerk 190kg, three times his bodyweight, a famous milestone. American fans went crazy when gymnast, Kerri Strug, won her team a gold with her last vault, with an injury that meant she had to do it on all but one leg, while Canada's Donovan Bailey won the 100 metres and anchored their team in the 4x100 relay. However, the most heart-warming moment of all came before the competitions began.

When, at the end of the Closing Ceremony, the moment came to light the Cauldron, swimmer Janet Evans, dubbed 'America's Sweetheart', handed the torch to a man who was and always will be, 'The Greatest', Muhammad Ali. A son of the south from Louisville, Kentucky, he was in a location that was significant for him. In 1970, after three and a half years, during which his heavyweight title was stripped from him for refusing induction into the US Army, Ali fought his first comeback bout in Atlanta. With his hands and forearms shaking from the effects of Parkinson's disease, he bravely accepted the Olympic torch and lit the Cauldron as the crowd erupted in appreciation of the man once considered the most famous person on earth. The Deep South, with its controversial social history about race, had recognised the man for what he was, '*The Greatest of all Time!*'

25
1998 Olympic Disgrace

During my years with the IOC, more than once, I heard Samaranch express concerns about the risks to which some weaker IOC members were exposed as a consequence of approaches by certain candidate cities offering 'favours' for votes. There were rumours and allegations but no evidence. As early as 1991, Samaranch had asked Marc Hodler, on whose loyalty he could rely, to lead a special committee to debrief the various candidate cities and try to gather some hard facts. Despite his commendable efforts, Hodler didn't succeed. For obvious reasons, anyone who may have been involved in dubious practice, or knew someone who was, preferred to keep quiet.

The IOC was left with insinuations which were unproven. The difficulty of the situation was aggravated by the status of the IOC members and by the nature of the law applicable to the IOC, namely Swiss law, which meant that IOC members were legally unaccountable in Switzerland. At the time, the act of buying votes in a non-public organisation like the IOC was not a criminal offence. It could be considered as unethical misconduct, but not as a violation of the law. It was definitely an uncomfortable and slippery environment, well known to the bidding cities striving to gather the votes required to be elected as host city for the Olympic Games.

Bidding for the Games had become a highly professional and lucrative activity. For many bidding cities, their governments and sponsors, very substantial budgets were allocated, usually scores of millions of dollars. The cities appointed very expensive consultants, spin doctors, lobbyists, public relations and communication gurus, as well as many other experts in various areas like venue architecture, accommodation, transportation, weather forecasting, information technology and sustainable environmental development to help them prepare their 'Bid Books', the formal presentation documents required by the IOC. It had become a highly profitable service industry. Other lobbyists focused directly on their 'targets', namely the IOC members themselves. In order to devise what they considered to be the best strategy to secure a member's vote, they gathered detailed intelligence on each member: his or her lifestyle, interests, ambitions, hobbies, family, entourage and professional and financial situation. And that is precisely where the slippery slope began.

During the investigations conducted during the Salt Lake City Winter Games scandal, the story of which I will outline below, I had access to the files of bidding cities, in particular their confidential reports on IOC members. They were just like detailed police detective reports, even entering into private details like preferred sexual behaviour. As you might imagine, the professional lobbyists used such intelligence to approach individual IOC members, who are, of course, human beings with strengths and weaknesses. One of the consequences of the universality of the IOC is that standards of conduct vary considerably depending on the traditions, religions, professions, education and social status of the members involved. While the conduct of the vast majority of IOC members is impeccable, the behaviour of some members has been shown to be far less than perfect. Indeed, it has been totally unacceptable, as was revealed by the Salt Lake scandal, which led to the worst crisis ever endured by the IOC.

It all began in strange circumstances on 24th November 1998, when allegations of unethical behaviour involving Salt Lake City bid officials and one African IOC member were reported by a local TV station based on a document which, curiously, was subsequently proven to be a forgery. However, the information it contained was accurate. The allegations were that a daughter of the IOC member in Cameroon, who had passed away a few months earlier, was receiving scholarship payments from the Salt Lake City Olympic Organising Committee (SLOC). On 1st December 1998, Samaranch wrote to the chairman of the IOC Judicial Commission, Kéba Mbaye, asking him to investigate the matter. At the time, I was under the impression that while seriously worried, Samaranch still hoped that the story could be kept under control.

A few days later, on 11th December, the Executive Board met in Lausanne. SLOC was due to present its progress report on its planning for the Games, which were still four years away. More rumours had emerged of allegations of unethical behaviour concerning other members of the IOC. The meeting was running normally, under the chairmanship of Samaranch. I was sitting next to him. The eleven or so members were sitting around the large table in the boardroom, with each member having an individual microphone in front of them. The discussions are normally quite informal, with members simply raising their hands to ask for the floor.

Nobody ever stood up, but on that morning, a bizarre and totally unexpected event took place. Marc Hodler, a senior member of the Executive Board had shown signs of agitation and suddenly stood up and struggled with the wire of his microphone to bring it up to his mouth. He then interrupted the discussion and asked in English in a loud voice, "May the gentleman from Switzerland be recognised?"

It was immediately obvious that Hodler was using very solemn parliamentary procedure to draw everyone's attention to what he was going to say. Samaranch was totally astounded and perplexed by the formal English expression and whispered to me, "What is this, what does he mean, to be recognised?"

I told him what I suspected, which caused Samaranch to raise his eyebrows and say to Hodler, "What do you mean, recognise the gentleman, of course I recognise you! I have always recognised you!"

Hodler, still standing and having difficulties with his microphone, kept insisting and demanding that the 'gentleman from Switzerland be recognised', and then proceeded to deliver a rather confused, pompous statement from which we gathered that he had seen corrupt agents in the lobby of the Lausanne Palace, where Samaranch lived and where IOC members stayed when in Lausanne. He went on to say that the members of SLOC were wonderful people but that that was not the case for some of his IOC colleagues who were corrupt. Samaranch tried to get him to sit down, but Hodler was visibly upset, and seemed strange and confused. By then, we were close to the end of the morning and the meeting was adjourned. Samaranch and I were to attend a press conference to announce a major new Olympic sponsor.

As we reached the entrance hall of the IOC headquarters, where the press conference was planned to be held, we noticed that Hodler was surrounded by a throng of journalists hanging on his every word in an impromptu press conference of his own. In a nutshell, he was telling the media that his friends at SLOC had been abused by some lobbyists and some of his IOC colleagues, that there was corruption afoot and that it was not confined to the Salt Lake City Games. The media were dumbfounded. There was a very senior Olympic leader openly declaring in the midst of an Executive Board meeting that there was corruption at the IOC!

As he was pressed with questions, he went on to make bizarre comparisons between the Olympic Games and the World Ski Championships. He told a strange tale that he knew that agents for bidding cities for the Olympics were offering cars in exchange for votes. He then said that the Italian resort of Sestrières had been awarded the World Ski Championships through a totally transparent process, but then said that it was thanks to the support of the Agnelli family, owners of Fiat and a major sponsor of Sestrières, that each national ski federation would receive a car if the championships were awarded to Sestrières, an outcome which had actually come to pass. As President of the International Ski Federation for many years, Hodler was trying to explain that his federation and his sport were not corrupt and much more transparent than the IOC, but he didn't seem to realise that openly promising a car to all voting delegations could also be considered as corruption. Things got even more weird when Hodler started to praise Gianni Agnelli, Italy's most prominent industrialist and the main supporter of Torino's bid for the 2006 Winter Games. Because of Hodler's confused explanations, his audience couldn't be sure whether he was praising Agnelli or criticising him. The leader of the Torino bid, an intelligent woman of distinction, was at the IOC that day. She burst into tears, convinced that Hodler, a Swiss, was attacking Agnelli and the Torino bid in an attempt to promote the competing Swiss bid of Sion. In fact, her tears turned to joy, because if anything, Hodler's action turned out to be a severe blow to the Swiss bid and, a year later, her city beat Sion to win the 2006 Games.

Hodler's rambling statement caused a perfect storm of media scrutiny as the press tried to come to terms with a senior and highly respected IOC member, international federation president, one of Samaranch's close friends and trusted advisers openly telling the world that the IOC was corrupt! It was also a golden opportunity for the IOC's critics to launch a major campaign, and because the allegations involved an American bid, the wheels of the US political and judicial systems began to turn and pick up speed rapidly. The IOC Executive Board did the same and appointed a Special Investigation Commission, chaired by Dick Pound and for which I served as secretary, to investigate the allegations of corruption and misconduct by IOC members.

I will always remember that December day in 1998 as a pivotal date for the IOC, as well as a turning point in my own professional life. Apart from serving as secretary to the Pound Commission, I was instructed by Samaranch to take overall responsibility for communications and public relations during the crisis. It was a logical decision as, being the spokesman for the IOC Executive Board, I already knew most of the main journalists who would be asking the difficult questions. However, my workload, which was already heavy, was multiplied by a factor of three or four overnight, so I decided to set up a small crisis task force within the IOC administration which was to meet early every morning to organise, co-ordinate and delegate the many tasks which were to be dealt with every day. As far as communication was concerned, I received valuable support from Kevan Gosper, Senior IOC member in Australia and chairman of the IOC Press Commission. I was also assisted in a very efficient manner by Michael Payne, then IOC Director of Marketing, who tackled the formidable task of dealing with the IOC's major sponsors, particularly in the USA. Dick Pound, who was supervising all IOC marketing operations as well the relationship with the major TV networks, was particularly active on the North American continent. In addition, I called on a talented young IOC staff member, Franklin Servan-Schreiber, who was, at the time, in charge of new media projects, and was thrown to the lions of the world's media about one year later when he became a press officer. To reinforce the team, he hired an intelligent French woman, Emmanuelle Moreau. Communication and public relations included public affairs, which implied a special challenge in the USA, so we appointed Hill and Knowlton, communications specialists, whose guidance was invaluable.

The IOC had become a target for a ravenous media, disgruntled sponsors and ambitious US politicians in search of notoriety. In the States, the IOC was a perfect political target: a foreign institution, dominated by Europeans, with no electoral weight in the US, yet wealthy and allegedly corrupt. For many, the time had come for the IOC not only to undergo fundamental reforms, but also to be taken over and controlled by different institutions, either by governments like the US, or by the UN, or even by those looking to make a huge profit.

The last weeks of December 1998 and January 1999 were the most crucial time, a period when the very survival of the IOC was at stake. Samaranch was under heavy personal attack for failing to prevent corruption and allowing the development of a so-called 'gift culture', which was particularly shocking when it came from those who were no more than hypocrites. There were many calls for him to resign; after all, he was seventy-nine years old and had been in office without interruption for nearly twenty years. During our many meetings and discussions at that time, I had no idea whether he contemplated resigning or not. Samaranch was a fighter and by the end of 1998, he was definitely up for the battle and determined to deal with the problems confronting the IOC. To that effect, he devised a clear and simple plan to be implemented within one year, namely by the end of 1999. It involved a rapid investigation of the allegations against IOC members, with possible sanctions by an extraordinary IOC Session in March 1999, just three months after the scandal broke out; the simultaneous adoption of a first set of reforms; the establishment of a special IOC 2000 Reform Commission, and of an Ethics Commission. The target for all reforms to be adopted was December 1999.

That meant that in 1999, the IOC would hold three Sessions: an extraordinary one in March 1999 in Lausanne, an ordinary Session in June in Korea and a third Session in December in Lausanne to approve all required changes and measures devised by the IOC 2000 commission. It was a very ambitious and hugely demanding project involving a monumental amount of work for all those directly involved. But we knew that we could count on Samaranch's unrelenting support. He assumed full responsibility for bringing the IOC's house back in order and felt that, if he could count on the support of the IOC membership, he should stay in office and carry out a reform project which had to be drastic and which no other IOC member could manage with such short notice.

The mission was clear; so was the roadmap and the timetable. All we had to do was get it done. The first thing we had to do was to understand how the judiciary and parliamentary procedures worked in the US so that we knew where the battlegrounds would be. It was obvious that in the US, public opinion, encouraged by many news reports and political statements, was led to believe that the bid committee for Salt Lake City had been the victim of a corrupt foreign organisation which should be investigated, brought to justice and punished. As a consequence, there were many leading figures in the US who thought the time had come for the USA to take over the Olympic Movement. After all, the financing of the entire Movement and of the Olympic Games still depended, to a substantial degree, upon the revenues flowing from US TV rights holders and sponsors.

Time was of the essence. Samaranch knew that in the face of intense pressure from various institutions and the media, the IOC had to demonstrate determination, efficiency and transparency. Thus, the IOC's own ad hoc commission, chaired by Dick Pound, which became known as the 'Pound Commission' worked tirelessly from the first day of its appointment, 11th December 1998, until the submission of its recommendations to the IOC Executive Board on 24th January 1999, just forty-four days, including weekends and Christmas. Remarkable!

The Pound Commission's task was particularly difficult because, as a body belonging to a private organisation, it had no legal authority to gather evidence or to subpoena witnesses. I remember discussing the legal situation with a personal friend who worked with the highest criminal authority having jurisdiction in Switzerland over the IOC. Regrettably, he quickly came to the conclusion that allegations of corruption could not be investigated under Swiss law. At that time, corruption was an offence only if it concerned public authorities. Thus, the IOC had to rely on evidence provided by other sources. To a large extent, those sources were in the US. First of all, we received substantial information from the Salt Lake City Organising Committee (SLOC) through the reports it delivered to the IOC Executive Board and the President. We were also in contact with the United States Olympic Committee (USOC) and the members of its Special Bid Oversight Commission, which was chaired by a distinguished senior statesman, Senator George Mitchell, whom Samaranch and I met in London.

Mitchell was widely recognised on the international political scene, in particular through a difficult peace mission that he'd successfully undertaken in Northern Ireland. He was subsequently engaged in peace talks between the Palestinians and Israel. Another source of information was whatever facts that, with the assistance of our US attorneys, O' Melveny & Myers, we could obtain from the US Department of Justice, which had launched its own investigation to determine if there had been any criminal activity. It soon appeared that it was much more difficult than we'd hoped to receive detailed information from the US authorities. It seemed to me as a European, that the IOC's situation was bizarre. We were told that the IOC was possibly a victim of potential crimes; yet we had no access to the FBI's files.

Our lawyers had to organise meetings with federal agents, during which only limited information was given to us and always reluctantly. Although the meetings were always courteous, we felt we were treated more like suspects than victims. The last source of information was, of course, anything we could obtain from IOC members, in particular those whose names were linked to potential acts of misconduct or corruption. The Pound Commission, with me as secretary, had begun work just before the 1998 Christmas holiday season and, based on our recommendations, on 11th January 1999, Samaranch wrote to all members who were suspects, informing them of the allegations against them and of the opening of investigations into them.

In the meantime, we had to review thousands of documents and travel to the US. The whole commission flew to New York to meet with FBI agents, and Pound went to Salt Lake City. They were frenetic and disturbing weeks, as it soon became obvious that a number of IOC members were guilty, at the very least, of gross misconduct, and had acted in a way unworthy of the IOC, behaviour which could lead to their expulsion by decision of the IOC Session. On 24th January 1999, following our recommendations, the Executive Board decided to propose that the IOC Session to be held on 17th/18th March expel six members and warn one, with three cases still pending. Subsequently, having considered the reports from the SLOC Ethics Commission and the Mitchell Commission which were received in February and early March, the proposals to the Session were such that on 17th March, during a dramatically tense meeting in Lausanne, the IOC Session decided, by particularly large majorities, to expel six IOC members: Agustin Arroyo of Ecuador, Zein Abdel Gadir of Sudan, Jean-Claude Ganga of the Republic of Congo, Lamine Keita of Mali, Charles Mukora of Kenya and Sergio Fantini of Chile. Ten other members were warned, four more had more or less spontaneously resigned, some of them under pressure from their national sports community, and one member had died.

On 1st March 1999, the Mitchell Commission released its own report which found deficiencies in both the IOC's and the USOC's procedures without mentioning specific names. It is interesting to note that one of its recommendations was to encourage the IOC to consider being declared as a public international organisation, which would lead to a future application to the Organisation for Economic Co-operation and Development (OECD) Convention on Combating Bribery of Foreign Public Officials in International Business Transactions. Since then, the IOC has sought in vain to obtain such status from the Swiss government, in spite of the existence of some Swiss legislation which, according to various opinions, would allow such a declaration. The IOC hasn't given up and is still lobbying to achieving such a status. While I haven't followed the latest developments on that particular topic, I imagine that being admitted to observer status at the United Nations General Assembly should enhance the IOC's position.

17th March 1999, the opening of the Extraordinary Session was both a very sad day in the history of the IOC and the beginning of a new era. The day had begun with a vote of confidence, by secret ballot, in favour of Samaranch; only one member cast a negative vote. The members knew that in these particularly difficult times, they had to stand behind their president, who was then the only person who could remedy the dreadful situation. The price to be paid was very high, but the IOC had no choice, it had to restore its credibility. It had to act drastically and swiftly.

I shall never forget the sense of shame and embarrassment throughout that entire day. One after the other, the indicted members were introduced in the hall of the Beaulieu Conference Centre in Lausanne. They entered through a discreet back door, protected from the hundreds of media crews and journalists who seemed to be everywhere. Each of them was given the opportunity to state his case (they were all men) in person from a stand in front of his peers. After they had made their case, each vote was simply a decision, under the vagaries of Swiss law, by an association of members to terminate the membership of some of its individual members. Before the day of the Session, I received several calls from lawyers representing members whose expulsion was proposed. I told them that they would not be authorised to assist their clients at the Session, which would be held in camera, and most of them expressed their disbelief and protested. A famous French criminal lawyer, Jacques Vergès, now deceased, rang me up and told me that he would, in any case, attend the Session, and if not allowed in, he would denounce it as a gross violation of due process and human rights to the international media and immediately sue the IOC. I advised him, as I did all the other protesting lawyers, to seek advice from an independent Swiss counsel and to check the status of our procedures with the counsel. Whether or not my recommendation was followed, I don't know. The fact is that no lawyer, including Vergès, ever appeared and the procedure which we'd used was never challenged. A few years later, the lawyer for one of the members who'd been expelled submitted a formal request to the IOC asking for rehabilitation for his client, which was denied. By then, the individual concerned was a man with no standing worthy of rehabilitation. We never heard from him again.

As it had lost approximately one tenth of its membership, the IOC had quite literally decimated itself. We all felt exhausted by the end. Some of the expelled members had been friendly and likeable personalities from poor and developing countries. In most cases, the evidence was not of real, tangible corruption, but rather of misconduct, which created the intolerable appearance of dishonesty. To this day, after much reflection, due to the extraordinarily short timescale and the difficult circumstances under which we had to work, I'm still not sure that we caught all the guilty members. Nevertheless, painful as this was, we showed the world that the IOC and Samaranch were serious about the necessity of a fundamental reform process. Interestingly, although Swiss law on associations is substantially the same today, I very much doubt that we would get away with the same summary procedure now, more than twenty years later. The influence of common law and the Anglo-Saxon legal culture is such that all forms of disciplinary procedures are conducted much more formally, according to the principle of due process.

Samaranch and the IOC had turned what had been a dark page in the history of the Olympic Movement. It moved on with the launching of a series of reforms, and an IOC Ethics Commission was established. An IOC 2000 Reform Commission was created, which included a number of prestigious outsiders like former US Secretary of State, Henry Kissinger, Italian industrialist, Giovanni Agnelli and former UN Secretary General, the Egyptian, Boutros Boutros-Ghali. Samaranch's objective was that before the end of 1999, a new Extraordinary Session would enact all the necessary reforms. The roadmap was clear, the deadlines tight and the challenge, once more, formidable.

There has been further serious collateral damage as a consequence of the Salt Lake City scandal. Paradoxically, the main victim turned out to be the man who should have been praised for his determination, Dick Pound. He had chaired the investigation commission diligently, efficiently and independently. Of all IOC members, he was one of the very few who had immediately understood the huge danger faced by the IOC. The biggest risk was that all major Olympic sponsors and partners, at that time essentially all US based companies, would withdraw all their financial support. There was also the real risk that US legislation in Congress would require US broadcasters to refrain from paying any fees to non-US organisations.

Worryingly, many IOC members were totally unaware of such risks and thought that the IOC should ignore the events happening in the US and simply refuse any form of co-operation with the US government, its broadcasters and its sponsors. Most of those members didn't understand or didn't want to understand the importance of Dick Pound's actions at the time and believed that he'd not served the best interests of the IOC, which was a grossly unfair assessment of the situation. They made him pay a heavy price in July 2001 in Moscow at the IOC's 112th Session, when he ran for president to succeed Samaranch. He got just twenty-two votes. Jacques Rogge won the ballot with forty-nine votes and became the IOC's eighth president. What was even more galling for Pound was the twenty-three votes for South Korean, Kim Un-Yong, one more than Pound, despite the fact that Kim had also been accused of dubious behaviour around the Salt Lake scandal. Tellingly, in 2004 in Korea, Kim was arrested for embezzlement and bribery and sentenced to two-and-a-half years in prison. He was deprived of all his IOC member privileges by the Executive Board.

26
A Taekwondo Assault and Attacks by US Politicians

While everybody at the IOC was hurrying to assist in the creation of the reforms that were to be considered by the 2000 Reform Commission, the crisis developed some other consequences. For instance, the Ordinary IOC Session, which was going to be held in Seoul in mid-June 1999, was a matter of concern. The senior Korean IOC member, Kim Un-Yong, was still under investigation by the Pound Commission, which was divided about his case. Some felt he should be excluded from the IOC, while others thought that his actions could be excused. The rumour was that he was being protected by Samaranch himself, which might well have been the case. I must say that, although I was secretary to the Pound Commission, had access to all its files and took part in all deliberations, and although I was meeting him practically every day to discuss all IOC matters, Samaranch never said a word about Kim, nor did he ask me anything about the deliberations of the Pound Commission.

Kim himself became increasingly angry and impatient, so much so that during the coffee break of a meeting of the Executive Board, of which he was a member, he lunged at me in front of several members of the international media. He had just learnt that the Pound Commission had instructed me to send him a letter asking for more information about his relationship with the Salt Lake bid. The journalists were shocked by Kim's sudden display of his martial arts skills, and so was I! I should point out that Kim was a taekwondo practitioner and had, in fact, been the first president of the World Taekwondo Federation. Kim also called me a bastard. I decided that I wouldn't tolerate being physically attacked and abused and immediately went to my car, left the IOC and drove to my office at my law firm.

I then called Samaranch, telling him that I would not return to the IOC in such circumstances. Very calmly, he told me that he fully understood my position and asked me whether I would be prepared to return to the IOC, and if so, what would be my conditions. I said that I required a written letter of unconditional apology to be signed by Kim in front of Samaranch. Ten minutes later, Samaranch called me back suggesting that I drive back to the IOC to meet with him and Kim, which I did. When I arrived, I was met by Samaranch and Mbaye, together with Pound, who had also been insulted by Kim. The latter signed two letters of unconditional apology, we shook hands, and the episode was over. The incident illustrates the tension felt throughout the IOC at the time. Incidentally, it also began the decline of Kim's Olympic career, his eventual fall from grace on the international scene and in his home country, Korea.

Apart from the work of the Pound Commission and of the IOC 2000 Reform Commission, which was discussing and preparing the substantial reforms to be submitted to the IOC Session, we had to be constantly available to answer the unending questions from the media. In addition, a new battleground was forming which required our immediate attention, namely the convoluted mechanisms of the US political and judicial systems. The IOC crisis had been triggered in the US through the bidding process that had ended with the award of the 2002 Winter Games to Salt Lake City. The US Federal and State authorities launched a series of investigations into what was characterised by the US Congress as 'The Olympic Site Selection Process'. This proved to be a golden opportunity, not only for the media and the investigators, but also, more particularly, for a number of politicians in Washington to enhance their profiles at little cost and without risk.

The subject matter, the Olympics, was attractive and had all the necessary ingredients for telling good stories and ensuring prime time TV coverage. Although the US members of the Salt Lake City Bidding Committee were involved in allegations of unpleasant corruption, they were often portrayed as the naive American victims of the real villains, who were unscrupulous foreigners, members of an unethical international club with an improper culture which needed to be rectified and, if possible, punished. It was also suggested that members of the IOC lived off extravagant amounts of money collected mainly from US broadcasters and sponsors, which could be better used to support deserving young American athletes. Our reputation in the US was rock bottom and the very existence of the IOC was threatened.

The hostile attitude of the US media and authorities prompted some very negative reactions within the IOC, in particular from some elderly members who advised Samaranch that the IOC should essentially ignore the US and refrain from co-operating with its authorities. It was, of course, bad advice, emanating from members who were totally unaware of the actual situation of the IOC in the real world. I was surprised to discover how quickly anti-American feelings arose, even among members whom I considered as moderate and balanced.

The tension reached a peak when the IOC was asked to co-operate with the US Congress' investigation into the Olympics Site Selection Process, in particular by asking Samaranch to appear in person to be heard by a committee of the House of Representatives. Many senior IOC members and close advisers strongly recommended that he should not go to Washington as it would be unacceptable for the IOC to be discredited by a parliament which had no jurisdiction over the IOC. On the other hand, some more realistic members, like Dick Pound, reminded Samaranch of the IOC's crucial interest in restoring its reputation and credibility with its US partners and sponsors. We could also count on the critical advice of one of the most influential diplomatic figures in the world, Henry Kissinger, who had agreed to serve as a volunteer member of the IOC 2000 Reform Commission. Samaranch didn't feel comfortable with the idea of appearing in person in front of the US Congress, especially as he would have to respond in English, his fourth language, the first three being Spanish, Catalan and French. But Samaranch was a pragmatist and decided, despite the advice of friends, mainly Latin sports leaders, that he would co-operate with Washington, and it was a great relief for me that he was following what appeared to be the wisest course of action.

In my daily contacts with the media, I could sense that the IOC's position would have been untenable had Samaranch decided to ignore Washington. He asked me to co-ordinate the necessary preparatory work with our advisers in America, and so the ensuing months became the busiest in my life and certainly the most fascinating, as I was to be submerged in the unique world of US politics.

What were the real stakes for the IOC in the USA? The answer could easily be found in some statements made by members of the Subcommittee on Oversight and Investigations of the Committee on Commerce of the House of Representatives. For instance, the influential Californian Congressman, Henry Waxman, made it clear that he considered that the IOC suffered from a culture of greed and corruption and that it was remarkably slow in taking the necessary steps to reform itself. Frustrated by what he considered to be the arrogance of the IOC, Waxman introduced a bill in Congress which would prohibit American corporations, including the television networks, from providing any financial support to the IOC until it adopted the Mitchell Commission reforms. The passing of the bill would mean a devastating blow to the financial and political independence of the IOC and its likely subordination to a major political power, the US government. It would also encourage other institutions and organisations in the world to gain control over the Olympic Movement and its assets. We were in a very precarious position.

After carefully considering his options, Samaranch became convinced that the IOC should co-operate fully with the US authorities. He told the US IOC members, Anita DeFrantz and James Easton, of his intentions, while also relying heavily on Canadian Dick Pound's experience and support. With the strong support of the IOC's Marketing Director, Michael Payne, Pound proved to be particularly effective in garnering the support of the IOC's American sponsors, broadcasters and other partners. It soon became clear that Congress wanted Samaranch to appear in person in Washington sooner rather than later, and to report on the reforms he was adopting to restore the IOC's standing and credibility.

With the assistance of our Washington counsel and other advisers, the first part of my work consisted in paying visits to some influential US senators and Congressmen to try and explain what the IOC actually was, as most of them had no idea, and to outline what was being done in terms of reform. I also tried to convince them to wait until the end of the year for Samaranch's personal appearance, so that his report could cover the measures actually finalised by the IOC. The reaction I received was negative, and there were even hints that Samaranch could be subpoenaed. However, after a couple more visits, I had succeeded in establishing a respectful relationship with the chairman of the Subcommittee on Oversight and Investigations, Congressman Fred Upton of Michigan. He eventually agreed to postpone Samaranch's hearing until December but demanded that some other IOC representatives, including myself, would have to appear earlier. We finally agreed that the appearances would take place in October, during the Subcommittee's first hearing, while Samaranch would appear on 15th December 1999 to provide the Subcommittee with a full report on the reform process within the IOC.

For a non-American, providing an under oath testimony to a politically hostile US congressional body was an unusual experience.

My own appearance had been prepared with the assistance of our Washington counsels, in particular Arthur Culvahouse, an influential lawyer who was then chairman of O'Melveny and Myers, the IOC's counsels in the US. The preparation included personal meetings with individual members of the Subcommittee, which were always courteous. On the other hand, during the hearing itself, the tone was far more aggressive, giving me the impression that I was thought to be more like a potential criminal rather than a witness. The harshness of some representatives was obviously intended for the consumption of the television cameras, which covered every minute of the hearing.

On the whole, I was struck by the level of ignorance displayed by most representatives regarding the Olympic Movement. They were individuals involved in a parliamentary investigation relating to possible new US legislation and had, presumably, been briefed by their assistants and had, supposedly, read some background material. Also, we had taken time to answer their questions in our preliminary private discussions. Yet, at the public hearing, their questions suggested that most of them knew little or nothing about international sports competitions. To me, the entire exercise was futile and a waste of energy, time and money. The purpose of the investigation was unclear, except perhaps as a public relations opportunity for the politicians arrayed in front of us.

Samaranch's December hearing was a repeat of October, except that there was far more media excitement and that he had to face much more aggressive and often discourteous questions. The American politicians looked happy. They felt they had admonished a foreign IOC president, and that was that as far as they were concerned. We never heard from the US House of Representatives again, with the details of the hearing recorded in a 570-page volume, which will probably never be read by anyone with any sense.

The Salt Lake City saga nearly brought the IOC to an end. But, after a few years of investigations by the Federal Department of Justice, for which millions of US taxpayers' dollars were spent, the whole matter ended as a judicial damp squib. Even so, the IOC and the US Olympic Committee had been made to reconsider their governance, which was an important consequence. Indeed, the standards of governance of both organisations had left a lot to be desired.

The IOC did make fundamental reforms, and changes were adopted. An Ethics Commission was established and, while co-option remained the basic principle for the recruitment of new IOC members, a Candidature Commission was established in order to diminish the risks of inappropriate choices being made. The majority of the members of the IOC's Athletes' Commission are elected by the athletes participating in the Olympic Games, which means that fifteen of the one hundred and fifteen IOC members have been selected through a democratic process. In addition, serious efforts were undertaken towards more transparency and better governance, although, in my view, there remains much more room for substantial improvements in all major international sports organisations, including the IOC.

The Salt Lake City Games scandal and ensuing crisis began a much-needed reform process, and as is often the case, a crisis turned out to be an opportunity. There are many lessons to draw from the Salt Lake farrago. First of all, the IOC did not have the procedures to meet such a challenge. Secondly, it's clear that whenever human beings are involved in making decisions which have substantial financial consequences, there is always a risk of improper conduct, including corruption. Such risks can't be entirely eliminated, which has been seen again in recent examples, in particular involving some IOC members concerning the awarding of the 2016 Olympic Games to Rio de Janeiro. Preventing behaviour that brings the IOC or another sporting body into disrepute, requires a permanent, adequate and vigilant governance, which is far from easy. Thirdly, in 1998, the structures and governance of the IOC were obsolete and required substantial reforms. A lot has been accomplished, but only the future will tell whether it is sufficient.

Furthermore, the sad episode of Salt Lake revealed that, at the time in the USA, the IOC, its representatives, its US members, regardless of their individual qualities, had little or no political weight or influence. Moreover, whenever an institution like the IOC is confronted with a crisis, it has to react very swiftly and not let the problem remain open for weeks or months. The Salt Lake issues were satisfactorily resolved because Samaranch acted very quickly. Finally, one should never underestimate the likelihood of interference from the US political or judicial institutions in any international sports organisation. Politics is never far away from sport.

27
The End of the Reign of Samaranch

In July 2001, exactly twenty-one years after he was first elected as IOC president, Juan Antonio Samaranch stepped down. The Olympic Charter had been amended in 1995, essentially to grant him an extension of his term beyond 1997. He was eighty-one years old. A number of observers and critics of the IOC, while recognising Samaranch's many achievements, felt that he should have retired much earlier, implying that he carried a serious responsibility for the IOC's recent crisis by having failed to act strongly enough to challenge some of his less than worthy members.

The end of his term was a very difficult and sad time for Samaranch. He had lost his wife, Bibis, in the middle of the 2000 Sydney Games, and by July 2001, was a lonely old man about to give up what had been at the core of his entire life. He personally oversaw all the details and rituals of his farewell Session, which he had wanted to be held in Moscow, just like his election twenty-one years earlier. The Russian authorities, including President Putin, and former president, Yeltsin, as well as the Russian Olympic community, with Smirnov at its head, saw to it that Samaranch, who had been the Spanish ambassador in Moscow when first elected as IOC president, received a well-deserved tribute.

Samaranch had always been a very popular and respected public figure in Russia, and he was very touched by the many gestures of friendship offered to him. He also had a moment of great satisfaction when the Moscow Session awarded the 2008 Olympic Games to Beijing, which was a decision he'd hoped for for several years. I remember his pleasure when I accompanied him to the majestic Chinese embassy in Moscow where President Jiang Zemin received us to celebrate Beijing's victory. Officially, Zemin was supposed to be in Moscow to meet Putin, but I'm sure his visit was planned in connection with the Beijing bid. A lavish party had been 'spontaneously' organised at the Chinese embassy and more than a thousand guests suddenly appeared. During our private meeting with Zemin, I was impressed by his personality. He was outspoken and very open and spoke excellent German, telling us that in his early years, he had worked as an engineer in Germany.

Throughout his last days in Moscow, Samaranch appeared very calm and relaxed. He paid several visits and I accompanied him on some of them, including a private tea party given for him by Moscow mayor, Yuri Luzhkov, on his huge country estate, where he was raising thousands of bees in scores of hives. Each hive was a miniature replica of a well-known historical palace or castle. Luzhkov was particularly proud of the many varieties of honey produced by his bees, and we had to sit for a couple of hours on the terrace of a modest hut in a field tasting endless spoons of his different honeys and sipping tea with him. The temperature was above thirty Celsius. I was sweating heavily, but Samaranch remained impeccably cool and stoical under the hot sun.

The closing of the 2001 Moscow Session marked the end of the Samaranch era. As the limelight faded and the celebrations and tributes came to an end, the time had come for Samaranch to conclude his presidency and leave Moscow. I was due to fly with him and his staff to Geneva. At Moscow airport, as we were waiting for our flight in the VIP lounge, Samaranch came over to me. He asked me to show him the antique postcards I had bought for my collection. There were probably twenty or thirty samples which he studied carefully. It was probably a symbolic way whereby he began to sever the links he had, not only with Moscow and Russia, but also with his past. During the flight to Switzerland, he slept, which was not surprising after two very hectic weeks. At Geneva airport, as he was getting into his car to go back to the Lausanne Palace, he shook hands with me and said with a gentle smile, "We have done some good things together, haven't we?"

Two hours later, while giving a live interview to Spanish radio at about midnight, he became seriously ill. Everyone feared for his life, but he recovered. After a few more years as chairman of Caixa, the main Spanish savings bank, and numerous other activities in various areas, after being ill for some time, he died of cardio-respiratory failure in April 2011 at the age of eighty-nine. Until then, he served as honorary IOC president, keeping track of everything in the Olympic Movement, but he never interfered with the work of Jacques Rogge, his successor.

The Samaranch presidency was an exceptional period in the history of the Olympic Movement and during his tenure, dominated the international sports scene. As a former politician, he was diligent in not only dealing with all the major world sports leaders, but also with leading politicians who had an involvement with sport. He was admired and popular in many parts of the world, in particular in Africa, Russia, the former communist countries and in China. The unity of the Olympic Movement was his obsession and he fought hard to maintain it. He knew that without the full support of all the National Olympic Committees and, even more so, of all International Sports Federations, the Olympic Games and the Olympic Movement could disappear rapidly. He also excelled at delegating tasks to people he considered more qualified than himself.

A typical example was the authority he gave to Dick Pound, who was in charge of all negotiations with the major US broadcasters and sponsors. Samaranch told me several times that he didn't understand North Americans and that it was much better to leave it to Pound, a Canadian lawyer, to take care of those relationships. In public, Samaranch was always cautious and low key. His speeches usually focused on his constant calls for unity and he thought press conferences were successful when nothing happened. In his permanent quest for unity, Samaranch paid special attention to the International Sports Federations, which wasn't always well received by the National Olympic Committees, who were concerned that they were being downgraded. Although he would never say it in public, privately, Samaranch told me and others on several occasions that, if necessary, he could organise the Olympic Games without the National Olympic Committees provided he could count on the Federations. He was equally careful in his relationships with governments. His past experience in the diplomatic service taught him that sports organisations should always maintain the best possible relationships with the sports ministries, while maintaining an acceptable level of autonomy and protection for the athletes. That particular challenge was, and still is, a very difficult one.

During his entire presidency, Samaranch was totally dedicated to his office and to the Olympic Movement and kept himself fully informed of any development, including in politics or business, that could impact on sport and the Olympics. He spent little time with his family, but during the summer, he would take a two-week holiday at his summer house in Catalonia, when I usually received more phone calls from him than when he was in his Lausanne office one floor above mine. He would focus on big issues with little interest in the details. He didn't like to elaborate on grand intellectual philosophy or espouse Olympic doctrines. In his own way, he was a visionary.

His vision was simple: to see the Olympic Movement grow, for it to be respected worldwide and to ensure that it stay united. He wanted the Olympic Games to be the most important event on earth and expected each edition of the Games to be better than the one before. Samaranch was neither an executive, nor a manager, he was a leader, and an exceptional one. However, that didn't prevent him from paying very personal attention to his staff. For instance, if one of his secretaries was hospitalised, he would discreetly visit her every morning before going to his office. He was an exceptional leader, but one with a caring heart.

28
The Presidency of Jacques Rogge

The Belgian orthopaedic surgeon, Jacques Rogge, succeeded Juan Antonio Samaranch as IOC president by an overwhelming majority in July 2001 in Moscow. His credentials were impressive: among many other things, he had been an Olympic athlete, competing in sailing, Belgian Chef de Mission at the 1980 Moscow Olympics, President of the Belgian Olympic Committee and of the European Olympic Committees, and had chaired the Co-ordination Commission for the 2000 Sydney Games, which were a great success. He was also serving as vice chairman of the IOC Medical Commission and demonstrated throughout his sporting career a particularly strong commitment to the fight against doping. His motto was 'Zero Tolerance', which he applied consistently during his entire presidency.

A very intelligent man of great culture, fluent in Ancient Greek and connoisseur of contemporary art, he was particularly diligent in his work, studying his files with extreme care. He spoke five or six languages fluently and was a true gentleman with very courteous manners. He was also lucky to have the full support of his wife, Anne, who matched many of her husband's qualities.

Rogge was totally committed to the Olympic Movement and its values and a man with the highest sense of ethics, particularly in terms of democracy, which he applied in all circumstances, even when it made it difficult for him to reach his objectives. As president, he kept a low profile, with a style completely different from that of Samaranch. He was very prudent and during the twelve years of his office, kept a tight control over the IOC and its administration which enjoyed very healthy finances. There were no institutional scandals and all the Olympic Games held during his tenure were successful.

On the other hand, it is regrettable that Rogge, although surrounded by a dedicated and competent staff, had a tendency to isolate himself and rule alone. His decisions were usually made without taking into account the advice or opinions of his staff, advisers or colleagues. That was particularly the case when, in 2007, he decided to launch the Youth Olympic Games. The idea arose from Rogge's justified view that the Olympic Movement should move closer to young people and emphasise the educational and cultural value of sport. The difficulty was that after some dazzling editions of the Games in Singapore and Nanjing, few people understood what the future would be of an event which didn't attract any serious media attention and seemed to be a burden for a number of IFs and NOCs. It is a shame, because Rogge's underlying vision was valuable, but, unfortunately, it wasn't shared and was thus difficult to implement. His prudent nature and the care he took in his public persona gave the impression that he was a rather dull, overly cautious personality, which would be unfair. Was he shy? Maybe.

Rogge deserves to be commended for the exemplary service he gave during the twelve years of his terms. He was totally immersed in his task, so much so that he endangered his health. During the last two or three years of his presidency, he was obviously weaker and spoke much more slowly, and occasionally with difficulty. His intellectual capacities remained perfectly intact, but he was clearly suffering.

It is difficult to assess yet how Rogge will be remembered in Olympic history. Officially and publicly, at all Olympic events and functions, he is spoken of as a great president and leader, credited with restoring the essential values of Olympism. But privately, many people familiar with the Olympic Movement, are more critical. They suggest that Rogge lacked authority and didn't measure up to the challenges the IOC was facing.

A typical example was that of his passive role in the absurd decision, taken in February 2013 by the IOC Executive Board under his chairmanship, to propose the exclusion of wrestling from the Olympic Games. Apparently surprised by the outcry that caused, he then followed a strange procedure, which allowed wrestling a second chance as an alleged new 'additional sport'. The whole episode was ridiculous and unnecessarily detrimental to the image and reputation of both wrestling and the IOC. It was also time consuming and costly. Instead of throwing his weight into the debate and objecting to the initial proposal of exclusion, Rogge felt that his role as president was to refrain from expressing any opinion and that he had to respect what he considered to be a democratic process. Those who are critical of Rogge's presidency recall that his predecessor, Samaranch, had a much firmer grip and that while the IOC progressed under Samaranch, under Rogge it was stagnant.

There is some truth in such assessments. However, it would be unfair to offer simplistic judgments of two personalities who both had their strengths and weaknesses. If I were to summarily rate the various IOC presidencies I have had the privilege to serve, I would describe Lord Killanin's presidency as like working for a country club chairman, where the club was actually ruled by its director, Monique Berlioux; the Samaranch presidency as an era of spectacular growth and the Rogge presidency a period of quiet consolidation.

As for Thomas Bach, elected in September 2013, it would be far too early to express an opinion. His personal style is very different from that of his predecessors; he is direct and open. His legal training, sporting experience as an Olympic gold medallist in fencing and as an administrator, as well as his business background, are important assets for a successful presidency. He is dedicated to adjusting the Olympic Movement for a new global society, and has already achieved considerable financial success to the benefit of the Olympic Movement, in particular by attracting new, powerful multinational partners and sponsors.

However, he is facing huge challenges from many different sides: an entirely new media environment, growing competition from different forms of entertainment, more sedentary lifestyles among young people, serious political tensions worldwide, significant environmental threats and, of course, the plagues of doping and corruption. In such a difficult environment, the task of the IOC president is monumental. However, he has launched major initiatives that show he has a solid understanding of the transformations happening in our society. For instance, the launching of the badly named Olympic Channel, which is, in fact, much more than a channel; it is a global multimedia digital platform which reflects new patterns of behaviour in modern times.

Bach has also grasped the need for a full renewal of the selection process for hosts of the Olympic Games. The concept of a single host city is being challenged by a broader concept of a host country, or even co-host countries. Also, the bidding process to become host of the Games is undergoing a fundamental transformation. Before Bach's presidency, the IOC used to wait for applicant cities to beg for the honour of being declared candidate cities. Now, the IOC understands that in a changing world, it can't simply sit and wait for candidates. Currently, it is proactively engaging in a preliminary phase of dialogue with cities that are potential bidders. That is an important change at a time when the staging of the Games raises more and more organisational, environmental, political and financial challenges. Another essential issue for Bach is to determine how the

Sports Programme for the Games should evolve in the future, which sports should be in the Games and which should not. And what form will the competitions take in terms of the number of athletes and how many events? Those and many others are the challenges that Thomas Bach is facing. Time will tell whether he will succeed in meeting those challenges.

29
Chairman of the FIFA 2016 Reform Commission

In late July 2015, when I was in Kuala Lumpur for the IOC Session, I got a call from Sepp Blatter, the president of FIFA, which came as a total surprise to me. We had known one another for many years, in fact since we were both studying at the University of Lausanne. Although we were never close friends, we always kept in contact, particularly when he was still Secretary General of FIFA, and I was Director General of the IOC.

During our conversation, Blatter explained to me that the FIFA Executive Committee had decided to set up a new committee charged with the task of re-drafting new FIFA statutes and that there was a consensus that I should be appointed as chairman of the committee, which would be called the 2016 FIFA Reform Committee. At the time, FIFA was undergoing the most serious crisis in its entire history. In a spectacular Swiss police raid, at the request of the US Department of Justice, several FIFA officials had been arrested at the luxurious 5-star Baur–au-Lac Hotel in Zurich. The culprits were accused of a number of crimes relating to corruption and the arrests, captured on camera, got immediate worldwide media coverage, including major networks like CNN and the New York Times, which had been tipped off and had a crew on the spot.

By the time of my conversation with Blatter, the crisis had developed into a major global scandal, with new allegations and accusations almost daily, directed not only at the arrested individuals, but also at the FIFA leadership, including Blatter himself. The criminal investigation initiated by the US Department of Justice was supported by a separate criminal investigation launched by the Swiss Federal Prosecutor. The offices of FIFA in Zurich were searched and all procedural and judicial steps were taken and controlled primarily by the US authorities, with their Swiss counterparts offering zealous support.

While there was no reason to question the US and Swiss authorities' right to proceed with the necessary investigations, many impartial observers, including members of the Swiss legal community and Swiss politicians, who had no sympathy for FIFA, were shocked by the lack of respect for Swiss sovereignty shown by the US authorities and were concerned by the indulgence of the Swiss federal prosecutors who appeared anxious to do anything to please their American counterparts. For instance, Janet Lynch, then US Attorney General, with the participation of the Swiss Federal Prosecutor, held a press conference dedicated to the FIFA case in Zurich. That was totally at odds with normal international diplomatic practice.

In view of all the incidents happening at FIFA during the summer of 2015, the atmosphere I found when I took up my mandate from FIFA was bizarre. All members of the staff were tense and fearful, and I paid my first official visit to Blatter's office in August to discuss my terms of reference. He was quite cordial and open but gave me the distinct impression of being isolated and lonely. My instructions were that the FIFA Executive Committee had decided to appoint a special task force, to be named the FIFA 2016 Reform Committee. It was made up of twelve members from the six continental confederations, which appointed two members each, and I was to chair such a committee. The mandate was to draft amendments to the FIFA statutes in order to reinforce the institution's governance and, as much as possible, address the gaps which had allowed misconduct and criminal acts to happen.

I was to submit a preliminary progress report to FIFA's Executive Committee in Zurich by mid-September, and my committee's final draft was to be submitted to the same committee for approval in December at a meeting to be convened in Tokyo. The final draft would then be sent to all FIFA member federations for deliberation and a final vote by the FIFA Congress in Zurich in February 2016. The same congress was to elect FIFA's new president to succeed Blatter. The timing was particularly tight and the challenge formidable.

As soon as my name circulated, I was contacted by representatives of some of the major FIFA sponsors. Their own reputation and credibility were at stake, and they wanted some sort of immediate, positive action, hoping, in particular, that Blatter might step down earlier and that the entire reform and electoral process might be accelerated. At the same time, a controversy had arisen, driven by an eager media and anxious sponsors, about the composition of the committee members, more specifically because they were appointed by the continental confederations, about their lack of independence. I was asked to require the right to appoint all members of the committee, or at least a majority of them.

By then, after I'd done my due diligence, a few basic facts were clear. First of all, the FIFA Executive Committee had already made up its mind and wanted the continental federations to appoint the members of the committee. They would allow me to appoint a couple of independent members, the names of whom would have to have the consent of the main sponsors. I was also aware that at least one independent panel, made up of distinguished senior international personalities, had earlier submitted a number of recommendations for reforms, and that FIFA had not implemented them. I also knew that from within, the chairman of the FIFA Ethics Committee, Domenico Scala, had been actively pushing for reforms and wouldn't welcome any intruders in what he considered to be his territory. The problem for him was that the FIFA leadership didn't like his style. Scala had a strong personality and a huge ego, which was perceived, rightly or wrongly, as indicative of unlimited personal ambition. That, among other things, was to be the reason for his rather abrupt firing at the ordinary FIFA Congress in May 2016 in Mexico, when Gianni Infantino was elected to succeed Blatter as FIFA president.

My analysis of the situation with which I was confronted was that, inasmuch as the mandate of my Reform Committee was to prepare new statutes and, more importantly, to have them approved by the FIFA Congress, it was necessary to be able to count on the support of the FIFA membership. To that effect, it made sense that the members of the Reform Committee be appointed by the continental confederations which, in turn, could convince the FIFA members to adopt and implement the proposed reforms. While my view appeared to be relatively well received by the Executive Committee and experienced insiders, it was not shared by many outsiders, including the international media, the sponsors and other critics who were demanding instant and drastic changes, beginning with the immediate removal of the FIFA leadership. Those views, although understandable, were unrealistic, as it would have been impossible, practically and legally, to bypass FIFA's legislative authority, its Extraordinary Congress, which had already been convened for February 2017.

In the light of that very difficult and complex situation, I decided that rather than include two independent members to my committee, and there was no agreement as to who they should be, I should have the authority to appoint an independent advisory board to which my committee would submit its proposals for review and advice. I managed to get the Executive Committee's approval for my plan and to convince the more reasonable critics of its validity.

This was in September 2015, and I immediately began to contact some senior international people of both genders and outlined a roadmap with a calendar which was tight but workable. However, my plan was unexpectedly derailed by two developments. First, Blatter was suddenly suspended and replaced by Issa Hayatou, FIFA vice president, an elderly African whose health required frequent medical treatment. Secondly, and more critically, by a sudden decision of the FIFA Executive Committee to bring forward its meeting to early December, thus taking away at least three weeks of my schedule.

It was obvious that my full plan had become mission impossible. I had to make a choice, either to resign, which would have added even more to the chaotic state of FIFA affairs, or to find another solution, which I did. In October, I abandoned my advisory board idea, in order to focus on my committee, so as to submit by late November a robust draft to the Executive Committee in preparation for the February 2016 Congress. I regretted that we didn't have more time before the Congress and suggested that it be postponed, possibly until May 2017, but to no avail.

In spite of the time constraints and the bizarre mood prevailing at FIFA headquarters in Zürich, my committee set to work diligently. My first decision, which shocked FIFA's leadership and staff, was that we would not meet at the FIFA headquarters in Zürich but in Bern, the Swiss capital. We chose old Bellevue Palace Hotel which is owned by the Swiss state and is a traditional gathering place for many Swiss politicians and other decision makers. I wanted to get away from FIFA's perverse atmosphere and also to signify my committee's independence.

After clearing some administrative resistance, I had to convince some of my colleagues who were used to Zürich and had never been in Bern. Some of their objections were caused by the fact that Bern, although being the Swiss capital, has only a very small airport, which serves a few domestic destinations but no intercontinental flights. Those of my colleagues coming from Africa, America, Asia and Oceania would have to arrive in Geneva or Zürich and join us in Bern by rail or road. Such mundane travel arrangements were new to them, as they were accustomed to being picked up in top-end VIPs' Mercedes limos in Zürich, where they had friends and knew all the best restaurants.

As I'd hoped, we did meet in Bern, and it did create a different mood. The committee members were as follows:

>François Carrard (Chairman), Switzerland
>
>Sheik. Ahmad Al Fahad Al Sabah, Kuwait
>
>Kevan Gosper, Australia
>
>Hany Abo Rida, Egypt
>
>Constant Omari Selemani, Congo DR
>
>Victor Montagliani, Canada
>
>Samir A. Gandhi, United States
>
>Gorka Villar, Spain
>
>Wilmar Valdez, Uruguay
>
>Sarai Bareman, New Zealand
>
>Dawud Bahadur, New Zealand
>
>Gianni Infantino, Switzerland
>
>Alasdair Bell, Scotland

As my colleagues knew nobody in the very old-fashioned Swiss capital, we became an isolated group. We took all our meals together, mostly at the hotel and sometimes at some typical local restaurants. The few FIFA administrative assistants at our disposal were mostly commuting every day between Zürich and Bern. All that contributed to establishing a team spirit, which proved to be very helpful for our task. The procedure I had defined was that there would be no minutes and no recordings, which allowed for a high degree of free speech and serious debate. Not surprisingly, many points were the subject of intense and sometimes heated discussion.

However, by the end, that method allowed us to adopt our entire document by consensus. Thus, after many meetings and weeks of hard work, and thanks to the great support of Marco Villiger, then head of legal affairs at FIFA, we managed to submit our draft to the FIFA Executive Committee at the end of November 2015. However, that left me with no time to convene and consult a high calibre advisory board. In an ideal world, I would have needed an extra month, but that would have made it impossible to comply with the statutory deadlines for sending our draft to all national federations in advance of the February 2016 Extraordinary Congress.

It was difficult for me to explain to the outside world, including the media and the sponsors who were very critical of the process, the practicalities which had forced me to give up the concept of an advisory board. Blatter had been suspended by then and his temporary replacement, Hayatou, was struggling with serious kidney problems. All in all, time was of the essence, and the atmosphere at FIFA was becoming more and more febrile against a backdrop of anxiety and fear. At the 2016 Extraordinary FIFA Congress in February, with some of my colleagues, I presented our draft. It was approved by an overwhelming majority of more than 85% of the votes, which would never have been achieved without the efficient lobbying of my colleagues. The final paragraph of our report read as follows:

'The reform process which shall be launched at the February 2016 FIFA Congress should be the beginning of a new era for FIFA. In order to assist the new leadership for the implementation of the reform process from its launch, the Reform Committee supports the proposal to have its Chairman appoint an Advisory Board of not more than five persons whose mission shall be to temporarily assist FIFA in the first steps of the implementation of its reforms'.

Let me close this chapter with an anecdote. When I was appointed, it had been envisaged that I could possibly serve as adviser to the new FIFA president for the implementation of the new statutes. The assumption was that a new president would not be familiar with the new statutes. That suddenly became unnecessary because of a totally unanticipated development. Gianni Infantino had been designated by UEFA to serve on my committee. Being himself a lawyer, he was one of the most active and instrumental members throughout our work. When we began, the official European candidate for the office of FIFA president was French legend, Michel Platini. However, in October 2015, for reasons which are well known, Platini was unexpectedly forced to step down because he was also caught up in the intrigues within FIFA. That led UEFA to nominate Infantino as its new candidate. I can testify that the circumstances caught him by surprise and that he had not been prepared for it. There were some discussions as to whether he should immediately resign from our committee. I strongly objected to that, as he was a key member of our group, and he continued to serve on my committee, even as he was campaigning for the presidency. In May 2016, he was elected FIFA president. Nobody, including himself, could have predicted that the new FIFA president would sit on our committee and had actually played a key role in the drafting of the new statutes, which explains why, while we remain good friends, he doesn't need me to advise him about statutes of which he was a major author!

30
Judges and Referees, a Major Risk for Sport

Tampering with results, match fixing and performance enhancing drugs are examples of the ever-increasing corruption that is polluting sport. But there are also other dangers. Some sports where performances like time, height, length or distance can be measured objectively with the assistance of instruments, are relatively isolated from cheating. However, other sports, in which results depend upon refereeing or judging, especially in those sports where subjective criteria apply, are at risk from influence beyond the field of play.

Unfortunately, the number of cases of alleged corruption by sports judges and referees has grown significantly in recent years and is a direct consequence of two factors, namely, the emergence of a sports society dominated by money and greed and the need by some political leaders to demonstrate the superiority of their regimes through international sport. Particularly exposed are martial arts and combat sports, gymnastics, figure skating, diving and synchronised swimming; but there are others. Winning a gold medal at any cost is a dream, not only for athletes, but also for politicians and wealthy sponsors. In many cases, corrupting a referee or judge has become a scourge which, if not addressed rapidly, could lead to the total loss of credibility of a specific sport. The phenomenon is not new and there have been notorious examples for many years in sports as diverse as boxing and figure skating.

Corrupting referees and judges may take multiple forms, beginning with apparently minor gestures and ending with full scale organised criminal acts. The first problem arises from the fact that, traditionally, most sports judges and referees have been, and still are, volunteers. That in itself shouldn't be a problem. However, historically, in many sports, judges and referees were recruited within the national federations participating in the event and each country had to provide a certain number of judges and referees in accordance with a quota laid down by the relevant international federation. Thus, many judges and referees were considered as part of their national teams, with whom they often travelled. So, while the rules made it mandatory for them to be totally impartial, being torn between their duties as judge or referee and their loyalty to their national teams, it is obvious that many of them were acting in a permanent state of conflict of interest. When Director General of the IOC, I was directly involved in a typical incident. The scene was the 2002 Winter Olympic Games in Salt Lake City, the sport was figure skating, and the episode was the pairs' final, an outstanding and strongly contested event between the Russian and Canadian pairs, Elena Berezhnaya and Anton Sikharulidze and Jamié Sale and David Pelletier.

Both had delivered remarkable performances in front of packed audiences. The judges' panel awarded the gold medal to the Russian pair, which caused a public uproar, partly, of course, because there were many more pro-Canadian than pro-Russian spectators in the crowd. However, it quickly transpired that one member of the panel, Marie-Reine Le Gougne, a French judge, had been given instructions from Didier Gailhaguet, the head of the French team, to vote for the Russians, because, in return, a Russian judge would vote for the French ice dance couple. Le Gougne turned out to be a rather fragile person and when confronted about her judging burst into tears and admitted her culpability. The International Skating Union (ISU) quickly decided to sanction Le Gougne for misconduct but to uphold the decision of the panel on which she served.

The public and the media, in particular the North American ones, were outraged by what appeared to be a totally unjustifiable decision. Common sense suggested that either Le Gougne acted wrongly, and thus the panel's decision couldn't stand, or that she was innocent, so, therefore, shouldn't have been sanctioned. The ISU and its Italian President, Ottavio Cinquanta, were put under a terrible pressure, and were at a loss. The incident also placed the IOC in an uncomfortable situation, as the pairs' gold medal award is a major moment in any Winter Olympics. The difficulty for us was that the results of any event, even at the Olympic Games, are at the prerogative of the relevant international federation. On the other hand, the medals, which symbolically confirm the results, are the remit of the IOC. We had to find an immediate solution.

I spent many long hours overnight with the lawyers and administrators of the ISU, which had placed itself in an untenable and absurd situation. It was out of the question to repeat the final; the Russians had already received their gold medals. Eventually, a solution was found to save the face of the ISU: taking into account the extraordinary circumstances of the case, they were to ask the IOC, as an exceptional favour, to accept the ISU's request, and, without questioning the gold medal awarded to the Russians, to award a second gold medal to the Canadians. The solution was adopted and brought an end to an episode which should never have happened. The Russians expressed some reluctance but, eventually, graciously appeared at the ceremony at which the Canadians received their gold medals. The crowd cheered and the media soon had other topics to cover.

To me, the sad lesson of that episode is that it is amazing that in the twenty-first century, there are deals done by the leaders of national teams to influence results for the benefit of their teams. I'm told that it's more frequent than one is led to believe. The figure skating incident in Salt Lake was a typical example of the weakness of a judging and refereeing system. At least in that particular case, there was no hint of money being involved, just reciprocal favours. Unfortunately, there are many other cases of what is alleged to be hard, money-based corruption. For instance, there have been, and there still are, numerous examples of match fixing in various sports like football, baseball and cricket. They don't only involve referees, but also players as well. I don't intend to elaborate on those events, except to say that they are criminal acts, but I want to underline the obvious threats to sporting integrity that they represent.

It is imperative that sports organisations find adequate solutions, but the challenge is formidable and concerns more or less all sports in which decisions are made by subjective human judgement and not by strict timing or measurement. For many sports or political leaders as well as sponsors, victories and medals represent incredibly important achievements. The stakes are high and the amounts of money involved are huge.

One answer to this plague may be found by establishing totally independent bodies of judges and referees. They would have to be qualified individuals without links to any teams, athletes or officials. I am fully aware that such solutions would require many additional human and financial resources, and it could be considered utopian. On the other hand, the current risks are growing every day, and responsible leaders should make every effort to overcome the threats faced by their sports. Thanks to the revenues from marketing, sponsoring and broadcasting, most international sporting organisations have the resources to fight against corruption. They should be used. It's a matter of life or death for sport. The equation is simple: if fans can't trust results, they'll find something else to enjoy.

31
The Future of International Sport and the Olympic Games

During the 19th century and a significant part of the 20th, sport was organised and governed by dedicated volunteers and widely ignored by legislators. That has changed completely over recent decades. Our habits have changed: sport has become a must for more and more people, going to sporting events has increased and watching them on TV and on new media is a major activity. New professional sports administrators and managers have replaced the volunteer leaders and sport has new stakeholders like broadcasters and sponsors.

Simultaneously, governments have begun to take a much closer interest in sport. New laws and regulations have been introduced. Sport is now big business and treated as such by national and international authorities like the European Commission. The importance of money has, inevitably, led to an escalation in contentious litigation, and traditional structures and practices are being challenged in courts and parliaments. Similarly, the governance of many international sports organisations is increasingly scrutinised and sometimes severely criticised. To add to its woes, in spite of the many efforts undertaken at various levels, doping remains an all but uncontrollable plague and a major threat to the future of a number of sports.

In fact, it is not unreasonable to suggest that apart from a few professionally run organisations, the world of international sport is not yet ready to cope with the new global challenges it faces. There is no such thing as a universal concept of governance applicable to international sports organisations. On the one hand, their legal structures are not comparable to those of the corporate world, where governance is more and more closely monitored. On the other hand, the differences between the multiple cultures, traditions, political and legal systems of the many national member organisations are such that it is often very difficult for the responsible leaders at world level to introduce and fully enforce a universally accepted state of the art form of governance.

Most international sports organisations are controlled, not by their membership, but by a small circle of individuals exercising tight control and supremacy over the entire sport worldwide. Those nongovernmental institutions are generally self-proclaimed 'supreme' authorities, even though their power is not based on any real legal basis but relies on a consensus reinforced by a long-standing tradition. Whether such a state of affairs has any legal validity is an unresolved question to be debated by the lawyers and judges of the world.

Interestingly, until rather recently, the European Commission had the wisdom to refrain from reviewing the disciplinary sanctions decided by sports organisations for violations of anti-doping regulations, considering that such sanctions, in effect suspensions of athletes, were purely sports-related matters. However, the European Court of Justice has adopted a different view and ruled that the Commission should review such decisions, not from the sports angle, but in order to determine whether they comply with the applicable rules of the European Treaty regarding the freedom to work. That is a clear reminder that sporting activities are not only governed by sports regulations but also by generally applicable national and international laws.

For many years, sports leaders, mainly in Europe, have attempted to obtain from governments a certain degree of autonomy for sports organisations. I've been involved in some of these negotiations with ministers and European Commissioners and was always struck by the double standard of governments. For example, for obvious reasons, many governments, in particular in Western Europe, pay lip service to the aspirations of the world of sport, which leads sports organisations to take for granted that some progress has been achieved and that their autonomy is officially acknowledged and endorsed. However, they don't, or don't want to understand that governments, except perhaps some Anglo-Saxon administrations, are reluctant to recognise any legal independence for sport.

So, sports leaders and administrators must understand that sport is governed by all applicable laws like all other human activities. That means that sport must acquire a new culture, new practices, new governance and an awareness and understanding that the fundamentals have entirely changed. Unfortunately, not all sports leaders have yet made those changes. This may be explained by the age of many leaders, by their lack of specific training in leadership and governance, by their lack of serious experience in any other areas than sport and by their naïve belief that the nature of sport allows them to depart from the laws that apply to all other human activities. A typical illustration of that naivety is found in the title of financial regulations recently adopted by the Union of European Football Associations (UEFA), which is viewed by many as a rather sophisticated organisation.

In view of the many deficiencies affecting the governance of European clubs, UEFA, a private institution based in Switzerland, decided to step in and issue its own complex financial regulations entitled, 'Financial Fair Play'. The intention behind the move certainly deserves credit. However, the reference to a sporting concept such as fair play as a headline of a set of regulations which are supposed to be mandatory and duly enforced by all members of UEFA, appears to be naive. The perception of such a reference is that UEFA doesn't want, or doesn't dare, to impose legally enforceable measures. While UEFA seeks to implement its Financial Fair Play, the whole system appears to be ambiguous. On one hand, the organisation wants to improve the financial governance of its sport, but on the other hand, it doesn't want to go as far as demanding that all applicable national laws, in particular as regards accounting and finances, be strictly enforced. That attitude is but one example of the survival of an obsolete and arrogant attitude. If UEFA really intends to be totally effective and serious in financial matters, it should require all its national federations, clubs, agents and other stakeholders to comply with all enforceable civil, criminal, corporate, bankruptcy and tax laws, just like any other type of business, with all the legal consequences. The example, in August 2017, of the circumstances and conditions of the transfer from Barcelona to Paris St-Germain of Neymar, for an amount exceeding US $250 million, is a perfect illustration of something far removed from 'fair play', which, by the way, is a phrase that only exists in English.

For the last few years, the world of sport has been confronted by a plague of corruption which may well be a far worse threat than doping. Two of its most damaging examples are match fixing and illegal betting. The financial stakes and possible benefits are so high that sports organisations alone are helpless against organised crime. The full involvement and support of public authorities, including criminal justice, is absolutely necessary to save sport and combat crime. This relatively new challenge doesn't only affect sport, it also impacts on society at large. I cannot think of a better example than the Lance Armstrong case. The latter had instituted a sophisticated system for cheating through doping, which enabled him to win seven Tours de France. He was never caught by the sports authorities acting autonomously. It took the support of the US authorities to enable the US anti-doping agency to establish Lance Armstrong's guilt.

The plague of corruption has also expanded to the actual purchase of the votes of decision-makers of sports organisations. This is best illustrated by a worldwide scandal that rocked FIFA. The allegations of corruption in relation to the decisions in the awarding of its major events were so serious that the US Attorney General and Department of Justice, with the full co-operation of the Swiss criminal authorities, had to initiate a major criminal investigation. Since then, FIFA has been exposed to the entire world as a fundamentally corrupt organisation. Despite that, the FIFA president, Sepp Blatter, was nevertheless re-elected with a substantial majority at the subsequent Zurich Congress, which in itself is shocking. Thankfully, for the future of the game, he later resigned. Perversely, and this is at the core of the problem, despite the fact that football has few moral virtues, it remains the most popular sport, its grounds are still full and money continues to flow into the game in enormous quantities.

Based on all the above, my personal conviction is that sport as we have known it throughout most of our lives is a thing of the past. The risk is that sporting competition will become nothing other than showbusiness, and that all the educational values carried by sport will be lost. I'm not sure that the major sports leaders are fully aware of and concerned by the seriousness of the situation. For many of them, the agenda seems to be 'business as usual': more and more competition, plus more events, plus more money equals success. The original spirit of sport, with its values like fair play, is fading away.

Decisions by referees or sports authorities used to be accepted. Now, athletes, teams, clubs and national organisations use regiments of international law firms to engage in fierce, expensive legal battles in front of arbitration panels, including CAS, and/or state courts to challenge any decision they don't like. In nearly all such cases, what is at stake is money.

Another major worry may be described as the politicisation of sport. A typical example is to be found in the way the 2016 Russian doping scandal is being handled by the sports organisations. There is no doubt that in Russia, there has been an organised and systematic doping policy, revealed after the 2014 Sochi Winter Games. There is also no doubt that harsh sanctions were justified. However, the matter becomes far more delicate when sanctions aimed at punishing an entire country also prevent innocent athletes from competing under their national flag and forces them to compete under a neutral or Olympic flag. That, in effect, denies the athletes their nationality and puts them in an uncomfortable position. It also makes it a highly political issue, particularly in the context of what is a new cold war between the USA and its NATO allies and Russia. It goes far beyond sport and touches the heart of nations. With such clearly political sanctions, sporting organisations are exceeding their boundaries and sailing into dangerous, uncharted waters. Let me be clear, in areas like doping and corruption in sport, I don't advocate unjustified tolerance or leniency; but I consider that collective political humiliation is not only wrong and dangerous, but contrary to the true spirit of Olympism.

There is no magic formula for ensuring the future success of international sport and that of the Olympic Games. But there may be a few operational guidelines. First of all, we should never forget that sport is about joy. Sport's main constituency is and should remain the youth of the world. Sport provides a fantastic educational opportunity to pass on the values of Olympism: essentially respect of oneself, respect of others and respect of the rules. Sports organisations must be run by honest, competent and skilled leaders and administrators, whether professionals or volunteers, and their governance must be state-of-the-art. That means full transparency, as required in the corporate and public world, as well as real accountability. I accept that leaves an open question: accountability to whom?

Answers to that question may be found in many directions. First of all, the athletes, secondly, the clubs at the grassroots and also the professional leagues. We should also consider the sponsors, the spectators, the viewers and the fans. All have a contribution to make. Good governance isn't rocket science; where there's a will, there's a way. It's time for action, not speeches.

As far as the future of the Olympic Games is concerned, the 'Olympic Agenda 2020', launched by IOC president, Thomas Bach, which includes 40 recommendations, provides a robust platform to address the issues that concern the survival of the Games. The challenges are formidable, in particular for the Summer Games. The first challenge lies in their sheer size and the number of events. If we were to start from scratch and suggest that we should attempt to create a global event that would consist of twenty-eight world championships, concentrated into one city over just sixteen days, with billions watching the spectacle, we would be ridiculed as crazy. But that's what the Games are. The justification from the IOC of the maintenance of the traditions of the Games goes back to Coubertin's dream to re-create the ancient gathering at Olympia. The Olympic village for athletes, the elaborate rituals of the opening and closing ceremonies, the symbolism of the rings, the torch, the cauldron; all are part of the unique package.

But the world has changed since 1896, let alone since the days of Ancient Greece, which opens up a number of questions deriving from the transition from the origin of the Games to the twenty-first century; the changes in our society, our interests and habits, quite apart from the extraordinary revolutions in technology and communication. We need a period of reflection so that we can decide about the future. It is clear that the Olympic Games must change, but to what, where and in what guise, is a matter for urgent debate. At stake is the survival of not only the Olympic Games, but also of the entire Olympic Movement and of the philosophy of Olympism.

Finally, even more fundamental is the formidable challenge of defining what is a sport. Without claiming to possess a learned definition of the word, I would suggest that according to a widely accepted, simple concept, sport may be considered as a predominantly physical activity, organised and practised in accordance with the rules provided for competition. However, in October 2017, a section of the European Court of Justice considered that bridge, which had been recognised as a sport in the United Kingdom, should not be considered as a sport for its lack of a significant physical activity. This definition is not shared by a number of international sports organisations like the IOC or the GAISF (Global Association of International Sports Federations), which recognise both bridge and chess as sports.

Over recent decades, there have been various controversies over the so-called 'mind' sports, which include, for instance, chess, a game widely considered as an important sport in the former Soviet bloc. Those specific controversies now appear to be secondary to the more recent appearance and fast growth of Esports (electronic sports in the form of video games). They introduce a totally new dimension because of the trends among younger generations and the arrival of social media.

Our society is changing so rapidly that it has become impossible to agree on a clear and uniform definition of which activities should be defined as sport rather than, for example, entertainment or show business. Once again, those responsible for the governance of sport need to get their act together. It's pointless to try to meet the challenges facing sport if we can't agree what it is.

32
Reinventing Olympism

Another major challenge to sport has recently emerged across the world. Driven by financial crises, the threats to the environment from consumer spending and the growth of both left-wing and right-wing politics, various groups have appeared which are highly critical of the size and costs of major events such as the FIFA World Cup and the Olympic Games. Such movements attract growing interest and sympathy from the media and from large portions of the public opinion. So far, the response from sports organisations has not been very convincing.

At the heart of these challenges is a lack of understanding of the real value of sport, which is far greater than the total cost of all the sporting events in the world added together. The time has come for a massive mobilisation of all constituents of all sports organisations, including the IOC, to convince, not only governments and politicians, but also educators and the public at large, that sport has real value. That means a fundamental worldwide change of mentality that will require a huge lobbying effort. I venture to say that the time has come for the Olympic and sports movements of the world to wake up and abandon their traditional political shyness and, based on its huge potential influence, to launch powerful campaigns for a new cause, the aim of which should be, 'One mandatory hour of sport per day for every child and student in every school or educational institution in the world'.

More than a project, it would be a new cause for the twenty-first century and would be directly related to and inspired by Coubertin's original message, which was essentially educational. Our society is suffering from a plague of violence, particularly among the young. More sport in schools is a response to the plague. Importantly, because the message would come from the world's sporting organisations, it would restore their credibility in the minds of the people of the world and convince them that major sports events will always be necessary and offer excellent value for money.

As the world of sport faces increasing criticism, it cannot remain defensive while its credibility diminishes. It must re-invent Olympism by simplifying Coubertin's educational message and adapting it to our times. The simple message of Olympism, the three fundamental forms of respect: self-respect, respect for others and respect for rules, should be taught in schools and would constitute a robust educational foundation for young people.

Having had the opportunity to attend many conferences and seminars dedicated to Coubertin in various parts of the world, I have reached the conclusion that his only contribution that might survive throughout the centuries to come is his inspired message of education through sport. That in itself justifies the importance of Olympism and must be cultivated and developed. Eventually, as in most areas of our society, the future success or failure of the Olympic Movement and international sport will be determined by the quality of its leaders. Thomas Bach, elected IOC president for eight years in 2013 in Buenos Aires, appears to be highly aware of all the challenges which confront international sport and the Olympic Movement. His ambitious project, 'Olympic Agenda 2020', is designed to tackle the many challenges and issues. His determination is impressive. Time will tell if he succeeds.

33
Glimpses of a Few People

Having emphasised the importance of the human factor in all aspects of our society and taking into account my own unwavering passion for all things human, I feel entitled to offer a few vignettes of some of the personalities I have encountered during my life. If anything makes it worthwhile to spend time on this planet, it is the people who inhabit it. During my more than fifty-year or so professional career, I have always been totally fascinated by all the people I've come into contact with. Apart from being interested in all the people I've actually met, I'm also fascinated by those thousands and thousands of people in my life of whom I've just caught a glimpse. They go their way and I go mine, and yet I clearly remember a figure, a dress, a look, a smile that are forever engraved in my memory. Those memories are never recorded elsewhere. I hate taking pictures, which directly ruin the scope and meaning of memories, and much prefer to leave it up to my own memory to sort out what should be kept and what should be eliminated. Memories should not be frozen forever but should be allowed to evolve as the people in those memories progress in life. To put it differently, those memories are my truths.

I am extremely fortunate to have met an extraordinary number of incredibly fascinating people all over the world. Many are very special individuals, quite a few are pompous idiots, but I'll refrain from mentioning those. I shall let my memory wander as it guides me, and I will limit myself to some anecdotes which may throw some light on them.

Nelson Mandela

If I was allowed to mention only one person in this book who impressed me more than anybody else in my entire life, I wouldn't hesitate for a moment to repeat what I have already said above, it would be Nelson Mandela by far. As I wrote, I had the privilege to meet him on several occasions and have many vivid memories. However, I will tell just two very different stories.

The first happened in May 1992, during Mandela's first visit to Switzerland, prior to his election as South Africa's president. He was staying at a very good old hotel near Montreux. Swiss security had posted two officers on permanent duty outside his room. They were middle-aged men wearing their prescribed dress of plain business suits with jackets and ties. On the first morning of his stay, Mandela suddenly stepped out of his room at approximately five in the morning. He was wearing his legendary baseball cap and full sports kit. The two officers, who were dozing on their chairs, jumped to attention, totally surprised. He greeted them with a broad smile and told them he was going out for a run. Of course, the two officers were under strict orders not to leave him,

As Mandela was quite fit, he ran down the staircase and began jogging along the shore of Lake Geneva in complete darkness. Both officers, sweating profusely in their suits, struggled to keep up with him. Thoughtfully, the great man waited for them and began a conversation, during which he apologised for waking them up so early and explained that during twenty-seven years in prison, he had got into the habit of waking up before dawn. He added that he still had the habit, except that no longer being a prisoner, he relished opening his own door and running past his 'guards' outside.

The second story involves a conversation at a dinner which took place in the same hotel around the same time. The party consisted of Mandela, Samaranch, Kéba Mbaye, Fekrou Kidane and me. The topic was the future South African government and its structure once Mandela was elected president, which was a racing certainty to happen soon. There was a long debate about whether the office of prime minister would be needed. Samaranch was of the opinion that once elected president, Mandela should have the South African parliament elect a prime minister who would act as a safety fuse in case of need. Mbaye shared Samaranch's view and considered that such a solution would strengthen the president's position.

Mandela agreed that a South African prime minister would make a lot of sense. However, he thought that his own election was already going to be considered by many as a form of revolution and that any proposal that required constitutional change would be viewed as an unnecessary political breach and unnecessarily provocative. He added that he would have to make huge efforts to promote reconciliation and unity and that that would be his priority rather than institutional reforms. The discussion lasted for more than two hours, during which what struck me most was Mandela's clear vision and his depth of political wisdom. Those qualities, added to his intelligence, kindness and ability to forgive were typical of a unique man.

A Bavarian Statesman in Lederhosen

The year was 1986, the place, Lausanne, the venue, its Palais de Beaulieu, the event, the IOC Session assembled to vote on awarding the 1992 Olympic Games, both winter and summer editions. The delegations of the various bidding cities included several high-level political leaders like Jacques Chirac, then French prime minister and mayor of Paris, and Felipe Gonzalez, the Spanish prime minister. Garmisch Partenkirchen was the German city bidding for the winter Games. Its delegation included the presiding minister of Bavaria, Franz Joseph Strauss, a famous German politician.

The IOC ritual, or protocol as it prefers to call it, is such that each delegation enters separately into the hall where the hundred or so IOC members are gathered and walks up to a podium from which the bidding delegation presents its city. While the dress code is optional, most delegations appear in business attire. When it was Garmisch's turn, the entire delegation dressed in traditional Bavarian costume. The sight of Franz Joseph Strauss, a rotund, red-faced man in long white socks, short leather pants and an alpine hat replete with a feather, was a sight to behold!

Strauss was a powerful and popular German statesman but he had little proficiency in any other language than his native German. Not only that, he had a somewhat harsh south German accent. Appearing in front of the IOC, which has two official languages, French and English, he had decided to deliver part of his presentation in French. He then proceeded, with great difficulty, to stumble through a written speech in front of him. At one point, he tried to explain that Garmisch was going to build an Olympic village which would welcome all 'Olympic champions', which in French is 'champions Olympiques'. Unfortunately, instead of saying 'champions', he solemnly proclaimed that the village would welcome all 'champignons', which meant Olympic mushrooms! To his surprise, and I don't think he ever realised what had happened, the audience roared with laughter.

The amusing Strauss incident illustrates the lengths to which politicians are prepared to go to convince the IOC to award them the Olympic Games. I've watched heads of states, kings, presidents or prime ministers: Obama, Putin, Mandela, Chirac, Lula, Blair, address the IOC membership to promote their national candidate cities to host the Olympic Games. Most of their speeches were boring, not helped by being delivered in a language with which they weren't familiar. On the other hand, I remember the brilliant address to the Session in Copenhagen in 2009 by President Obama in support of his city of Chicago for its bid for the 2016 Games. However, despite his excellent delivery, the outcome was terribly disappointing for the US delegation: Chicago was eliminated in the first round, and eventually the Games were awarded to Rio. In truth, the IOC's decisions are not usually determined by the quality of the speeches delivered by politicians, but by other considerations, including, in particular, the contents of the evaluation reports submitted by the experts. Are they always right? I leave it up to the reader to make up their own mind.

Primo Nebiolo, 'The First'

Primo Nebiolo, who died in November 1999, was an extraordinary character. His entire life was dedicated to sport: first to the Universiades (World University Games), which he chaired for many years, and, most importantly, to athletics. President of the International Association of Athletic Federations (IAAF), he ruled athletics unchallenged for almost twenty years. He made a huge contribution to the success of track and field, and he deserves great praise for his achievements.

Mind you, his colourful personality left behind a string of most amusing anecdotes. While recognising his qualities, many remember him as a tyrant, obsessed with his status. It was reported, for instance, that when attending sports events like the Olympic Games, he gave orders to ensure that the suites allocated to him in the official hotels should never be smaller than those of anyone else. He demanded the use of the largest limousine and was particularly keen to be treated at least as well, if not better, than Samaranch. After a lobbying campaign that had lasted for years, the obsession persisted after he was admitted as an IOC member in 1992. A native of Turin, he was a man of small stature, with a passing resemblance to Mussolini, a likeness accentuated by his gestures and his hoarse voice. Whenever he tried to speak in English, which was often, his pronunciation was so disastrous that he was incomprehensible. Even so, he couldn't have cared less and somehow managed to get his message through by force of personality.

Among the countless anecdotes which illustrate Nebbiolo's uniqueness I will offer you just one. It was 1992, at the Barcelona Olympic Games. The entire IOC was housed at the Hotel Princessa Sofia, where I also had my office. The weather was beautiful and very hot and every morning I would walk through the hotel's lobby to see Samaranch, who had his office on the top floor of the bank he chaired, the Caixa, a few hundred metres away. He would hold a daily briefing there. One morning before I left, I found in my mail an elegantly printed formal invitation card. It came from President and Mrs Nebiolo, incidentally, a most charming woman, and was an invitation for that day to attend a formal luncheon, 'in honour of their Majesties King Juan Carlos and Queen Sofia'. I informed Nebiolo's office of my acceptance and proceeded to my daily visit to Samaranch. While walking through the hotel's lobby, I noticed several IOC members and their wives discussing the invitation, obviously looking forward to the opportunity to meet the Spanish royals.

During my meeting with Samaranch, I told him I thought I could talk to him at length during lunch. 'What lunch?' he asked. So, I told him about the Nebiolo lunch in honour of the Spanish royals, assuming that, as IOC president, he would be invited. Samaranch was surprised and knew nothing about it. Then he began to laugh and told me that he'd just spoken on the phone to the king who was in Madrid that day and would not be coming to Barcelona, nor would the queen.

We both laughed and realised that it was a typical Nebiolo stunt. Knowing perfectly well that the royals wouldn't be there, Nebiolo had chosen not to invite Samaranch. Later that morning, as I passed through the hotel's lobby, I heard the growing excitement and noticed the elegant dresses and hairstyles of the IOC members' wives. 'We're going to meet the King and Queen of Spain' was the gist of all the talk. At the venue, a beautiful old palace, a lively crowd drank champagne, and the ladies discussed whether or not to curtsey. After more than an hour, we were all invited into the dining room to take our seats.

Everybody assumed that the royals would arrive at any moment, and many had their cameras at the ready. I could hardly contain myself. Suddenly, Nebiolo, who was in the middle of the centre table, stood up and gave a speech in which he thanked everybody for having accepted his invitation to celebrate the King and Queen of Spain. He asked everybody to stand up and, as the guests looked around expecting a royal entrance, simply proposed a toast in honour of their majesties. He then asked everyone to sit down and said, 'Buon appetito'! As usual, Nebiolo got away with his ruse. The guests had drunk lots of champagne, the food was excellent and nobody would admit to having been fooled. Needless to say, Samaranch enjoyed my report later that day.

That's just one of the many stories which could be told about Nebiolo, whose first name was Primo, the 'First', a rather fitting moniker. He was certainly a tyrant and with an ego to match, but he was also a sports leader with a powerful vision for his sport. He also had a heart and a sense of humour capable of self-ridicule, qualities which are all too rare nowadays.

Lee and Lee

A couple of years ago, when I was a member of the board of directors of Bank of China Switzerland, a meeting with some very senior Chinese bank officials was to take place in my law firm's office in the heart of Lausanne. Prior to the meeting, we had lunch at the Beau-Rivage Palace, a luxurious grand hotel, the best hotel in Lausanne, many say the best in Switzerland. As I've mentioned before, I am the chairman of its board, which is relevant to this story.

At the end of the lunch, we prepared to be driven to my office. As we were going through the hotel's lobby, I was escorting one of our Chinese guests, who happened to be the most senior one. I didn't clearly hear his full name, except that 'Lee' was part of it. As we went through the hotel's main door, we found ourselves in front of a huge black Maybach limousine. Maybach limos have been designed by Mercedes to be the most lavish of luxury vehicles. They cost a fortune and are quite rare. That day, the sight of such a limousine was exceptional, even in front of a hotel busy with Ferraris, Rolls-Royces, Bentleys or Mercedes. Mr 'Lee' walked straight to the Maybach, the chauffeur immediately opened the right rear door and my guest sat down in the right back seat. Without any thought, I automatically followed and sat next to my Chinese guest.

I gave my office address and the chauffeur drove off. My guest and I exchanged some banalities, but, after a while, I noticed that the chauffeur seemed uneasy, constantly looking back at us in his mirror.

He suddenly addressed my neighbour and asked him whether he was Mr Lee. I found his question odd, why would a chauffeur have to identify his boss? Obviously, Mr Lee nodded, but as we drove on, the chauffeur's unease was clearly growing, and I asked him if there was a problem. He answered that he'd been told to wait for Mr Lee and drive him not to my address but to Geneva airport. Somewhat alarmed, I said that I assumed he was driving for the Bank of China, at which point he looked horrified and immediately stopped the car. He told me that he had nothing to do with the Bank of China but had been ordered to pick up Mr Lee, chairman and major shareholder of Samsung!

There had been a huge misunderstanding, and the poor chauffeur was terrified that Samsung would sack him. I immediately called the hotel and cleared up the incident. We quickly drove back and picked up another car, this time an ordinary Mercedes, and on the way to my office, my guest and I managed to make sense of what had happened. When my 'Lee' saw the Maybach, he assumed that it was the Beau-Rivage chairman's car, my car, and got straight into it. I followed him, convinced it was his car, waiting for him. We both had quite a laugh about it.

Funnily enough, it so happened that I knew the chairman of Samsung who had been a member of the International Olympic Committee for many years. A secretive person, his health had always been precarious, and I do not think anybody ever dared to tell him how his Maybach had been so easily borrowed. The members of his entourage were afraid of possible sanctions, so I never told him. He passed away in 2016 after a long illness, when Samsung was facing major worldwide problems with its Galaxy 7 cell phones catching fire because of faulty batteries. The other irony was that my 'Lee' was Chinese, but Samsung's 'Lee' was Korean.

Mink Coat Diplomacy

Samaranch had a charming wife, Maria Teresa, whose nickname, to all their friends and family, was Bibis. She was smart, elegant, lively and had been highly important in her husband's career, particularly as Spain's first ambassador to the USSR. She was also the first lady of the IOC and, as such, very supportive of many of Samaranch's activities. She travelled a lot across the world on her own, acting as a perfect Olympic ambassador.

One cold winter morning in the early nineties, I got an urgent call from Samaranch. He told me that, returning from a trip to New York, Bibis had just landed at Geneva airport, where she was being delayed by Swiss customs officials and being questioned about the origin of her fur coat. As usual, Samaranch didn't go into much detail, he simply told me to fix it. I immediately called the airport's customs office and was told that indeed, Señora Samaranch was being questioned about a potential attempt to import into Switzerland a highly valuable brand-new mink coat. The officer I spoke to was very polite and was aware that Bibis held a Spanish diplomatic passport. He then passed the phone to Bibis, who explained to me that the coat wasn't new, that she'd received it from her husband several years earlier. She also said that she had several mink coats, having lived for a while in Moscow, and that she didn't remember where or when her husband had bought it.

Of course, she wasn't carrying any form of document concerning that coat, but knowing her as I did, I knew that her story was perfectly true. I resumed my discussion with the customs officer and explained to him that Señora Samaranch was perfectly credible and that she should be allowed to go immediately so as not to create a diplomatic incident. I added that, as I was not only the IOC Director General but also a registered lawyer called to the bar, I was willing to guarantee any fine which could be due to the Swiss authorities. The officer was embarrassed but told me that there was a problem since customs had absolute proof that the coat was brand new, contradicting what Bibis told me.

I was very surprised and asked him what the evidence was. His answer came as a total shock. He explained that, as there were many fraudulent imports of fur coats, the Swiss customs used expert officers who could distinguish new coats from old ones. So, I asked him what method they applied. I will never forget his answer. Apparently, the so-called expert could tell a new coat from an old one by sniffing the inside of the coat at the junction of its sleeves and its body, and could, if there was no hint of sweat, be sure the coat was new! I couldn't believe my ears.

I cut short the conversation and immediately called a senior customs official in Bern, the Swiss capital, who fortunately understood how ridiculous the situation was. A few minutes later, I received a call from Bibis, who was in her car on her way to Lausanne, to tell me the matter was closed. She burst out laughing when I told her the detail of the conversation about armpits and sweat, a bizarre olfactory test that nearly turned her into a smuggler. We never heard any more about it, nor did I ever meet the nasal expert.

The King and I

In the late nineties, following some preliminary meetings in Sydney for the 2000 Games, Samaranch and a few of us made a stopover in Bangkok, where we were to be received by King Bhumibol, who carried the grand title of, 'might of the land, unparalleled brilliance'. Importantly, Thailand, a sport loving country, was contemplating submitting a bid for the Olympic Games. Our visit was regulated by protocol and the king was to receive us in his summer palace, in a resort located on the southwest coast of Thailand.

We received strict instructions about how to dress. Dark suits were a must, even in the middle of an extremely humid, hot day and we were reminded that, when seated, we should never cross our legs, as lifting a foot could show dirt on a shoe and thus imply a serious insult. We were also told that, when in the presence of the king, we should at all times face him and never turn our backs to him. With those requirements and a few more very formal recommendations, we were flown in a squadron of military helicopters over the beautiful coastline for an hour, before landing close to the seaside palace, located in the middle of a beautiful park, and guarded by a warship.

We walked through the park, escorted by scores of servants dressed in traditional Thai dress. To my pleasant surprise, the palace appeared to be a very comfortable summer residence with covered terraces, and not the type of extravagant place one might have expected. We were taken into a pleasant living room, adorned with typically European mountain paintings. Suddenly, just before the king's arrival, a dozen servants, carrying trays of refreshments, entered the room on their knees, at which point, the king arrived with his entourage. During the entire function, the servants stayed on their knees, while the king, known for his passion for science, in particular botany, conducted himself like a very quiet, distinguished gentleman in his late seventies, which, apart being a king and the richest monarch in the world, is exactly what he was.

I knew that he'd been educated in my city, Lausanne, where some of his family lived, and where he attended the law faculty of our university. I knew he was fluent in French, and I was also aware that his family had been frequent guests at the Beau-Rivage Palace. Even more importantly for me, I knew he was a great jazz fan, and a decent saxophonist. It was also well known that he had his own big band with whom he used to play on Saturday evenings. So, when Samaranch introduced me to him, telling him that I was the chairman of the Beau-Rivage and of the Montreux Jazz Festival, the king was silent for a moment before saying, "Ah, yes, Lausanne, the Beau-Rivage…, those were nice times indeed." Then, as I offered him a few CDs of Montreux, he looked at them and added, "Nice times indeed."

The officials in charge of protocol were disconcerted. Our exchange had apparently exceeded the norm allocated for a simple introduction, and they'd lost control of the narrative, as the king had spoken in French, which they obviously didn't understand. During the entire encounter, in full compliance with the protocol, all the other guests were turned towards the king and me. Simultaneously, the servants were still wriggling around among us, and I noted that they were particularly skilled at moving backwards, so as not to insult their supreme ruler. It was at that moment that I remembered the 1956 Yul Brynner and Deborah Kerr classic musical, 'The King and I'. I hadn't thought about those famous scenes or the wonderful music of Rodgers and Hammerstein for many years, but all of a sudden, it was as if I was on the set of the movie.

Nelson Paillou, the Chain Smoker

Nelson was the charismatic president of the French Olympic Committee in the eighties and nineties, a period during which he was the most important sports leader in France. He was outspoken, friendly and totally committed to his mission. A man of short stature, he didn't look like a sports person. He chain-smoked cigarettes, which he rolled himself, during every waking hour of the day.

During the 1996 Atlanta Games, knowing that I tolerated smokers in my conference room, he would visit me every morning. The ban on smoking was already strict in the USA, and he was obviously delighted to have found a safe haven where he could satisfy his addiction. It was always a pleasure to see him as, apart from sport, he was a man of great sophistication. He was a perfect incarnation of the best of French Olympic panache. I always believed that he should have been chosen as an IOC member for France, but, unfortunately, he never got the chance. the French seats on the IOC were successively occupied by highly prestigious personalities like Count Jean de Beaumont, a senior aristocrat and banker, and Maurice Herzog, world famous alpinist and former sports minister under de Gaulle. They were followed by Jean-Claude Killy, the glorious skiing icon, and later Guy Drut, the 110-metre hurdles winner at the 1976 Montreal Games, who became France's sports minister under ChiracChirac, Jacques. During many of those years, Paillou continued to act as a dedicated French administrator.

Before the 1998 Nagano Winter Olympics, I remember flying with Paillou from Paris to Tokyo via Anchorage on Air France. The purpose of the trip was to attend meetings in Tokyo in preparation for the Nagano Games. We were sitting close to one another in the first-class cabin on a night flight that was distinctly memorable for me. First of all, during the entire flight, Paillou smoked one self-rolled cigarette after another, discharging myriad flickers of burning fag paper, so that the cabin was lit up like an airborne volcano. The other passengers were alarmed, so was I, but the crew didn't take any action out of respect for Paillou's notoriety and VIP status. We were all eventually released from the pyrotechnics when we finally landed smoothly at Tokyo's Narita airport.

Apart from Paillou's fireworks, the flight was also memorable for another reason. The seat next to mine had remained unoccupied until the very last minute before to take-off. I was looking forward to spending the long night with an empty seat next to mine, when an Air France official unobtrusively escorted an elegant woman, who was to be my companion for the flight, to the seat. To my delight, my neighbour was the legendary French star, Catherine Deneuve. The unexpected encounter gave me a wonderful opportunity to chat with her. She was in her early fifties, still stunning, absolutely charming and very down-to-earth.

An amusing coincidence was that the first-class passengers had been given a copy of Paris Match, the famous weekly magazine, which carried a large picture of her, which she kindly autographed for me. The next morning in Tokyo, I went to a meeting with various international sports officials. As we were sipping coffee before the meeting, we were telling one another about our experiences in Tokyo the night before. When I was asked what I'd done, I was proud to say that I'd spent the night with Catherine Deneuve!

Sometime later, I had to go to a meeting with Paillou in Paris. It was a session of a French government committee of which he was a senior member. By then, the French government had instituted a very strict ban on smoking in all public buildings. Smoking was only allowed in specially designated areas called 'espace fumeur'. As a guest, I had a seat in a back row of the room, while Paillou was sitting on the front row. Although smoking was not allowed in the room, Paillou began his usual routine, rolling and lighting a cigarette. The committee's chairman, a distinguished senior official, reminded Paillou courteously that smoking was only allowed in designated areas, and that the committee's room was not one of them. Paillou replied just as courteously, apologised for his oversight and pulled out of his pocket a piece of cardboard on which the words 'espace fumeur' were printed. He placed the sign on his desk and said to the chairman with a smile, "Now, Mr Chairman, I am in order."

The whole room burst out laughing and the chairman smiled as Paillou puffed away in his self-proclaimed smoking area. Unfortunately, Paillou passed away some years later, not surprisingly from lung cancer. He had been one of the most popular figures of French sport and he is greatly missed.

Robert Badinter

Having just recalled one French sports leader, I must pay tribute to another. He is the man who has impressed me most other than Mandela. Robert Badinter is a distinguished French lawyer, former French minister of justice, former president of the French Constitutional Council and member of the Senate. He is the man who succeeded in convincing the French National Assembly to abolish the death penalty in 1972 and I believe him to be a remarkably distinguished defender of human rights. Without making concessions on principles or values, he seems to always find ways and means to promote human dignity.

I first met Badinter in the early seventies in our firm's offices in Lausanne. He was then one of the most famous and prominent lawyers in France and was co-operating with one of my partners on a most difficult criminal case involving a famous Canadian scientist accused of murdering his wife while living in Switzerland on a sabbatical year. The scientist had been arrested after landing in Paris and was extradited to Switzerland, where he was finally tried and acquitted. A couple of years later, I came across Badinter again in

Paris. I'd been instructed by a client to seek damages for defamation from a famous French weekly magazine.

My client, a Swiss resident, was an art collector who had had problems with the tax authorities. The magazine had published an article describing my client as dishonest, which was untrue. Having written to the magazine, I received a phone call from Badinter. He was the counsel for the magazine and its owner and offered to meet me to discuss the situation. My client told me to accept, so I went to Paris and visited Badinter in his office which was on Rue Faubourg Saint-Honoré. The meeting was cordial, constructive and fascinating for me. Badinter had done his homework; not only had he checked the facts, but he'd also done his legal research. He went straight to the point and told me, without any reservation, that my client was absolutely right and that he had no doubt that, if we went to court, my client would win. The important point was what would my client be granted by the French court which had jurisdiction over the matter. What Badinter suggested was that we would be given a declaration, according to which my client's honesty would be confirmed. As damages, we would obtain the symbolic one-franc as moral compensation in accordance with the applicable French law. We would pay our own costs and fees; such was the law at the time. The magazine and its owner would be ordered to publish the judgment, which they would be entitled to do in small print. All that would happen a couple of years after the end of the trial, during which time Badinter would be instructed, as a matter of principle, to deny my client's claims. It would be a Pyrrhic victory.

Badinter noted my gloomy mood and offered me what he considered to be a better solution. The owner would write a personal letter of apology to my client, without referring to the incriminating article. The magazine would publish, during the year, a story covering my client's cultural activities and presenting them in a positive manner. The magazine would nevertheless retain full editorial control over the story. In addition, Badinter's clients would pay a contribution to my client's costs. My client agreed to what turned out to be a win-win settlement and very quickly obtained a private written apology from the media magnate. The magazine subsequently published a positive story about my client, but never had to publicly retract the untrue allegations it had published. Also, my client didn't have to spend too much on the case, which was settled very quickly.

Thanks to Badinter's simple and direct approach, the case will always be remembered by me as one of the most intelligent settlements I ever reached as both sides ended as winners. By the way, I didn't know then, but about ten years later, Badinter's client appointed me as his counsel in a major international arbitration case. What goes around, comes around.

Jean-Claude Killy

If the entire Olympic Movement, including the IOC, was forced to be reduced to a single individual who would be its trustee and embody all its values, Jean-Claude Killy would be that person. He has achieved all that can be achieved and held all the positions that count within the Olympic Movement and has been a shining light of Olympism throughout his life. As an athlete he was the triple alpine Olympic gold medallist at the 1968 Winter Olympics, a unique achievement. In 1992, he successfully co-chaired, with the French politician Michel Barnier, the organisation of the excellent Albertville Winter Olympics. Additionally, since 1995, he has always been a dedicated and particularly loyal IOC member, even when, now and then, he had to keep to himself his personal convictions, which are very strong.

His last major Olympic challenge, which was particularly difficult, was to chair the Co-ordination Commission for the Sochi Olympics, where his contribution to the great success of the Games was widely acknowledged and considered decisive. When he reached the age of seventy in 2014, although he could have stayed until the age of eighty under the rules, he resigned as an IOC member, because he wanted to set an example and comply with the revised age limit which applies to new members.

Jean-Claude Killy was also, and still is, successful in his professional career. He is one of the first athletes who successfully capitalised on his fame, creating his own brand and serving on the boards of several prestigious multinational groups. In private, he seems prudent and reserved, and to those who don't know him, he appears shy or even sombre. On the other hand, those who know him appreciate his devastating sense of humour. In short, Jean-Claude Killy is the best embodiment of the true Olympic spirit and of the Olympic values. He is now an IOC honorary member; I hope that his example will shine a light for others long into the future.

Fidel Castro

I met Fidel Castro on three occasions: in Havana in 1990, in Barcelona in 1992 and in Lausanne in 1998. The first occasion was during the Pan-American Games. I'd been invited to an official dinner that he was giving to a few sports leaders. The function began with a delay of nearly two hours, during which we'd enjoyed a number of excellent mojitos. When Castro arrived, dressed in his usual khaki battledress, he started by shaking hands with every one of the fifty or so guests, which took another thirty minutes. As he sat down, a few journalists and TV crews were allowed in, at which point, the leading Latin American sports figure, Mexican, Mario Vasquez Rana, presented him with an ostentatious gold wristwatch.

The obviously very expensive present was in stark contrast to the cheap black plastic watch worn by Castro. Perfectly aware that the whole scene was being covered by the media, 'El Comandante' took off his watch and put the glittering gift around his wrist, which he flaunted for the cameras, saying, "You all know that all presents given to me belong to the people of Cuba. This beautiful watch will be no exception. I might be tempted to wear it for a while, but you are all witnesses to me proclaiming that this jewel is the property of the Cuban people, and if anyone has any doubts, you will be able to verify the accuracy of what I say at the reading of my last will and testament."

There was an explosion of laughter, and the meal began. According to protocol, it was supposed to last for an hour and a half. In fact, we had to stay for nearly three hours, until Castro decided to leave. As he did so, I noticed that he was again wearing his old black plastic watch. Many years later, in 2017, I met Castro's son who remembered that his father had brought the gold watch home and told his family about the episode. He also remembered that the watch was sold at a very high price by the Cuban administration and the money used to buy medicines for Cuba's hospitals.

I met Castro for the third time in Lausanne in 1998, when he visited IOC headquarters for a meeting with Samaranch to discuss a Cuban bid to host the Olympic Games in Havana. He was accompanied by the Cuban minister of sport, the Cuban ambassador in Bern and a few advisers and assistants. Samaranch was joined by a couple of members of his administration and me. As the meeting began, Castro asked Samaranch about his daily routines. Samaranch, slightly surprised, politely answered that he usually began his day's work by arriving at his office at nine o'clock.

I then saw that Castro was writing with a pencil on a white sheet of paper something like 'arrival at 9:00 am'. As the talks continued, Castro wrote down all the details in line after line of notes. At the end of the discussions, there was a photo opportunity and an exchange of gifts, during which both delegations mingled. At that point, I saw that Castro's sheet of paper was still on the table and I decided to pick it up as a piece of memorabilia for the Olympic Museum. However, as I moved towards the table, a beautiful young Cuban woman took the paper and said with a charming smile, "I do this all the time, it's part of my job."

The incident had an unexpected follow up many years later in Havana. I was visiting Cuba with the late Claude Nobs, founder and CEO of the Montreux Jazz Festival, of which I am the chairman. We were to attend some jazz events and visit pianist, Chucho Valdés, a jazz icon. When we arrived at Havana airport, we were greeted by an official delegation of the Ministry of Culture. The interpreter was an elegant Cuban woman with greying hair. We both looked at each other, realising that we'd met before and suddenly remembered that it was in Lausanne when I attempted to snatch Castro's meeting notes. Claude Nobs was amused when he heard the story. We then learned that, not only was our charming host in charge of protocol for the minister of culture, but also that she was still meeting the aging Castro nearly every day. He'd retired from office but was still writing for the daily newspaper, 'Granma', the official newspaper of the Cuban Communist Party, which she translated into French.

Since our visit, many changes seem to be under way in Cuba. President Obama has at last changed the US policy towards its traditional enemy, and President Raul Castro appears to have understood that fundamental reforms are unavoidable in a country that has been kept in communist isolation for decades. Cuba is an extraordinary, beautiful country, and Cubans are wonderful, proud people who deserve that whatever changes take place over the coming years neither undermine their fascinating culture nor hurt their dignity, which they have maintained even under the highly questionable rule of Fidel.

Following the election of Donald Trump as president, it appears that, as in several other areas, the opening made by Obama with Cuba has unfortunately been reversed and that, under pressure from

Trump's Florida supporters, US policy is, at least temporarily, back to the old days of boycott.

A Brandy with a Cardinal, and Keeping the Beat with a Pope

At the end of May 1990, Samaranch sent me to Rome with a double assignment: to visit a senior cardinal at the Vatican in order to pass on a message on behalf of the IOC, and to represent him at a ceremony during which the Polish pope, John Paul II, was to bless the city's renovated Stadio Olympico. The first part of my mission was to visit the French cardinal, Roger Etchegaray, who was the equivalent of the senior minister of foreign affairs for the Vatican. The purpose of my visit concerned an initiative which the Vatican wanted to explore in relation to a major event for young people.

At that time, the Vatican was successfully developing and promoting large international gatherings of the Catholic youth of the world. That inspired the church's leadership to investigate whether their initiative could be connected to the Olympic Movement. My instructions were to politely inform the Vatican that the IOC had to decline any link with an event which was inspired by any religion. Any such connection would be a form of religious discrimination and thus constitute a breach of the Olympic Charter.

I had wondered why, of all the possible messengers among the IOC leadership, including senior Latin IOC members who were Roman Catholics, Samaranch had picked me. My guess was that because the message was to decline a proposal from the Vatican, Samaranch didn't want to choose a Catholic messenger, for whom the mission could have been embarrassing. It was far simpler to send an agnostic Swiss director general.

I was very well received by Cardinal Etchegaray, a most distinguished French gentleman, in his private apartment, which also served as his office within the Vatican. As we both sat in his relatively modest but cosy living room, an elderly Catholic sister came with a bottle of French brandy and two small glasses which she filled. It was an unexpected welcome on a warm, sunny afternoon at what must have been around four pm, the time at which lunch often ends in Rome. The cardinal, a warm personality, told me that, after lunch, he liked to take a sip of a favourite brandy from his homeland, the Basque country. I immediately felt at ease with that kindly and erudite man. We then discussed the matter at hand. As I told him about the IOC's negative position regarding the Vatican's initiative, he indicated by a gracious gesture that it was expected and was of no importance. He immediately changed the subject to other questions about sport and the Olympics. We took a few more sips of his brandy and our relaxed conversation continued. He even talked about life at the Vatican, which I found fascinating, and I spent a delightful afternoon. As I left the cardinal's office, I was almost ready to sign up for the Vatican's famous corps of Swiss Guards!

At the end of the same afternoon, I was driven to the Stadio Olympico for the pope's blessing. When I arrived, the stadium was completely full, with an enthusiastic young crowd being entertained by an excellent international rock band. The atmosphere was like a great musical festival. As I was representing Samaranch, I had an excellent seat on the second row, right behind the Italian prime minister, Giulio Andreotti, and not far from the pope's ceremonial chair. When he arrived, the crowd cheered wildly as he sat in his gilded chair, at which point, the ceremonials began with a piece played by the rock band.

From my seat, I could see the pope, who was wearing a long cassock, and noticed his red leather papal shoes. Then to my great surprise, I noticed what no one in front of him could see, that he was marking the music's rhythm with his feet, just like any young fan. I suddenly felt that I'd been 'blessed'. I'd been drinking brandy with a cardinal and sharing the beat of a rock band with a pope! It was great fun, but I remain an agnostic to this day.

The blessing of the stadium also provided me with an interesting lesson in political communication. The Italian prime minister was due to deliver a speech to the crowd in the stadium, and before the ceremony, the giant screens in the stadium were showing the usual pictures of the fans in the crowd waving and screaming. At certain points, they also showed snapshots of various personalities, including the politicians. As was often the case in Italy, the crowds began to boo as soon as Andreotti's face appeared on the screen. As I was sitting not far from him, I could see that he was talking to an assistant while gesturing towards the screen. The assistant had a mobile phone and was obviously passing on instructions to someone. I then noticed that Andreotti's face appeared again two or three times and each time it was greeted with loud boos. Andreotti, who was very calm as always, ordered his assistant to go and talk to the master of ceremonies with the result that Andreotti didn't make his speech, but nobody seemed to care.

I was told later that his assistant always had specific instructions from his boss to test the mood of large crowds in public venues before Andreotti decided whether to speak or not, which explained why his face was shown several times. It was a test as part of the prime minister's communication planning.

Helmut Kohl

During the spring of 1993, I accompanied Samaranch to Bonn, then still the German capital, on a visit to the German chancellor, Helmut Kohl, who, we were told, was planning to appear a few months later in front of the IOC Session in Monte-Carlo to present the Berlin bid for the 2000 Olympic Games. The bid had been launched before the fall of the Berlin Wall and had been based on a wonderfully idealistic idea, to bring together the youth of the world in Berlin for a special edition of the Olympic Games, jointly organised by East and West Germany.

In 1993, that very special bid had lost all its momentum as a consequence of the dismantling of East Germany, and, following unification, had thus become a West German bid. However, it had little chance of success against its main opponents, Sydney, the eventual winner, and Beijing. Therefore, the purpose of the meeting with Kohl was, as diplomatically as possible, to inform him of the bid's prospects, so that he could make a decision about whether to go to Monte-Carlo or not. Kohl quickly understood the message and, in fact, didn't go to Monte-Carlo, where Berlin got only nine votes.

Kohl then changed the topic of the conversation and told us of the consequences of the German reunification and of the future of Europe. During approximately one hour, we heard a fascinating account of his views. He didn't speak English, and, as I spoke German, Samaranch told Kohl that I would speak on his behalf. Kohl told us very succinctly that German reunification would involve very substantial sacrifices but was a necessary prerequisite and prelude to the future of Germany and of Europe. He explained that the European Community, it was not then named 'Union', would expand to the east and include new members like Poland. He also said that the political centre of gravity of Europe was moving eastward and that the capital of Europe would be Berlin, the new capital of Germany. Having witnessed what has since happened in Europe, I can only admire Kohl's foresight.

George W. Bush

Shortly after the tragedy of 9/11, in New York, two months later, in October 2001, a meeting was arranged for new IOC President, Jacques Rogge, to meet President Bush at the White House in Washington. The topic to be discussed was whether the upcoming 2002 Winter Olympics, which were to be held in Salt Lake City, would still take place. Rogge asked me to accompany him. The meeting was held in the Oval Room. The IOC delegation was small and included our leading US counsel, Arthur Culvahouse, who had made the necessary arrangements. President Bush had just one adviser with him and no files. He quickly came to the point and told us that, despite the appalling aftermath following 9/11, the US government wanted the Games to be celebrated as planned. He added that he would allocate some additional funding for security.

As the subject matter of the meeting was thus swiftly settled, the conversation drifted to other matters which were not on the agenda. At one point, while referring to subsequent Games which would be held in 2004 in Athens, Bush said that there were many Greeks who seemed to dislike the USA, and that it was very difficult to understand Greece and the other countries of that area. I then spoke, saying that the same difficulty was shared by many North Europeans. I added that I had read a very interesting geopolitical book on the Balkans by an excellent American author, at which point he interrupted me to say, "You mean Balkan Ghosts by Kaplan? A very good book. I know the author."

I was quite surprised that the man who'd been described to us as rather limited culturally was perfectly aware of the existence of Robert D. Kaplan, whose books appeared to me to be reserved for intellectuals. What had also struck me was his spontaneity. The whole meeting, which had lasted about an hour, left me with the feeling that, as in many other cases, the superficial portraits of many personalities widely disseminated by the media are often not as accurate as most people believe.

Vladimir Putin

Even though I've been introduced to him on several occasions at various meetings and functions from 2001 in Moscow to 2014 in Sochi, I can't in all honesty say that I know Vladimir Putin. Yet those various occasions gave me the opportunity to observe him, sometimes closely. I don't speak Russian, but I know some of his advisers and other members of his entourage. He is sometimes described as an unreachable man, and he is certainly an enigmatic character. My view of his behaviour leads me to think that he's always on his guard, and that his cool demeanour is a form of shyness.

It's obvious that he doesn't like to speak in public and, in particular, that he hates reading prepared speeches in his relatively high–pitched voice. In such situations, he looks uncomfortable and is obviously eager to bring the occasion to an end. Putin is a man of action and power, not a speaker. His ambitions are probably without limits. Politically, it's clear that he wants the Russian Federation of Russia, the largest country in the world, to fully recover the power and status of the former Soviet Union. He hasn't forgotten the humiliations that Russia and the Russians have endured for about twenty years since 1991. Most of the western states, and many of their leaders, didn't understand or care about the Russian frustrations and their deep desire for some form of revenge. I don't think that Putin trusts anyone. He certainly doesn't trust the Americans. At the same time, the Americans and most of their allies don't realise that the way in which they currently disparage Russia and Putin is counterproductive.

Putin loves and plays sport, in particular martial arts and winter sports. I believe that, just as in politics, his vision of international sport is that Russia should play a leading role, not only in sports performances, but also in sport administration. That wasn't the case for many years, but the global scene is currently changing. I am not a political analyst, and it would be preposterous for me to express an opinion on the future of the international situation. Such reflections belong to the remit of world leaders like Henry Kissinger. However, just as Kissinger showed his personal interest in international sport, it's worth mentioning Putin's personal interest in sport. As the world slips into a new and dangerous cold war, may I dare to express the hope that sport, and more particularly Olympic sport, might perhaps mitigate the risks of conflicts. Sport opens different channels of communication, and I believe that, by using their sporting links with

Putin, international sports leaders could play a more active role in reducing tensions. That may sound naive but, after more than forty years of involvement in international sport, I've been struck by the growing closeness of the political and sporting worlds. I wouldn't have dared to venture such an opinion forty years ago, but today's world is very different.

Claude Nobs and the Montreux Jazz Festival

There are many personalities in areas beyond sport that I've had the privilege to meet during the last fifty years or so. In particular, I have fond memories of artists like the unique new realism French sculptor, César Baldaccini, a good friend, Jean Tinguely, the Swiss painter and sculptor and Tadeusz Kantor, the great Polish theatre figure. However, of all the people I have had the pleasure of knowing in the arts, there is one extraordinary personality I'd like to mention, Claude Nobs, the founder and CEO of the world famous Montreux Jazz Festival.

Nobs created Montreux in 1967 and led it without interruption until his tragic death, following a skiing accident, in 2013. Nobs was the son of a local baker near Montreux. He took an apprenticeship as a hotel cook and then became an administrator with the Montreux Tourism Office. He had a passion for jazz and decided to launch a jazz festival in Montreux. It began as a small, local event, but Nobs had a burning desire and a very strong will. The turning point in his life was a meeting in New York with Nesuhi Ertegun, the famous boss of Atlantic Records.

Nobs had succeeded in pushing his way through Ertegun's door and that unplanned meeting marked the beginning of a friendship that would last for nearly fifty years. It also gave him access to all the top jazz musicians and singers. Over the years, Montreux became one of the most famous musical events in the world. A few years ago, Time Magazine listed Nobs as one of the 100 most important people in the world. He lived near Montreux in two extraordinary chalets on a mountain overlooking the fantastic landscape above Lake Geneva.

Nobs was not only the soul of the festival but was also amazingly curious about everyone and everything and had hundreds of friends throughout the world. When he wasn't travelling the globe, the major stars of music and art would visit him in his chalets. When he decided to privatise the festival, which he had been managing on behalf of the Montreux Tourism Office, surrounded by a few close friends, he established a foundation to restructure the festival and asked me to become chairman of the board, a position I still occupy. One of his closest friends was Quincy Jones who often visited him in Montreux. His friendship with Nesuhi Ertegun and Daniel Filippachi, the French press magnate and jazz expert, lasted forever.

Until his last day, Nobs was totally dedicated to the organisation, development and promotion of the festival, his festival. He was never satisfied, always launching new projects and testing new ideas. His accidental death, following a fall on Christmas Eve 2012, during a cross country skiing trip, was a great loss and caused much grief around the world. During his life, he was always supported by his life partner, Thierry Amsalem, who, as Nobs' inheritor, is dedicated to preserving Nobs' cultural heritage. As CEO of the festival, Nobs was succeeded by a very talented young man, Mathieu Jaton, whom he selected and who embodies Nobs' spirit.

More than ninety concerts are performed each summer in Montreux during the festival's two weeks in July. The greatest artists of all time have performed on the Montreux stages: Prince, Santana, Herbie Hancock, Stevie Wonder, Grace Jones, Lady Gaga and Elton John. And, year after year, Quincy Jones is still a major supporter of the festival, in particular by bringing new talent to Montreux. Having the honour to chair its board has been one of the most rewarding and inspiring experiences of my life.

34
What Else?

For the last forty years, apart from my law firm and a number of corporate directorships, I have been mainly focused on international sport administration. However, I've strived to keep my independence and to avoid being totally absorbed by sport, which is, after all, a very peculiar world. I have always wanted to keep very close links with what I consider to be the real outside world. That's why I never gave up my legal practice and still advise a number of clients who are decision makers in areas like industry and finance, and I've served on various boards. Those contacts and experiences have been of considerable importance in helping me to appreciate the real issues in our society. So, I managed to keep one foot in international sport administration, which I loved, and another one in the rest of the world, which I loved just as much, and which, I hope, helped me come to balanced judgements, in the best interests of the institutions and individuals I served. The learning curve is never ending and permanent.

Thanks to the confidence of its main shareholders, the extraordinary Sandoz family, for many years I've been the chairman of the board of directors of the Beau-Rivage Palace, a five-star hotel established in 1861 in a wonderful park in Ouchy, the small harbour of Lausanne on the shore of Lake Léman, the local name for Lake Geneva. It is currently rated as one of the very best hotels in Europe and enjoys worldwide fame. It has a unique position in a 40,000 square metre park with breathtaking views from most of its 160 beautiful rooms and suites. During all my years with the Beau-Rivage Palace, I have had the good fortune to experience a number of extraordinary moments, some of which I'd like to share here.

US president, Richard Nixon, loved the Beau-Rivage. After his presidency ended in rather sad circumstances in 1974, he stayed with us several times. At that time, the hotel's general manager was the charismatic Bodo von Alvensleben, who had previously served for a number of years as manager of the Waldorf Towers in New York, where he had developed a significant social network and knew Nixon personally. One afternoon, as I was attending the hearing of an international arbitration tribunal in Geneva, I was handed a message saying that I should call Alvensleben at the Beau-Rivage as soon as possible, which I did during a short recess. He told me that Nixon was arriving at the hotel that afternoon and that it would be nice if I could greet him as chairman of the board.

It was agreed that, at the end of the day, when I was back in Lausanne, I would drop by at the Beau-Rivage and pay a short courtesy visit to Nixon in his suite. I went back to my hearing, then an hour later, I was again asked to call Alvensleben, who told me that the plan was being changed and that I was expected to greet Nixon not at the hotel, but in a restaurant where he was going to have dinner with some friends. As much as I considered it an honour to greet as former US president, I didn't see the point of doing it when he wasn't in our hotel. As I was trying to think of a way out of what appeared be a futile exercise, I asked Alvensleben which restaurant Nixon had chosen. To my surprise, the place was the Auberge du Raisin in Cully, a well-known restaurant in my village and right next to my home.

So, I told Alvensleben that, while it wouldn't make any sense for me to greet Nixon outside of the hotel, I would be honoured to welcome him and his party for a pre-dinner drink at my home. I was certain that the reply would be negative for all sorts of reasons, including protocol and security, and I would thus be honourably discharged of my duties. I then got a third call, informing me that Nixon was delighted to accept my invitation and that he would arrive by six pm with a party of four, and that Swiss security and the US Secret Service, six agents, would be at my home one hour earlier to inspect the premises. By then it was approximately three pm, the hearing wasn't over, and I was about an hour's drive from home, where nobody had any idea about Nixon's arrival. I managed to reach my wife, who wasn't at home, and told her that she had to urgently prepare snacks and drinks because we were going to host former President Nixon. She first told me that I'd made better jokes and that I must be very tired or very drunk! I eventually succeeded in convincing her that it wasn't a joke, and that, in addition, she would have to accommodate a number of Swiss and US security agents, who were about to invade our home. I managed to drive home and, as I arrived at my door, a US Secret Service agent stood in my way and asked me to identify myself, which I did.

By then, our two daughters, who were six and eight years old, were arriving home from the village school with our au pair, to by greeted by a posse of police officers. As my home is a very old house on a narrow street in the heart of the village, the unusual activity had aroused the neighbours and passers-by who gawped at a couple of black limousines as they delivered their passengers: President Nixon, one of his close friends, two ambassadors and Alvensleben. They were in a great mood and, instead of staying for an hour as planned, remained for more than three hours, consuming all the snacks and quite a few bottles of champagne.

The conversation was very interesting, and Nixon clearly had a deep understanding of the current geopolitical situation in Europe. By nine-thirty pm, the chef of the Auberge du Raisin called up, concerned that his guests hadn't arrived. Escorted by their security agents, our guests then walked to the restaurant while our neighbours, who had recognised Nixon, looked on in astonishment.

One of the many important international conferences held at the Beau-Rivage was the peace talks for Lebanon in 1984. Lebanon had been torn apart by war and terrorism and the situation was very tense and complex between Christian Lebanese, Syria, Palestinian refugees and the state of Israel. The official Lebanese delegation, led by President Amine Gemayel, the brother of Bachir, who had been assassinated two years earlier, was staying at the hotel and I had had the opportunity to greet him, a most elegant young statesman just forty-two years old. The Swiss president, Pierre Aubert, had announced his intention to visit the conference and it was agreed that I would welcome him. President Gemayel also wanted to greet him, so both of us were ready at the door.

As we were chatting, President Aubert's official black Mercedes arrived and out stepped Aubert, his face covered with plasters and bandages. He immediately apologised for his appearance, explaining that he'd had an accident with his bicycle, leading Gemayel to say with a broad smile, "It seems that the roads of Switzerland are not any safer than those in Lebanon."

Aubert was well known for his passion for cycling and for spending his holidays cycling around the country incognito with his wife. A story he liked to tell was about the end of one of his tours when he and his wife arrived covered in dust at a fine hotel, where they were turned down because of a lack of rooms. They then rode on until they reached a phone box from which he called up the same hotel and, after identifying himself as the head of state, asked if there was a room available for him. The answer being positive, still covered with dust, they rode back to the hotel where they were warmly welcomed by the manager in person who had no idea that his staff had just turned away the head of state!

Very little came of the peace conference and the Lebanese War continued until 1990 at the cost of over 120,000 fatalities. Gemayel served as president until 1988, when, facing threats to his life, he went into exile for twelve years, He returned to Lebanon in 2000 and re-entered his country's multifaceted political landscape, but not at a senior level. Sadly, his son, Pierre, a cabinet minister, was assassinated in 2006. His brother, Samy, is currently a member of the Lebanese parliament.

During the eighties on Saturday evenings, the bar of the Beau Rivage was a popular spot late into the night. On one occasion, following the annual dinner of the Bar Association, many lawyers, wives and friends were gathered around the crowded bar. The alcohol flowed and couples were dancing to an excellent combo. The place was packed and noisy and the mood very happy. I was pleased to see many of my colleagues enjoying themselves, and, as is often the case, nobody paid any serious attention to the band and the music. It was about one in the morning, and, after a short break, the musicians had resumed playing.

I was standing at the bar when I was struck by a different sound from the band and a voice which sounded familiar began singing, "You are the sunshine of my heart…" It was not the voice of the combo's usual singer, so I walked towards the band and realised, despite the darkness of the place, that the pianist had changed. As I got nearer to the piano, I found, to my very pleasant surprise, that the artist singing the famous hit song was none other than Stevie Wonder himself, who'd taken over the piano unannounced.

I couldn't believe my eyes or my ears and rushed back to the bar to tell my friends that, in that dark corner, the singer was actually Stevie Wonder. Soon the entire attendance became aware of that extraordinary moment and spontaneous applause broke out. He went on performing for about half an hour in front of what had become an enthusiastic crowd until, escorted by his bodyguard, he left the bar as unobtrusively as he'd arrived.

In the meantime, I'd spoken to the duty manager to find out how this could have happened unannounced. The answer was simple, Stevie Wonder was staying the night at the hotel because Diana Ross was getting married the next day. He'd arrived at around midnight and asked for a piano so that he could practise. As there wasn't a piano in his suite, the management told him that the only available piano would be at the bar, where the resident band was playing. He immediately went down to the bar to give us all a moment of magic none of us will ever forget.

Epilogue

Throughout the first seventy-seven years of my life, I mostly did it my way. Of course, we can't pick our parents, our place of birth or our country and, in my case, I was very lucky compared to the billions of people who are born into a life of little or no prospects. I had a good education and my parents were thoughtful and tolerant. When I decided, at the age of seventeen, to go to California, although I was their only son, they didn't object.

This was the major turning point in my life. The rest was a succession of choices I made when offered certain opportunities. Did I make the right choices every time? I don't know, and I really don't care. Regrets, I have a few, but too few to mention. I've met extraordinary people, seen most of the world and have a wonderful family. I'm not rich, but I'm not poor either and I live comfortably.

Above all, I love people. Every morning, I feel happy to be alive and I look forward to the day ahead, which will bring me new experiences and new opportunities. I have a rather good memory, which keeps me away from nostalgic flashbacks. I'm not interested in the past, but in the future, and I'm convinced that the future will provide extraordinary opportunities for future generations. Such optimism may appear naive in the light of the numerous conflicts, dramas and tragedies occurring in today's world. However, in order to assess our prospects for the future, we must consider two fundamental universal issues: religious extremism and globalisation. These two factors, while they are very different in nature, are at the heart of the world's current critical geopolitical dilemma.

Religious extremism has for centuries been a major source of conflict and remains a global problem in the twenty-first century. Most major governments are more and more concerned that growing numbers of their young people are joining the forces of religious extremism. But I remain convinced that better systems of education, including Olympic education, could help prevent the trend to extremist views.

Globalisation is an ongoing process, which began centuries ago, and is now being accelerated thanks to technological and scientific progress leading to the world becoming a global community almost overnight. The world is shrinking like never before, boundaries are disappearing, but as they do, many of us want to make them stronger. Migration is an issue which will only be solved globally. Current political leaders are desperately trying to find solutions, but I'm convinced that they will never succeed until they address the root of the issue, which is none other than fundamental human freedom, the right to move freely and to make a decent living. It is a formidable challenge, with all kinds of social, political and human consequences, and I'm worried that our current political leaders are only interested in short-sighted unilateral, nationalistic solutions. We need global visionaries, and perhaps the world sports community, with its huge networks, might have a useful role in creating a peaceful global community.

There's no doubt that there will still be many more conflicts, criminal acts and other horrible tragedies before our planet is unified, but I'm convinced that, eventually, unification will be achieved. That's why, despite the many ordeals that lie ahead, I feel resolutely optimistic. The next generations will face extraordinary challenges which they must view as opportunities to build a new world, one that, ultimately, will be a better world.

Cully, Switzerland, July 2016.

The IOC members stand in tribute to François Carrard, 2022

Index

3M 76

A

ACOG (Atlanta Centennial
Olympic Games Organising
Committee) 178–181
Adidas 70–71
Agnelli, Giovanni 185, 191
American Express 75
American Field Servicve (AFS) 17–
18, 28–29
Amex" \t "See American Express
75
Apartheid v, 147–148
Armstrong, Lance 219–220
Armstrong, Louis 8
Arroyo, Agustin 189
Automobile Club of Switzerland
(ACS) 49

B

Bach, Thomas vi, vii, 66, 72,
163, 174, 205–206, 221, 225
Badinter, Robert 237
Baltic republics 135
Barnier, Michel 91
Beau-Rivage Palace 14, 78, 87–
89, 231–232, 234–235
Beaumont, Count Jean de 84
Beitz, Berthold 82–83
Berlioux, Monique 51–52, 54–55,
64–65, 70, 77, 80–86, 96–97,
205
Bhumibol, King of Thailand 234
Biden, Joe 31

Blatter, Sepp 207–210, 212,
220
Boutros-Ghali, Boutros 191
Bush, George W. 180, 245
Buthelezi, Chief 149

C

Caballé, Montserrat 87, 145
Carrard, Alba 46
Carrard, Erica (née Godall)
2, 3, 6, 8–9, 12–13, 15–
17, 19, 34, 88, 97
Carrard, Jean 2, 3, 12–13,
16–17, 29, 34, 45–46
Carrard, Maud 96
Castro, Fidel 239–240
Cercle des Nageurs de
Lausanne (CNL) 9
Chevallaz, Georges-André 64
China 10, 51–55, 57, 128,
137, 163, 172–173, 201,
231–232
Chirac, Jacques 85, 87–91,
228
Cinquanta, Ottavio 215
Coca Cola 70, 171
Coubertin, Pierre de 141–
142, 160, 164, 168, 171,
173–174, 222, 224–225
Court of Arbitration for Sport
47, 60–62, 220
Court of Arbitration for Sport
(CAS) 47, 57, 59

D

Dassler, Adolf 70

Dassler, Horst 70–72, 76

Dassler, Käthe 70

Dassler, Rudolf 70

de Klerk, F. W. 148–149

Delamuraz, Jean-Pascal 64, 88

Dennis, Brian F. 39

E

Estonia 130, 138

F

Fairfield, Peg 19

Fantini, Sergio 189

FedEx 75

FIFA vi, 23, 60, 71, 191, 193,
195, 207–212, 220, 224

FIS (International Ski Federation)
159

Furgler, Kurt 64

G

Gadir, Zein Abdel 189

Gafner, Raymond 67–68, 84–85,
92, 96, 98–101

GAISF (Global Association of
International Sports Federations)
222

Ganga, Jean-Claude 189

Gonzalez, Felipe 228

Gorbachev, Mikhail 131, 133–134

Gosper, Kevan 149, 186, 211

Grand Prix Drivers' Association
(GPDA) 49

H

Hayatou, Issa 210, 212

Heiberg, Gerhard 154, 160–161

Herzog, Maurice 84

Hodler, Marc 159 160, 182, 184
185

Hsu, Henry 51, 53–54

I

IAAF (International Association of
Athletic Federations) 229

Infantino, Gianni 209, 211–212

International Olympic Committee
(IOC) v–vi, 47, 51–57, 59, 62–
79, 81–100, 128–130, 132–133,
135, 137, 141–145, 147–151,
153–156, 158–200, 203–205,
207, 215, 221–222, 224–225,
228–230, 232–233

International Ski Federation" \t
"See FIS 185

IOC" \t "See International Olympic
Committee (IOC) vi

ISU 215

J

Jean Carrard 2

Jewell, Richard 179

John Muir High School 20–23,
25, 35

John Paul II 242

Johnson, Ben 94, 97

K

Kéba 227

Keita, Lamine 189

Kidane, Fekrou 150, 227

Killanin, Lord 54–55, 65, 81, 205

Killy, Jean-Claude 91, 239

Kim Un-Yong 192–194

Kissinger, Henry 191, 195

Kodak 75

Kohl, Helmut 244

Kozlovsky, Alexander 'Sacha' 140

Kwaśnicwski, Aleksander 132

L

Landsbergis, Vytautas 137–138
Latvia 130
Lausanne Palace 14, 65, 81, 184, 200
Lausanne, University of v, 4, 23, 33, 35, 37, 207
Le Gougne, Marie-Reine 215
Lithuania 130, 137
Luzhkov, Yuri 200

M

Magdaleno, Paul 25
Mandela, Nelson 148–152, 226–228
Mbaye, Kéba 59–60, 67–68, 82–83, 148–150, 183, 194, 227
McSweeney, John 20
Mercury, Freddie 145
Mérode, Prince Alexandre de 96–97, 128
Meylan, Philippe 34–35
Milosevic, Slobodan 143
Mitchell, George 188–189, 196
Montreux Jazz Festival vii, 10, 235
Moreau, Emmanuelle 186
Moses, Edwin 149
Mukora, Charles 189
Mutko, Vitaly 141
Mzali, Mohamed 87–91

N

Nebiolo, Primo 229–231
Nelson Mandela 226
Nicolaou, Lambis 161
Nixon, Richard 249
Nobs, Claude 10, 241, 247

O

Obama, Barack 30, 228–229

P

Paillou, Nelson 235
Payne, Billy 176–177
Payne, Michael 70, 186, 196
Platini, Michel 212
Pound, Dick 71–74, 185–189, 191 196, 201
Procter & Gamble 39–41, 45
Puma 70
Putin, Vladimir 137, 141–142, 162, 199, 228, 245

R

Rebollo, Antonio 145–146
Rochat, Maurice 88
Rogge, Jacques 65, 72, 137, 155, 167, 172, 192, 200, 203–205
Rudolph, Eric 179
Rusak, Ivan 128, 134–135, 140

S

Samaranch, Juan Antonio v, 47, 55–57, 59–61, 63–65, 67–68, 70–75, 77–79, 81–90, 92–93, 95–101, 129–133, 136–140, 144, 147–151, 153–156, 159–160, 167, 172, 176–178, 181–205, 227, 229–235
Samaranch, Maria Teresa 232
SANOC (South African National Olympic Committee) 147
Scala, Domenico 209
Schamasch, Patrick 176
Schmitt, Pal 129
Servan-Schreiber, Franklin 186
Shefler, Stanley 64
Siperco, Alexandru 67–68
Sjöström, Henning 42–46, 48

SLOC (Salt Lake City Olympic Organising Committee) 183–184, 188–189

Smirnov, Vitaly 130–133, 135, 140, 199

Strauss, Franz Joseph 228

Stupp, Howard 100

Sweden, King of 153

T

Taipei 51, 53–56

Taiwan 52–54, 56

Toor, Art 25

Tröger, Walter 81, 83

Trump, Donald 30–31

U

UEFA 212, 219

Ullmann, Liv 154

University of Bologna 17

V

Vergès, Jacques 190

Villiger, Marco 211

Visa 75

W

Weider, Ben 137

Wonder, Stevie 252

World Anti-Doping Agency (WADA) v, 57

Worrall, James 67–68

Wurzburger, Alain 53, 57

Y

Yaryan, Bill 25

Yeltsin, Boris 133–134, 136–137, 141, 199

Yugoslavia 29, 143–145, 155

Z

Zweifel, Françoise 85, 100–101

BV - #0040 - 090424 - C26 - 229/152/19 - CC - 9781916556225 - Gloss Lamination